Chinnagounder's Challenge

6/4/00
To Professor Alan and Nicole
Brew
Whose lives and minds
are dedicated to The
love of nature.

Warm regards,

Deane Curtin

Chinnagounder's Challenge
The Question of Ecological Citizenship

Deane Curtin

Indiana University Press

BLOOMINGTON AND INDIANAPOLIS

This book is a publication of

Indiana University Press
601 North Morton Street
Bloomington, IN 47404-3797 USA

http://www.indiana.edu/~iupress

Telephone orders 800-842-6796
Fax orders 812-855-7931
Orders by e-mail iuporder@indiana.edu

The paper used in this publication meets the minimum requirements
of American National Standard for Information Sciences—Permanence of Paper for Printed Library Materials, ANSI Z39.48-1984.

MANUFACTURED IN THE UNITED STATES OF AMERICA

Library of Congress Cataloging-in-Publication Data

Curtin, Deane W.
    Chinnagounder's challenge : the question of ecological citizenship
    / Deane Curtin.
        p.   cm.
Includes bibliographical references and index.
ISBN 0-253-33576-0 (cloth : alk. paper). — ISBN 0-253-21330-4
    (pbk. : alk. paper)
1. Environmental ethics. 2. Postcolonialism.   I. Title.
    GE42.C87   1999
    179'.1—dc21   99-25161

1 2 3 4 5 04 03 02 01 00 99

To

Rita, Evan, and Ian,

who know this book by heart

CONTENTS

PREFACE AND ACKNOWLEDGMENTS

Since at least the seventeenth century, philosophers have used the metaphor of lenses to describe how we know "the external world." But, as anyone of a certain age knows, lenses can obscure as much as they reveal. Those designed to help you read this book may turn distant sites into a deep fog.

Imagine that our moral lenses have much the same effect. Suppose they make it possible for us to recognize the "fine print" of our own culture, but that they systematically obscure and distort the texts of distant cultures. There would then be two very different kinds of disputes, disputes *in* ethics and disputes *about* ethics. Disputes in ethics which might be called *in-context moral disputes* are "normal" in the sense that the parties all function within a common moral framework, or, at least, an overlapping set of frameworks. We feel "at home" in such disputes. When we disagree, we at least understand each other. *Out-of-context disputes* are disputes due to the fact that the parties' moral frameworks do not neatly converge. We have the feeling that "these people" organize their moral lives differently. Their lives are foreign to us. These are "disputes," if they can even be called that, in which we "talk past" one another.

One type of out-of-context dispute is particularly evident in cross-cultural disputes over "the environment," where the size and texture of the moral domain is in question. The green revolution, for example, was the revolution in agricultural production that began in the late 1940s. It used new "miracle seeds" to achieve dramatic increases in agricultural production. One of its effects, however, was to displace traditional farm economies that had evolved over centuries producing local foods for local markets. The moral product of the Western Enlightenment, the revolution assumed that the boundaries of the moral coincide with the boundaries of the *human* community. In "target" countries, however, the domain of the moral is often far more extensive. It typically includes whole *ecological* communities.

In India, for example, one of the earliest sites for the green revolution, cows are indeed sacred, but so are many other animals, insects, and plants. The shift to a new mode of agricultural production meant heavy dependence upon pesticides and herbicides, chemicals invented to eradicate the sacred. The rapid industrialization of agriculture was not simply a technological innovation, as it is often viewed from "our side," but a fundamental challenge to the dimensions of local moral knowledge. What counts as having moral standing, and needs to be treated with respect, often fails to cross over from one moral domain to another. What appears from our side to be ethically neutral, a "technology transfer," may have grave moral import on another side. It may threaten the fabric of the moral community.

A second issue at stake in moral boundary disputes is over moral personhood. The tradition of Western liberal individualism assumes that the moral person is defined prior to engagement in culture. One's culture is an accidental trait that surrounds a core of essential traits, those one has *willed* oneself to be. In many non-Western cultures, however, one is a person to the extent one already has a place in the community.

To an outsider, for example, the ritual enacted daily at a Japanese train station may seem bizarre: a younger man bows to his superior; an older man bows in return. The younger man bows again, but more deeply. The older man bows again, but not as deeply. This spasm of mutual respect borders on the humorous to the outsider, but to the insider it is a ritual that sets the conditions of speech. Communication cannot occur until relative position is established.

It is typically a frustration to Americans who travel in Asia that they are treated, first, as a representative expression of their culture and only secondarily, if at all, as a unique individual. We feel that our moral identities have been effaced, that we have not been judged fairly, as a cultural free-agent. Sometimes our having been "misunderstood" causes us to imagine what it might be like to organize moral experience in a profoundly different way.

The distinction between in-context and out-of-context disputes, however, is probably too simple to take us very far without qualification. For example, it is not clear whether this distinction marks different kinds of disputes, or merely disputes that differ in degree of communication. In chapter 9, I will finally conclude that there are no truly intractable disputes in the sense that, in principle, they cannot be mediated. With sufficient training and sensitivity, we may become a "partial insider" to a profoundly different moral world. We might learn to translate from one world to another.

Furthermore, cultures can be highly diverse. Basic failures in communications may occur, not just in cases of great geographical distance, but between groups within a culture. Some feminists argue, for example, that women's moral experience tends to be quite different from men's experience. Recent events in the United States—the O. J. Simpson trial is the most celebrated case—have caused some to ask whether race tends to play an important role in the organization of moral experience.

It may even be that the failure of understanding does not go both ways. If we experience a culture as almost unspeakably foreign, this does not imply they lack the tools to understand us. On the one hand, for example, when a culture has been colonized, it may be intimately aware of the moral world of its colonizer. To colonize another culture, on the other hand, it may be necessary to distort it, to shape it to a particular moral agenda that is not its own.

Finally, as the globalization of capital occurs, geographically distant subcultures are trained to speak the language of capital without borders. Stock traders in New York and Hong Kong may have more in common with each other than with their geographically local culture.

The provisional distinction between two kinds of moral disputes is useful, however, if it allows me to focus on an unsettling possibility. It may be that certain systematic features of the ways we in the West, as products of the Enlightenment, tend to organize moral experience encourage us to believe we have understood profoundly different cultures when we do not. A consequence of this is that sometimes when we try to help profoundly different cultures, we fail.

Today, moral boundaries are not stable. The late twentieth century is marked by two powerful movements: the increasingly global reach of Western liberal individualism, and the resistance to this movement in traditional communities. Most of us are familiar by now with news of the eclipse of biological diversity. We are in the midst of only the sixth period of massive species extinction in all of biological history, occurring at a rate approaching 100 times what biologists consider normal. We hear less frequently about the parallel loss of human cultural and genetic diversity. Of the world's 6,000 linguistically different cultures, the great majority, some 4,000–5,000, are classified as indigenous. In terms of numbers, these cultures tend to be small, at most, 625 million people out of a world population of roughly 6 billion.

These cultures are often fragile. One-third of the original North American languages have been lost, two-thirds in Australia. Eighty-seven tribes disappeared in Brazil alone in the first half of this century (Durning 1992: 81–83). Yet most of the world's cultural and genetic diversity reside in these small, unique cultures. At a pace that only increases, these cultures face the tragic choice of living in a homogeneous global culture, or being eradicated altogether.

Although these kinds of disputes are particularly acute when industrialized first world cultures come into conflict with so-called fourth world, or indigenous, cultures, they also affect much larger population groups. These are often described as conflicts between the so-called first world and third world. Many of these cross-cultural disputes—international arguments over the GATT (General Agreement on Tariffs and Trade) and the NAFTA (North American Free Trade Agreement), biodiversity, third world population control, first world levels of consumption—usually hide deep conflicts over local definitions of *nature* and *culture*. Most of these disputes never get to the point of being genuine disagreements that can be subjected to mediation. They remain out-of-context.

Economic and military dominance means that we in the first world can insist on a mono-lingual moral world, but this invites both logical and moral difficulties. Logically, this begs the question by assuming that the moral language of liberal individualism is the language in which disputes about liberal individualism must be mediated. Morally, this claim to a monopoly on moral rationality *itself* risks something dear to our self-understanding: the understanding that we are a democratic culture. This book is about the meanings of freedom in the late twentieth century, and the consequent need to rethink familiar understandings of culture in relationship to nature.

Chapter 1 begins by asking whether the conceptual resources we have developed in the United States for speaking about the relationship of culture and nature can be exported. Not only are these uniquely American resources difficult to export, I find that social and environmental justice in one context may become injustice in another context. This "phase shift" in moral perception is a puzzle I return to frequently. How can a social system appear—perhaps *be*—just and nonviolent from within, yet unjust and violent when transported elsewhere? How can there be such a profound shift in moral perception from insider to outsider? I suggest that one sort of violence is easily recognized within the moral traditions of Western liberalism: individual violence. But other sorts of violence are exceedingly difficult to identify, given common liberal assumptions: institutional and systemic violence.

Chapter 2 opens by calling for an act of the moral imagination. Could it be that progressive forces working for social justice in the first world become regressive when applied to the social context of the third world? The British utilitarians are justly celebrated for their roles in challenging the authority of tradition (common law) and replacing it with a critical conception of liberal equality based on statute law. John Stuart Mill's role in fostering equal rights for women, for example, has long been noted, and rightly so. While not disparaging Mill or his role in the development of Enlightenment thinking about equality, this picture of his legacy must be balanced against the fact that Mill and his father, James Mill, spent their entire working lives in the service of the East India Company. John Stuart Mill was groomed by his father to write the civil and legal correspondence with India, effectively functioning as the British governor of India until the day the British government instituted direct rule.

To understand the dilemmas that confront contemporary conceptions of freedom, we need to understand how British utilitarians reconciled their support for liberal democracy at home with their active support for colonialism in India, Ireland, and elsewhere. This dual legacy is not just historically significant. I find contemporary importance in the conception of "development" that follows from utilitarian definitions of culture and nature. In utilitarianism, we get an almost fully articulated version of the developmentalist project: development is the extension of a calculus of individual preference satisfactions from a moral/rational "center" to the periphery.

Chapter 3 examines the twentieth century causes of first world/third world conflict over definitions of culture and nature. I focus primarily on events since World War II, when the United States became interested in blunting the spreading influence of communism among third world peasants by transferring a free market model of development to the third world. The foremost vehicle for this transfer was the green revolution. Its intentions were not simply technological; its goals were couched in terms of world peace. I ask whether the green revolution has been the vehicle of peace. My conclusion is that its systemic violence encourages us to confuse peace with pacification.

In chapter 4, I move to the contemporary impact of development on the third world, considering the social and ethical issues that underlie the GATT and NAFTA free trade agreements on traditional communities. I also consider the defense against development arising from traditional farmers in India and from the descendants of Mayan people in southern Mexico. The GATT raises new issues concerning the access of first world companies, and third world economic elites, to biological and cultural diversity. Most of the world's biological and cultural diversity is found in third world rainforests. New forms of trans-national capitalism require access to this diversity. Protests to development from indigenous communities are not the last gasp of a historically outmoded peasantry, as both Marxists and capitalists would have it, but voices from the cutting edge of global conflict over culture and nature.

Chapter 5 extends these arguments concretely to women's knowledge of their ecocommunities. I ask, "In what sense is women's knowledge of their communities privileged?" I begin to develop an account of what it means to function within a practice. Those who function as insiders to the practice "know the rules." They possess expertise that demands recognition in authentic human development.

Having brought forward the types of situations I am concerned to understand in part 1, part 2 regards whether first world "radical" environmental philosophy advances our understanding of cross-cultural disputes over nature and culture. In chapters 6 through 8, I focus on two features of first world radical environmental philosophy. The first is the idea that environmental philosophy *is* the project of establishing a theory of intrinsic value, or inherent worth, for non-human entities. More generally, these views are examples of the idea that it is the job of philosophers to provide unified theories of universal moral considerability. I reject both these assumptions about the purpose of environmental philosophy, and contend that it is precisely these commitments which account for the failure of first world radical environmental philosophy to produce concrete results that can inform public policy debates. In chapter 8, I begin to consider explicitly pluralistic approaches to environmental ethics.

My second concern in these chapters is with the ways first world radical environmental philosophy treats the "Other," whether this means women, the third world, indigenous cultures, or the Orient. In many cases, I find that first world radical environmental philosophy projects the same prejudices onto the rest of the world as does liberal individualism. And it has done little to advance a global understanding of environmental conflict. Neither economic liberalism nor most versions of Western "radical" environmental ethics help us to set aside familiar, neocolonial prejudices about the ethics of nature and culture. We need to begin again.

Part 3 presents my constructive response to the issues raised in part 1, and an alternative to the positions examined in part 2. I argue for a form of pragmatic ecocommunitarian pluralism: many communities, particularly those long established, already reveal a localized sense of community that is more-than-human. No philosophical demonstration will make this more real. The role of a public environmental philosophy is to facilitate nonviolent cross-community discourse through which goods internal to a community may be preserved or gradually transformed.

Starting from the premise first intimated in chapter 5 concerning the authority of insiders to a practice, I argue in chapter 9 for the authority of local communities to maintain traditional relationships to place, and for the local expertise that is assumed by such relationships. This obviously raises the question of how to mediate conflicts among communities, particularly when we live in a deeply pluralistic world. Instead of assuming that serious moral conflicts are always due to ill will (that is, that they are cases of conscious, in-context individual violence), I start by asking how moral communication goes wrong. I draw a distinction between what it means to function within a practice (in a larger sense, a community) according to the goods internal to that practice, and what it means to operate according to a set of external goods.

I propose that all genuine development begins with what Michael Walzer calls a "thick" description of a culture; it must begin from a cognitive sympathy for the internal goods that constitute the community. Talk of utilities, or, to refer to the other great Western moral tradition, talk of individual rights, only comes later, when thick descriptions have "thinned out" in the process of cross-cultural moral communication. True human development is not just the abstract guarantee of rights, nor is it reducible to the satisfaction of individual preferences. It is the actual ability to function within an ecocommunity in such a way that one can participate in defining, achieving, and transforming the internal goods of one's practice.

The final chapter begins with the story of Chinnagounder, a man who has witnessed more than one hundred years of change in India. His story challenges us to look back at contemporary American culture from its borders, asking how we can draw out aspects of American traditions that will give new meaning to freedom, and to the reconciliation of culture with nature. The debate about "the environment" becomes a question of the character appropriate to ecological citizenship.

It is emphatically not my purpose to essentialize the first world and blame it for all the problems suffered by the third world. There is violence within all communities. Some third world countries were never colonized by the first world. Third world governments and communities perpetuate violence against themselves. Nevertheless, this is a book written primarily for a first world audience in the hope of mediating differences in moral vision. My concern is not to admonish, but to understand. The principal conceptual tools I bring to this task are not intended to lay blame with intentional (individual) violence. They expose categorical features of our worldview that make it difficult to perceive certain sorts of violence.

This is a book written by a philosopher for a broad audience. I hope that my professional colleagues will find the book valuable. However, the kinds of questions I engage require that I write for a more inclusive audience. I am concerned not only with philosophical theories, but with the impact that philosophies have had on people's lives and on the fate of nature. This is a work of public philosophy. Readers with little patience for philosophical debates might focus on parts 1 and 3. The chapters in part 2 begin and end with summaries that should be sufficient to a bridge between earlier and later chapters.

I have benefited immeasurably from several professional relationships during the time I was writing this book. Concerned Philosophers for Peace (CPP) provided me with the opportunity to present versions of chapters 3 and 9. My friend and colleague Duane Cady encouraged my participation in CPP as a friendly place to try out the ideas. He was right. Rick Werner and Jim Sterba were particularly insightful in commenting on chapter 9, which I regard as the key philosophical chapter. Bob Litke and I worked together on a collection of essays on institutional violence. Readers will have no difficulty in recognizing the impact my work with Bob has had on this book. Some of what we wrote together for the introduction to the anthology has found its way into this book's definitions of violence in chapter 1. Joe Kunkel deserves recognition as the principal force behind CPP for as long as I have been involved.

A second organization that has been important is the International Development Ethics Association (IDEA), whose president is David Crocker. I attended IDEA's international conference in Tegucigalpa, Honduras, where I presented a version of chapter 5 just as the ideas in this book were beginning to take shape. I have benefited from enduring relationships with David Crocker, Peter Penz, and Natalie Dandakar.

I read a version of chapter 4 at a meeting of the Radical Philosophy Association. Alison Jaggar commented helpfully on that occasion, and also provided an extensive written review of chapter 10. I deeply value her critical reactions.

Several environmental philosophers have been among my closest and most valued friends and colleagues over the last several years. David Rothenberg has been a constant source of support and encouragement. Andrew Light has read as much of this book as anyone except myself, and has offered extensive critical comments on several chapters. Bob Sessions read the original manuscript proposal to Indiana University Press, and articulated the core concern in the book: the culturally variant relationships of nature and culture. Chapter 7 is evidence of the constructive response Arne Naess has provided to my work. Greta Gaard has been a constant ecofeminist friend and conversation partner. Karen J. Warren has supported my work in environmental philosophy from the beginning, and published several of the chapters in earlier versions. Bryan Norton and Paul B. Thompson share many of the concerns discussed in this book, although perhaps not my conclusions, and I value their friendship. I also acknowledge Shari Collins-Chobanian's support and help. Gary Snyder read and responded to an earlier version of chapter 7, a particularly rewarding experience given my admiration for Snyder and his work for more than twenty-five years.

Much of my firsthand knowledge of India derives from several extended trips there, including a semester I spent in residence at the Centre for Research on a New International Economic Order in Chennai (CReNIEO), formerly Madras. Dr. K. Rajaratnam, director of CReNIEO, and Dr. P. J. Sanjeeva Raj, academic dean, opened many doors for me, and frequently shared their intimate knowledge of the development process in India. I extend my thanks also to Dr. Desmond D'Abreo and Margaret D'Abreo, whose integrity and dedication to real Gandhian development has been a benchmark for this book. Professor Ramjee Singh of the Gandhian Institute of Studies in Varanasi kindly published an earlier version of chapter 4. I also mentored an extraordinary group of American students during a semester in India. Their post-India lives have been a great joy to behold.

At Gustavus Adolphus College, I gratefully acknowledge the support of Raymond Sponberg and Florence Sponberg, who endowed the Raymond and Florence Sponberg Chair of Ethics, which I hold. It provided much-needed support for the completion of this book. I have also received extraordinary support from President Axel Steuer; from my dean, Elizabeth Baer; and from my colleagues in the Department of Philosophy: Douglas Huff, George Georgakarakos, Lisa Heldke, and (at least in spirit) Laurent Dechery. Friends and colleagues in the Gustavus environmental studies program have furnished an irreplaceable intellectual home. These include Don Scheese, Mark Johnson, Tim Sipe (now at Franklin and Marshall College), Bob Douglas, and, especially, Claude Brew.

At Indiana University Press I have enjoyed the wise counsel of

Joan Catapano, Jane Lyle, Toni Mortimer, LuAnne Holladay, and Grace Profatilov.

This book can only be dedicated to my family. With my children, Evan and Ian, I have shared expeditions in search of the Nilgari Taar, and played in crocodile-infested rivers. Without Rita, my wife and best friend, I cannot even imagine where, and who, I would be today. Their love, encouragement, and support made this book possible.

Several chapters are significantly revised versions of previously published articles and essays. My appreciation goes to the editors and readers of these journals and collections.

Chapter 3: "Making Peace with the Earth: Indigenous Agriculture and the Peace Politics of the Green Revolution," *Environmental Ethics*, vol. 17, no. 1 (1995): 59–73.

Chapter 4: "Gandhian Legacies: Indigenous Resistance to Development in India and Mexico," in *Mahatma Gandhi: 125 Years*, ed. Manmohan Choudhuri and Ramjee Singh (Varanasi, India: Gandhian Institute of Studies, 1995), 24–34. (To commemorate the 125th anniversary of Gandhi's birth.)

Chapter 5: "Women's Knowledge as Expert Knowledge: Indian Women and Ecodevelopment," in *Ecofeminism: Women, Culture, Nature*, ed. Karen J. Warren (Bloomington: Indiana University Press, 1997).

Chapter 7: "Dogen, Deep Ecology, and the Ecological Self," *Environmental Ethics*, vol. 16, no. 2 (1994): 195–213, and "A State of Mind Like Water: Ecosophy T and the Buddhist Traditions," *Inquiry*, vol. 39, no. 2 (1996): 239–53 (special issue in honor of Arne Naess).

Chapter 8: "Toward an Ecological Ethic of Care," *Hypatia*, vol. 6, no. 1 (1991): 60–74.

Chinnagounder's Challenge

Part 1
Nature and Culture

Living at the Margins

1

Turning South

THE AMERICAN INVENTION OF NATURE

This book began to take shape before dawn on a crowded public bus headed west out of Kathmandu, Nepal. As night gave way to the faint hint of morning light, I began to notice my traveling companions: women with bulging cloth satchels marked out their territory in the aisle in preparation for a long journey; chickens stirred in their cages, waking with the rest of us. As we entered a long series of switchbacks climbing out of the Kathmandu Valley, I noticed children leaning out the windows, suffering queasy stomachs.

Our arrival at the top of the ridge was greeted with the sunrise seeming to explode over the entire Nepali Himalaya. It also meant plunging down another series of switchbacks on the far side of the ridge. As the rear of the bus swung out at each turn dislodging rocks that tumbled into a deep gorge, I noticed the bus seemed to be without brakes. It was a long, harrowing trip: a "six hour" ride turned into twelve.

I had no trouble locating my destination, the Terai, a dense jungle at the southern border of Nepal where the Himalayan plateau falls off into the heat and dust of India. Everyone on the bus had somehow learned where I was going; almost everyone turned to communicate that I had arrived. As I stumbled off the bus, giving thanks that my journey was over, I quickly sensed that something was wrong. Tadi Bazaar was a dust-choked trading village and bus stop miles from anywhere I wanted to be. The "jungle camp" was another two hours by oxcart across dry river beds. After the hours in the bus I decided to walk, covering several miles of cracked earth, a mosaic shaped by the last monsoon rains.

Finally, I arrived at the camp: six canvas tents arranged in a semi-circle. Three teenage boys presided as hosts. Still, there was no jungle. After a hasty dinner I asked—in a carefully controlled voice—where I might find the jungle. My hosts slowly pointed west, down a road that disappeared into a dusty haze. Again, I decided to walk.

Looking to my right, I saw one ancient tree, the only vegetation in sight. Straight ahead, the sun was already setting, appearing to set the dusty road ablaze. It was then that I noticed sounds, faint in the distance, the sound of bells: animals returning to the village at night. Then, I heard the sound of human voices—women's voices. At last, the figures of women began to appear out of the sun. First one, then small groups, and eventually many women. Each walked under heavy bundles of neatly bound wood carried aloft on their shoulders.

I had found the jungle.

I realized quickly that *I* was one reason for the destruction I was witnessing: tourists expect hot meals; some demand hot showers. I also understood why I had seen only boys back at the jungle camp. Gathering firewood is "women's work."

The advertisements for a "jungle camp" were not false, strictly speaking. At one time, the area had been a jungle. Under pressure from foreign conservation groups, the Nepalese government created the nearby Chitwan National Park to attract high-paying foreign tourists. Indigenous people had been relocated to marginal lands on the park's borders to create a "wilderness" within the park. They were now surviving on low budget tourists, like myself, by illegally cutting away at the edges of the receding jungle. There, they risked their lives daily by sneaking tourists into the jungle past King Birendra's royal guards. At the time of my arrival, the guards had recently flown in on military helicopters to check on the king's herd of elephants, which were about to be shipped to zoos around the world.

I later discovered that my experience in the Terai was not unique. Indian sociologist Ramachandra Guha has questioned Project Tiger, an international project designed to save rare tigers at the expense of indigenous people. As Guha has written,

> Because India is a long settled and densely populated country in which agrarian populations have a finely balanced relationship with nature, the

setting aside of wilderness areas has resulted in the direct transfer of resources from the poor to the rich. . . . The initial impetus for setting up
parks for the tiger and other large mammals such as the rhinoceros and
elephant came from two social groups, first, a class of ex-hunters turned
conservationists belonging mostly to the declining Indian feudal elite and
second, representatives of international agencies, such as the World Wild-
life Fund (WWF) and the International Union for the Conservation of Nature and Natural Resources (IUCN), seeking to transplant the American
system of national parks onto Indian soil. (Guha 1989: 75)

My experience in the Terai along with Guha's reading of recent Indian
ecological history raise an unsettling dilemma for us in the first world,
for environmentalists and friends of economic "development" alike.
What makes sense as a preservation strategy in the first world often
has disastrous consequences in the third world. Wilderness preservation may seem logical in sparsely settled areas of North America,[1] but
it often benefits neocolonial elites and disenfranchises the poor in the
densely populated third world. As Guha implies, well-intentioned environmentalists who do not check their first world biases toward nature conservation typically end up working with the most regressive
social forces in third world countries. In defending justice for the environment, they often play unwitting roles in causing gross violations
of human justice.

The classic American environmental dispute, one that still shapes
our thinking about the environment, occurred in the first decade of
the twentieth century over the fate of the Hetch Hetchy Valley in California's Yosemite National Park. It pitted John Muir, singer of praise
to wilderness, against Gifford Pinchot, who advocated damming the
valley to provide a constant water supply to the city of San Francisco.
Pinchot was a utilitarian. He believed natural resources must be developed scientifically for human benefit in a democratic society. A
populist, he feared the European tradition that reserved access to the
environment for the wealthy. Pinchot's academic training was in forestry; he described his profession as "tree farming" (Worster [1977]
1994: 267). To his environmentalist critics, it is severe criticism to say
that Pinchot brought an "agricultural mind" to the question of wilderness.

Reflecting Pinchot's utilitarian influence, to this day national forests are overseen by the Department of Agriculture. Congress requires that they are managed to produce the maximum sustainable
amount of timber each year. As Pinchot said, "'The purpose of Forestry, then, is to make the forest produce the largest possible amount
of whatever crop or service will be most useful, and keep on produc-

ing it for generation after generation of men and trees'" (quoted in Worster: 267).

Muir, Pinchot's lifelong critic, insisted that nature has value in itself, apart from human uses. It has value even if never experienced by human beings. Muir was instrumental in establishing the national park system, which is run by the Department of the Interior with its own legislative mandate, not the Department of Agriculture. Logging and mining are prohibited in national parks.

Although Pinchot won the battle—the valley was dammed—the shock over this use of one of America's first and greatest national parks has worked in favor of natural preservation in the long term. In 1964, Congress passed the Wilderness Act, which gave the legal definition to the (immigrant) American concept of wilderness. The act makes clear that the need for formally designated wilderness areas was in response to "an increasing population, accompanied by expanding settlement and growing mechanization." Since wilderness is necessary as a brake to the rapid growth of American economic culture, the most famous words of the act come as no surprise: "A wilderness, in contrast with those areas where man and his own works dominate the landscape, is hereby recognized as an area where the earth and its community of life are untrammeled by man, where man himself is a visitor who does not remain" (Wilderness Act 1964: sections 2a and 2c).

From an American perspective, the alternatives Muir and Pinchot represented seem exhaustive: nature either exists as a resource for human use, or it has value in itself, apart from permanent human settlement. In fact, however, the act was a series of political compromises that continue to frustrate efforts to both protect integrated ecosystems and respect cultural integrity. Despite its apparent separation of nature from culture, it also defines wilderness as an "enduring resource" for present and future generations of Americans.

The focus of the act was on scenic value rather than ecological value. Only when it comes to the last of its management goals does it mention that wilderness areas "may also contain ecological, geological, or other features of scientific . . . value" (section 2c). Critics of the wilderness system often point out that the arbitrary borders of national parks and officially sanctioned wilderness areas typically are not designed to protect entire ecosystems. The slaughter of bison leaving Yellowstone National Park in search of food during the winter of 1997 is only the latest of many such examples.[2]

In addition to its ambiguous ecological legacy, many Native American critics of the wilderness system contend that it is a neocolonial attempt to enforce the legal separation of tribes from their traditional lands. As with so many American legal and moral traditions, the act represents as universal, definitions of nature and culture that are, in fact, culturally specific reflections of a dominant population.

Given this history, we can understand why the Muir/Pinchot debate looks to Guha like a local dispute, not a debate about global environmental ethics. The debate was an attempt to establish moral limits to economic growth using the most familiar categories of Western moral philosophy: extrinsic and intrinsic value. The utilitarians and their contemporary incarnations, neoclassical economists, attempt to reduce all value to extrinsic value. Immanuel Kant and his heirs in the human and natural rights traditions emphasize intrinsic value as the foundation of all value.

Granted, since moral standing in the Enlightenment tradition was intended to apply almost exclusively to human beings (and then, not to all human beings), the Muir/Pinchot debate does mark an important extension.[3] Nature was often the philosopher's standard example of something that could not have moral standing. However, as Guha points out, the debate over the moral standing of nature is "radical" only as a new direction within the oldest categories in Western moral philosophy.

If we attend carefully to Guha's challenge to American definitions of nature and culture, we will see that neither Pinchot nor Muir allow us to understand the problems environmentalists face in India, and in many other third world countries. The concern Guha highlights is not captured by Pinchot's utilitarian philosophy of wise use for capitalist interests, either as an economic resource for capital development or as a refuge from urban life. It is also not captured by Muir's vaguely Kantian philosophy of separation of nature from (capitalist) culture. Recall that Guha began, "Because India is a long settled and densely populated country in which agrarian populations have a finely balanced relationship with nature." Guha's interest in traditional agriculture as a central ecological problem derives from his overriding interest in how to maintain traditional *relationships* between nature and human culture, relationships to land that are disrupted when *either* first world attitude intrudes. For very different reasons, both Pinchot and Muir assume that nature and culture are categorically distinct.

Guha's observation should cause us to question whether the terms of the American debate are truly exhaustive. If we shift from narrow Western perspectives on the environment to a more inclusive set of perspectives, the critical environmental problem is not wilderness[4] preservation in the distinctively American sense, although I do not deny this is a critical issue in many contexts, especially if wilderness preservation really means biodiversity preservation. The critical problems have to do with local reconciliations of culture with nature: biologically diverse agriculture and fishing, traditional access to land and water, and social forestry.[5] The critical environmental issue for the great majority of the world's people is the struggle to maintain traditional relationships to particular places: their ecocommunities.

Close to 80 percent of the world's people do not live in the first world; most lead agrarian lifestyles. Despite our images of its crowded cities, 80 percent of India's population is rural. Most of these people are poor, despite the glowing reports on India's new middle class that regularly appear in the Western press. Unless we are satisfied to project the biases of a small minority of the world's people onto the majority, we need to subject our Western, often urban, industrial assumptions about the relationship of nature and culture to rigorous scrutiny. We need to examine *both* the first world defense of wilderness, to the extent that it is a reaction to first world economic urbanism, and the idea that nature exists only as a resource. If we want to reconcile environmental justice with justice for the disenfranchised people of the world, we must learn from the daily lives of third world women and their communities as they mediate between nature and human cultures.

THE AMERICAN INVENTION OF CULTURE

Just as we unknowingly project first world definitions of *nature* onto the third world, so we project first world definitions of *culture*. Such tensions often boil over at international conferences. The International Conference on Population and Development (Cairo, Egypt, September 5–13, 1994) was one such conference.

Conflict over commas and brackets in the so-called Cairo Document, the official document of the conference, was widely reported in the Western press. The press depicted the conference as a showdown between first world liberal feminists, who wanted to secure language guaranteeing a woman's right to an abortion, and the determination of the Catholic Church to prevent any such language, even at the expense of the conference itself.

Not so widely reported were the objections of third world women to the very terms of this debate. They charged that it falsely polarized the conference, silencing the concerns of women in Asia, Africa, and Latin America, where population increases shape the daily patterns of women's lives. Despite its title, which promised equal discussion of population *and* development, the conference tilted toward a one-sided dispute over reproductive rights and contraceptive technology. The broader issues connected to family planning, issues that affect the ability of women to function effectively within their communities—the right to development and environmental and economic justice—went largely unreported.

Indian social and environmental activists, Vandana Shiva and Mira Shiva, were prominent among those who expressed their frustration at being caught in the crossfire between first world liberals and conservatives. They condemned the liberals, whose concern for "individual sexual freedom," as they put it, fostered the image that "women's rights" are "antithetical to the rights of children and women's freedom as based on neglect of the family." "By ignoring the social, economic and family responsibilities that third world women carry, the exclusive focus on 'sexual and reproductive rights' is disempowering, not empowering, for third world women because it makes women appear socially irresponsible" (Shiva and Shiva 1994: 16). In turn, the Shivas argued, the appearance of a vacuum in social responsibility allows conservative forces to press for a "family values" agenda which forces women back into oppressive social structures and makes truly effective family planning choices difficult.

Caught between such forces, technological advances are often turned against women: the "right" to an abortion combined with the increasing availability of prenatal sex testing, for example, often results in disastrous consequences for third world women. Amartya Sen captured the dimensions of this problem when he compared actual female births with "normal" birthrates and found that "more than 100 million women are missing" (Sen 1990). In India alone, the sex ratio of women to men has declined from 972 women per 1,000 men in 1901, to 929 in 1991 (India 1993: 16–17). It is not at all clear that either the right to an abortion, or the church's "family values," significantly help third world women to function effectively within their communities.

It has become commonplace in development *theory,* if not yet in practice, that recognition of women's roles in their communities is critical to the long-term success of locally-based community development. The Shivas' reaction to the Cairo conference should make us pause, however, as we consider the just relationship of population and environmental policies for the next century. Their point is fundamental: liberal individualism, which we might think of as being allied with the goals of third world women, systematically misreads the complex web of social connections that position such women within their societies. It rewrites their social and moral identities according to a first world narrative of women's progress. This means that critical terms in the liberal narrative of progress are themselves contested. The very terms of the international population debate, they assert, are colonizing.

We can see that many of the Shivas' objections derive from five general features of Western thinking about ethics. All tend to systematically misrepresent traditional social patterns in the third world, particularly in indigenous communities. These are:

1. *Universalism* about ethical claims (sometimes combined, strangely, with the idea that moral choice is simply a matter of maximizing one's subjective preferences). We will witness one version of this position in the next chapter in Jeremy Bentham's insistence that ethics is a matter of abstract rules that reduce to "a common standard" and are prior to culture, so that, as far as ethical discourse is concerned, "all places are alike." This might easily account for the tendency to "talk past" the third world, to think that the particularities of third world cultures do not count.

2. *Individualism* about the moral subject, which increasingly corrodes the possibility of community and the moral standing of non-individuals. Communities then become merely a "fictitious *body*," in Bentham's words. This distinctively Euro-American construction of moral personhood contrasts starkly with Asian and African cultures where a person's social identity is often primary (Kasulis 1981: chap. 1). One functions fully as a person only to the extent that one has a role within a culture. Cultures are then hardly "fictitious"; they constitute what it means to be a person.

3. The conception of moral judgments as issuing from an autonomous *will.* Moral rationality, if it is still understood as inquiring about human goods, is reduced to instrumental reason. It is understood as the "scientific" ability to calculate over quantities of discrete individuals. In other versions of political liberalism, the moral will does not engage the good at all.

4. The priority of *right* over the substantive goods of diverse communities. It follows, therefore, that there is a distinction between ethics proper, and mere culturally specific social arrangements.

5. Finally, out of these deep assumptions about ethics comes the conception of *progress* defined in terms of the replacement of culturally specific practices and social identities with a culturally "neutral" moral rationality.

These five commitments cover a diverse set of positions in Western moral philosophy. Ethics courses in American universities are built around the disputes engendered by the expansive distinction between teleological, or utilitarian, approaches to ethics, and deontological, or Kantian, approaches. It is easy to see why disputes between these two approaches would be vigorous. Broadly, the first approach says, "In determining the good, consider only the consequences of our actions." The second says, "In determining the right, never consider consequences; only universal principles or the intentions of an autonomous moral will count." These positions are, indeed, different. However, if we step back and view them from an outsider's perspective, we can see that both are characteristic of a uniquely Western angle of moral vision. They are both variations of *political liberalism*.

Moreover, one can easily appreciate that several of the above features might encourage problems when either variant of political liberalism turns its moral gaze to the rest of the world. Despite their differences, they share deep theoretical expectations about the function of ethics. The danger inherent in liberalism's universalist and monist moral stance, for example, is expressed in James Mill's confident declaration: "Exactly in proportion as *Utility* is the object of every pursuit, may we regard a nation as civilized" (Mill [1817] 1858: 2:105).

Far from making cross-cultural ethical disputes more transparently situated in today's "global village," the deep assumptions that political liberalism makes about moral personhood and community actually function to obscure moral communication. They encourage us to treat deeply out-of-context disputes as if they were in-context. If the Shivas are right, the impact of such expectations is felt concretely, not just in theory.

I am not suggesting that we in the West have no concern for community. Community relations have become ever more problematic principally when they impinge on individual freedom. In the United States, especially, Alexis de Toqueville's fears in the nineteenth century for the fate of community have largely come true. Toqueville admired the ways early Americans found to enliven the bonds of community without resorting to the hereditary hierarchies of Europe. He found that we balanced individualism with commitment to community, particularly through volunteer organizations and a lively public press. But he worried that our strength, when pressed too far, would become weakness, that healthy individualism would become corrosive. Writing in the 1830s, Toqueville warned, "Thus, not only does democracy make every man forget his ancestors, but it hides his descendants and separates his contemporaries from him; it throws him back forever upon himself alone and threatens in the end to confine him entirely within the solitude of his own heart" (Toqueville 1945: 99).

These misgivings about the role of community in public life have sparked an energetic and important debate between liberals who support a deontological form of political liberalism and their communitarian critics over the role of community in shaping moral identity. The teleological form of political liberalism has not been a major player since both sides in the current debate took shape in reaction to an earlier debate over utilitarianism.[6]

Contemporary deontological liberalism finds its most distinguished contemporary expression in the work of John Rawls. According to the position as originally articulated by Rawls, justice requires impartiality. It requires that we operate from behind a "veil of ignorance" which prevents us from knowing who we are, where we are located in our community. We cannot know our race or sex, for example, because the basic commitments of a democratic society cannot be racist or sexist. As Rawls says, from behind the veil, "parties do not know their conceptions of the good." While not egoists, neither are we "conceived as not taking an interest in one another's interests" (Rawls 1971: 13).

Rawls intended his description of the original position to be precultural. The original position is the hypothetical framework from which the principles of any democratic society may be established. Rawls needed to assume, however, that rational agents in this position are individuals who operate according to an economic model of rationality: "the concept of rationality must be interpreted as far as possible in the narrow sense, standard in economic theory, of taking the most effective means to given ends" (Rawls 1971: 14).

Rawls's concern was that in a deeply pluralistic society, where different individuals have different conceptions of substantive social goods, justice must remain neutral between competing claims. The right precedes the good. Justice is procedural, not substantive. It requires that we set aside all the moral sentiments that bind a community together: benevolence, altruism, and care for others. Moral rationality is modeled on "economic rationality," in which the individual maximizes his or her own self-interest.

Rawls's position in A Theory of Justice has been challenged by communitarian critics. One criticism is that it appears to beg the question of moral personhood in favor of a narrowly liberal conception of the moral self. Despite his claim to identify the original position of any moral agent concerned to establish a democratic society, Rawls's account of moral rationality describes the economic rationality of the political liberal (Sandel 1982). Pluralist critics, whether communitarians such as Michael Sandel and Michael Walzer, or liberals such as Richard Rorty, tend to believe that even this minimalist account of rationality is biased in favor of a Western account of rationality. Universalism begs the question when it assumes its own account of moral rationality as part of its proof of universalism. In other words, there is no "moral Esperanto" (Walzer 1994: 7).

Rawls has always been concerned to accommodate legitimate pluralism in a theory of political liberalism. However, his critics have driven him to clarify his earlier project. In his more recent book, *Political Liberalism*, Rawls distinguishes between a "comprehensive" liberalism of the sort one finds in Kant or Mill, and a more cautious kind of political liberalism based merely on the idea of an "overlapping consensus of reasonable comprehensive doctrines" (Rawls 1993b: 134). Unlike Kant or Mill, who try to establish the ontological reality of the liberal individual, Rawls in his later view depends only upon a practical consensus among diverse people with a variety of interests.

The accommodation of pluralism has become an important concern for liberals who are basically sympathetic to Rawls, but who do not think Rawls went far enough, and for critics who reject liberalism altogether.[7] These are extremely important debates about the future of democratic practice. However, the concerns of political liberals in extending a Rawlsian framework are often irrelevant to my concerns here. Their concern is to accommodate pluralism within the framework of societies with traditions of political liberalism that face increasing demands for recognition of cultural difference from within those societies. These debates are largely in-context. My concern is usually with out-of-context debates: trans-cultural debates, often between the first and third worlds. Here, one side comes out of the tradition of political liberalism. The other side, as the Shivas demonstrate, if it experiences political liberalism at all, typically experiences it as the voice of colonialism.[8]

I am open to the suggestion that some formerly colonial contexts have benefited from political liberalism. In fact, it is hard to imagine where India would be today without its commitment to a secular state. However, this does not negate the distinction between liberalism as an expression of Enlightenment culture, and liberalism as an artifact imported from another cultural context. The major point of the next chapter is to illustrate historically the problems of transporting liberalism from one context to another.

Since my concern is frequently as much with the historical impact of philosophical views on real people as with the subtleties of contemporary philosophical debate, critics may point out that I often run together two importantly different forms of political liberalism. Chantal

Mouffe, for example, defends a new ideal of "radical democracy." She grants that, "One objection to a strategy of democratization conceived as the fulfillment of the principles of liberal democracy is that capitalist relations constitute an insuperable obstacle to the realization of democracy." Mouffe understands Rawls's later position as recognizing just such a distinction between the principles required for democracy and capitalism. "Political liberalism and economic liberalism," she contends, "need to be distinguished and then separated from each other" (Mouffe 1992a: 2).

I am sympathetic to the need for debate within politically liberal societies on the meaning of democratic practice. In the final chapter I return to this idea, arguing that we require a new, distinctively American, debate on the relationships of nature and culture. If it is *our* debate, and does not simply appropriate the terms of the debate elsewhere, we must see it as consciously engaging new possibilities for the liberal tradition. However, most of the debates considered before the end of the book are out-of-context. They are debates where we cannot simply *assume* a common tradition of liberalism.

In addition to addressing a different set of issues from those that usually concern the liberalism/communitarianism debate, I am also skeptical of the possibility of extending political liberalism to cover the sorts of deeply cross-cultural debates that concern me here. I doubt, for example, whether the political liberal can specify a concept of the moral individual, even understood as a practical consensus, without begging the question in favor of a Western conception of individualism and moral rationality. Recall the Shivas' objection: "By ignoring the social, economic and family responsibilities that third world women carry, the exclusive focus on 'sexual and reproductive rights' is disempowering, not empowering, for third world women because it makes women appear socially irresponsible" (Shiva and Shiva 1994: 16). When the liberal separates "the right" from substantive conceptions of "the good," questions of justice are divorced from women's culturally specific social identities.

Although we may modify political liberalism to further accommodate pluralism, no version of liberalism can fully address the concerns that arise in ensuring cultural integrity. Liberalism, for example, may be able to justify affirmative action quotas as *temporary* measures designed to equalize access to social goods. But, given its pre-cultural theory of justice, it cannot endorse *permanent* measures designed to secure cultural survival. Laws mandating that schools teach in the language of a minority culture as a way of preserving cultural integrity, for example, violate liberal assumptions about the cultural neutrality of justice. Of course, liberals deny that the state has any obligation to provide such guarantees. However, the argument for this appears to assume political liberalism.

I am still concerned, furthermore, with the model of moral rationality that liberalism offers. According to all versions of liberalism, rational choice is purely *preferential* or *voluntaristic:* Why do we choose certain life plans over others? Well, "we just do" because that is what we prefer. Choice is merely a psychic inventory of the wants and preferences we already happen to have. It does not prescribe how we *ought* to live together. Yet, this is often the sort of concern at the heart of cross-cultural disputes.

Another concern involves questions of what it means to explain a culturally thick moral reason for action. Liberalism is committed to a reductionist theory of explanation according to which thick, culturally resonant self-interpretations of moral behavior are really premoral, or reducible to abstract, culturally neutral sets of moral rules. Even when it is taken to be nothing more than a practical consensus, it is perfectly possible that an insider to a practice can be silenced in his or her own account of life goals. Unless there is a neutral standpoint from which to judge people's self-explanations, it is always dangerous business to conclude that they are mistaken. How can we ever be in a position to decide that ours is the only available hypothesis?

Most important, however, is the fact that in many deeply cross-cultural disputes there is no relevant state. Disputes over the GATT agreement, for example, go to the World Trade Organization (WTO), which was set up to adjudicate free trade disputes. Few would claim that the WTO, which is governed by business executives appointed by heads of state, is a democratic institution. These are not disputes within the political culture of liberalism. They are *about* the scope of liberalism.

Aficionados of the liberalism/communitarianism debate will not find these reasons convincing, briefly stated as they are. However, this book might best be thought of as an experiment in envisioning another alternative, rather than as an extended response to liberalism. The alternative proposed here rests on respecting the fact that many cross-cultural disputes are deeply out-of-context. They are disputes in which communication has not yet begun because basic convictions diverge. Moreover, this book attempts to imagine the possibility that there are ways to foster "democratic discourse" without assuming a moral Esperanto. The alternative approach assumes that, for the most part, people are experts about their own lives, as well as their culturally specific relationships to nature. It resists the temptation of powerful cultures to tell other cultures "what they are really saying." Rather than placing the autonomous, judging will at the center of all moral discourse, the alternative approach sees self-understanding as the goal of cross-cultural moral communication. Rather than erasing the Other, it requires the Other, now conceived as a conversational partner through whom one's moral identity can be elucidated.[9] Since the purpose of this form of moral conversation is to open the ground for discussion of substantive goods of the community, this is not a form of cultural relativism.

In the years since my experience in the Terai, I have come to believe that there are, indeed, *many* ways to understand the relationship between human culture and nature. Traditional people, for all their diversity, do tend to distinguish—in a variety of ways—between nature and culture, but they often understand the borders to be vague, provisional. Typically, the sense of community goes beyond the boundaries of the human community to include a sense of the relationships between people and a particular place.

As the women emerged from the sun carrying the remains of the jungle, I began to understand why women are so regularly caught "at the borders" between worlds that do not seek mutual understanding. When the biological commons that many poor third world women depend upon for food, fuel, and medicines is taken over and "developed," often by economic development programs that sound unimpeachable to Westerners, poor women and their communities suffer. Women are the world's farmers; they are the world's medical practitioners; and they are primarily responsible for child care. All these responsibilities depend upon a healthy environment, as well as political access to the environment. When inappropriate attitudes, whether foreign or domestic, are imported into contexts where they do not belong, women and their communities are most vulnerable to marginalization. Because of what poor women do, they usually have the most sophisticated knowledge of local environments. Yet, they are often the last to be consulted when change ("development") occurs.

The dilemma is that while these practices of caring for nature are typically experienced as oppressive by women and the world's poor, we—humanity, the planet—cannot do without them. The future of the planet urgently requires a global practice of localized care for the environment. Caring for the environment must, therefore, be transformed. Genuine caring cannot be "women's work," although women, because of their traditional roles, can take the lead in defining a new environmental practice.

We all live in ecocommunities. We all live in relationship to a particular place. However, it is a characteristic of "development" to obscure this, for example, through efforts to build a world network of food exports. While third world women and their communities live within very narrow ecological niches, it is common for wealthy elites, in the first and third worlds, to regard the entire planet as their ecological niche. To be dependent upon only local produce is considered "primitive," "backward"—an earlier form of production that is uncomfortably close to the border between nature and culture.

The fundamental issue is whether we can foster democratic, or at least relatively non-coercive, discourse about global change. We cannot simply assume that relationships between culture and nature are exclusively economic. Real cross-cultural communication requires that the moral and social dimensions of these relationships come to the forefront. This is important, not just for "them," but for us. Just as traditional communities are under pressure from change they cannot control, so it has often been noted by first world writers that rapid change tends to erode the sense of community here as well. Inner cities are breaking down; family relationships are failing in the suburbs. Family farms are being lost to large corporations at an alarming rate. Jobs are being exported to the third world for the sake of lower production costs. All these problems raise the hard capitalist question, "Who, and where, will the consumers be in the next century?" Despite vast differences between the first world and the third world, it may be that there is something we can learn from each other. Distance sometimes brings self-understanding. The common issue is how to maintain and foster the ecocommunity—familiar, enduring relationships to people and place—in the face of global change.

As Indian writer Ashis Nandy says, "a theory of freedom today must seriously consider and build upon the civilizational perspectives of those who, in their defeat, even when stripped of their autonomy, dignity and means of survival, have dared to reject the values of masculine achievement, productive work and technocratic expertise to protect and nurture, however clumsily, alternative concepts of compassion, freedom, justice and dissent" (Nandy 1987b: xvi). Nandy is correct; our freedom is at stake. The refugees from the Terai are not an isolated aberration. They are the avant garde, a new kind of refugee. They are not simply political refugees, although they are that. We in the first world have procedures for processing political refugees. They are environmental refugees,[10] people who are forced to migrate because their traditional environmental niche has spiraled off into chaos. The environmental crisis is a crisis of citizenship.

"SOLUTIONS" FOR THE THIRD WORLD

Before we can consider *moral* views about the relationships between "worlds," however, we must first examine the powerful and familiar intuition that such relationships are not moral at all. Garrett Hardin's proposed "ethics of the lifeboat" is among the most celebrated of these solutions. His now infamous image of the lifeboat has done much to polarize the first and third worlds. Hardin depicts first world people as occupying a few precious seats in a lifeboat. They are surrounded by third world hordes floundering in rough seas, begging for a hand. He argues that the only "realistic" thing to do is to let them drown. To "Ted Kennedy liberals" who recoil from Hardin's suggestion, he proposes that they give up their own seat in the lifeboat (Hardin [1974] 1994: 284).

Hardin is typical of the first world environmentalist for whom third world population growth, and preservation of first world wilderness areas, are critical, interconnected issues. He is correct, at least, in seeing that first world conceptions of development are causing the circumstances for the environmental refugee. His solution, however, is Malthusian, the same Thomas Malthus whose colonial ideas were implemented in India in the eighteenth century and *caused* the modern phenomenon of the environmental refugee.

Hardin's deftly chosen image of the lifeboat forces us to accept several assumptions that are helpful to his argument. The very image of separability—we are either warm and dry in the boat, or struggling in the seas—encourages us to think that the two "worlds" are separate, conceptually and ethically. Since they are separate, we cannot raise the important issue of whether there is a third world *in* the first world. Our task is self-defense, defense against beings who are depicted as utterly different. The "real world," as Hardin tells the story, eliminates ethics. His message is that we in the first world are fools for the sake of ethics if we allow the first world to be engulfed by the problems of the third world. We should cut off all food aid and close our borders to prevent the third world's overflow from destroying our wilderness areas through their demands for land. "Complete justice," he concludes, "complete catastrophe" (Hardin [1974] 1994: 284).

The lifeboat image is bolstered by Hardin's equally famous account of "the tragedy of the commons," the biological commons. There is no problem as long as population density is low. Each family can graze its animals without having an impact on other families. But inevitably, someone will decide that they would be better off grazing more than need requires. When one family does it, others follow, and quickly environmental and human tragedy occur. This, according to Hardin, represents what is actually happening in a world of increasing population when no one owns the biological commons. It makes hard economic sense to convert the commons to private property to limit access to the land. If people starve, well, we are back to talk of lifeboats.

Hardin's logic is enticing to first world residents and wealthy third world interests who know nothing of, or simply do not care about, traditional communal methods of environmental protection.[11] It rings true to those who believe that rugged individualism and the institution of private property will solve problems of social and environmental conflict. Hardin's perspective also appeals because it resonates with the Western idea of realpolitik: politics and ethics must be held apart. To those who point out that the private property interests of colonialism were part of the *cause* of overpopulation and increasingly desperate use of the environment, Hardin conveniently responds that he cannot be morally responsible for the past. He was fortunate to be born among the victors, and has no inclination to change places with the vanquished (Hardin 1968: 284).

Hardin is characteristic of a group of contemporary first world writers who depict relationships between communities as non-moral, as requiring hardheaded economic and political calculation for the sake of survival in the first world. While Hardin sees himself as defending the first world environment, and this has made him a hero to certain self-styled radical American environmentalists, his claim to a hardheaded, rational, non-ethical stance has much in common with those who want to exploit the third world's environmental resources for the sake of first world economic growth.

Lawrence Summers, U.S. secretary of the treasury, once chief economist of the World Bank (the principal agency the first world created to "develop" the third world), argued in an infamous World Bank internal memorandum that the third world may be "under-polluted." It would make sense, he said, to shift highly polluting industries from the industrialized first world to the developing third world. The first of the three reasons he offered for this transfer of wastes provides the clearest example I know of what might be called the "commodotization" of the third world:

> The measurement of the costs of health-impairing pollution depends on the foregone earnings from increased morbidity and mortality. From this point of view a given amount of health-impairing pollution should be done in

the country with the lowest cost, which will be the country with the lowest wages. I think the economic logic behind dumping a load of toxic waste in the lowest-wage country is impeccable and we should face up to that. (Summers, p. 66)

According to Summers's "economic logic," the worth of a person's life is determined by his income. Since third world residents already have shorter life expectancies, the least (economic) harm occurs in killing them with toxic waste. The lives of first world residents are literally worth more because we make more money. Although they would regard their goals as different, there is an undeniable echo between Hardin's image of the drowning third world hordes to whom we have no ethical connection and Summers's calculation of a person's worth.[12]

Hardin and Summers are not alone in arguing that, when it comes to relations between the first and third worlds, economics trumps ethics. Consider the exceptionally candid opinion of Jim MacNeill, principal advisor to Maurice Strong, who organized the 1992 United Nations Conference on Environment and Development, the Rio Summit:

Economic activity today is concentrated in the world's urban/industrial regions. Few if any of these regions are ecologically self-contained. They breathe, drink, feed and work on the ecological capital of their "hinterland," which also receives their accumulated wastes. At one time, the ecological hinterland of a community was confined to the areas immediately surrounding it, and that may still be true of some rural communities in developing countries.

Today, however, the major urban/developing centres of the world are locked into complex international networks for trade in goods and services of all kinds, including primary and processed energy, food materials and other resources. The major cities of the economically powerful Western nations constitute the nodes of these networks, enabling these nations to draw upon the ecological capital of all other nations to provide food for their populations, energy and material for their economies, and even land, air, and water to assimilate their waste by-products.

This ecological capital, which may be found thousands of miles from the regions in which it may be used, form the "shadow ecology" of an economy. The oceans, the atmosphere (climate), and the other "commons" also form part of this shadow ecology. In essence, the ecological shadow of a country is the environmental resources it draws from other countries and the global commons. If a nation without much geographical resistance had to do without its shadow ecology, even for a short period, its people and economy would suffocate. . . . Western nations heavily engaged in global sourcing should be aware of the shadow ecologies and the need to pursue policies that will sustain them." (Nelson 1993: 7)

"Global sourcing" of "ecological capital" is a new expression for an old reality. For all the modern-sounding language ("The major cities of the economically powerful Western nations constitute the nodes of these networks"), sadly, little has really changed from the days of the East India Company. Progress in the first world depends upon the expropriation of resources—human and natural—from the third world. To justify this, the third world must be conceptually and ethically distant, a "hinterland."

Finally, consider the "solution" proposed by Edward Luttwack in his book *The Endangered American Dream*. He warns that the United States cannot survive a complete globalization of labor, a world in which a day's work at the computer pays as much in Botswana as in New York City. Before Americans see their standard of living eroded, industrialized democracies will turn fascist and militarist in their defense of first world economic privileges. Put bluntly, first world democracies must choose between perpetuating their own democratic institutions and justice for the third world (Luttwack 1993).

Does social justice in the first world *require* exploitation of the third world's people and their lands? Are first world wilderness advocates really allies of those who would exploit the third world? Is first world "wilderness" a luxury bought at the expense of the lives of third world people whose land we exploit instead of our own?

Hardin's lifeboat ethic and Luttwack's suggestion that the first world must exploit the third world to survive are strikingly concordant with the position called "war realism." War, this position holds, is neither morally good nor bad, but simply an inevitable fact of life.[13] The purpose of war is to protect one's nation, to effect a shift in power, and to win as quickly and convincingly as possible. Ethics has nothing to do with it. This modern sense of life perhaps began with Niccolò Machiavelli during the Renaissance as newly organized trade unions searched for a powerful response to royal and clerical power.

At least in its contemporary expressions, however, I contend that the strength of this view is a matter of self-deception. While it denies the applicability of ethics to cross-cultural discourse, this view is nothing more than a reiteration of one variant of political liberalism. It is a form of utilitarianism that has learned to emphasize utilitarians' scientistic claims about moral rationality so that its ardent individualism becomes the only way of conceiving moral agency. It reduces moral rationality to one kind of economic rationality. In the following two sections I draw out the moral underpinnings of this view, and define the kind of violence that occurs when the moral dimension of our lives becomes unspeakable.

THE INEVITABILITY OF ETHICS

Much of the language underpinning this retreat from ethics comes from the discipline of economics. Former U.S. presidential economic advisor, Charles L. Schultz, expressed this boldly when he said, "Market-like arrangements . . . reduce the need for compassion, patriotism, brotherly love, and cultural solidarity as motivating forces behind social improvement. . . . Harnessing the 'base' motive of material self-interest to promote the common good is perhaps the most important social invention mankind has achieved" (quoted in Daly and Cobb, Jr. 1989: 139). Such language has a powerful appeal in modern life. Many people, perhaps without understanding fully what they are committing to, accept the idea that the quality of life can be reduced to quantities. If this is assumed, the basic issues of this book cannot even be raised.

The economic model of life seems inevitable to many because it is self-referential. It admits no counterexamples. One way to open up such a system to the ethical dimensions of an issue is by carefully examining the terms of the position claiming to be non-moral, asking whether its own "story" is complete and consistent. This is what Herman E. Daly and John B. Cobb, Jr., do in their book *For the Common Good.*

Daly and Cobb point out that among the social and humanistic disciplines, economics has argued most effectively for a quasi-scientific status. It has made the most progress in defining economic "laws" from which human economic behavior can be deduced. Just as the physical sciences require a physical domain that acts in a consistent and orderly way, modern economics posits *Homo economicus:* the self-maximizing individual. As the authors say,

> The key assumptions [in economics] have to do with *Homo economicus,* that is, the understanding of the nature of the human being. Economic theory builds on the propensity of individuals to act so as to optimize their own interests, a propensity clearly operative in market transactions and in many other areas of life. Economists typically identify intelligent pursuit of private gain with rationality, thus implying that other modes of behavior are not rational. These modes include other-regarding behavior and actions directed to the public good. (Daly and Cobb, Jr. 1989: 5)

Classical economic theory has no place for the public good as something more than the collection of individual goods of autonomous individuals. Choosing to buy food from local farms in support of one's community instead of export crops from Central America (even if this costs more) is regarded as irrational. In technical terms, such irrational choices are "externalities."

> Whenever the abstracted-from elements of reality become too insistently evident in our experience, their existence is admitted by the category "externality." Externalities are ad hoc corrections introduced as needed to save appearances, like the epicycles of Ptolemaic astronomy. Externalities do represent a recognition of neglected aspects of concrete experience, but in such a way as to minimize restructuring the basic theory. As long as externalities involve minor details, this is perhaps a reasonable procedure. But when vital issues (e.g., the capacity of earth to support life) have to be classed with externalities, it is time to restructure basic concepts. (Daly and Cobb, Jr. 1989: 37)

Localized externalities, such as black lung disease, can be internalized and assigned a cost. The disease exists only in the coal industry among miners and their families. The operators of the coal mine and plant can be directed by the government to address the health costs of their industry, and the cost can be passed on to customers. Unfortunately, this is not the case with *pervasive* externalities. The greenhouse effect and acid rain cannot be traced to a "single localized activity" (Daly and Cobb, Jr. 1989: 55). Such pervasive externalities require major institutional changes, and the moral commitments of whole communities. Economic theory does not really provide an argument for the complete reduction of qualities to quantities. It simply refuses to recognize the existence of dimensions of life that cannot be explained within the theory.

Economics has also achieved the cultural standing of a science based on its assumption that "preferences" can be measured. That is, the rational system that will replace normative questions in our lives is based on the idea that we can canvass subjects on the question of how much they are willing to pay to have certain preferences satisfied. A group of American economists, for example, showed subjects pictures of their regions with varying degrees of air quality. They then asked how much the subjects were willing to pay in addition to their normal electricity bills to achieve various levels of air quality (Rowe, D'Arge, and Brookshire 1980; Brennan 1992; Sagoff 1988).

Such an experiment does show *something*. No doubt, quantifiable preferences often count in decisions concerning what we should do. The problem occurs when, as with Schultz, we begin to think that preferences exhaust what there is to say about rational decision-making. As Socrates pointed out long ago, there are preferences we should not have. I may prefer that my enemy cease to exist, and I can certainly put a price on what it would cost to effect that preference. Whole communities sometimes have preferences that they should not have, yet these preferences are treated in neoclassical economics as equal to other preferences.

At a deeper level, as Bryan Norton points out, there is a peculiar set of values that resists *any* attempt at quantification. He calls these "transformative values" (Norton 1987). Norton gives the example of a teenager who is forced to attend a concert of classical music. We assume that she prefers other kinds of music, and would never have gone to a classical concert on her own. To her surprise, she is engaged by what she hears. She begins listening to Mozart and develops a taste for classical music. Such transformative values, as Norton argues, are completely unpredictable. The intensity of impact on a person's previous preferences cannot be gauged in advance, and it varies widely from person to person. In short, there can never be a calculus for transformative values.

If Norton is right, there is always the possibility of a transformative experience that puts previous preferences into perspective. Such experiences are "externalities" that, in principal, cannot be quantified and internalized. In such cases, we do not simply reapply the "normal" moral categories. Transformative values often arise precisely in disputes on the borders between cultures that do not share basic assumptions about the language of morals. Because basic assumptions are questioned, a phase shift in moral understanding can be effected. With transformative values, we come to see and experience whole sets of "just" practices in a new light.

A TAXONOMY OF VIOLENCE

Out of a concern for inherently qualitative aspects of life, Daly and Cobb write with a sense of anguish for our future if economic theory is not transformed:

> We human beings are being led to a *dead* end—all too literally. We are living by an ideology of death and accordingly we are destroying our own humanity and killing the planet. Even the one great success of the program that has governed us, the attainment of material affluence, is now giving way to poverty. The United States is just now gaining a foretaste of the suffering that global economic policies . . . have inflicted on hundreds of millions of others. (Daly and Cobb, Jr. 1989: 21)

As an economist, and former staff member of the World Bank, Daly does not suggest that economics should cease to exist. Instead, he proposes a shift from the current conception of economics, which he calls "chrematistics," understood as "the manipulation of property and wealth so as to maximize short-term monetary exchange value to the owner," to an older meaning of "oikonomia," understood as "the management of the household so as to increase its use value to all members of the household over the long run" (Daly and Cobb, Jr. 1989: 138). Oikonomia, in short, is economics in service to community.

Homo economicus is the model of the human being that makes chrematistics possible. The shift to oikonomia, Daly and Cobb point out, will require a shift to the conception of the person as person-in-community. Unlike the ethically neutral self-maximizer, person-in-community is defined relationally, as an inherently social being.

Daly and Cobb call our attention to the death of our humanity and the planet which *Homo economicus* causes. The transformative shift they encourage to the idea of person-in-community is also a call for a new kind of language. It calls forth the ability to say what cannot be said, what is, at least, dismissed as irrational and marginal in the language of chrematistics. They point to the violence that occurs when the quality of one's life becomes unspeakable, and they call for the reemergence of the normative dimension of life.

If a dialogical space can be opened up in which such normative questions emerge, then I submit that two questions are critical: "What are the character and causes of violence in the contemporary world?" and "What are the effects of violence on the abilities of communities, in particular, to sustain, perpetuate, and transform their distinctive sets of values?"

It will take the entire book even to begin to answer these questions. I start here by offering a taxonomy of violence that will shape much of what I have to say in later chapters. The taxonomy provides an analytical structure for chapters 2, 3, and 4, chapters that examine a set of concrete issues ranging from the history of colonialism in India to agricultural change and the rhetoric of international debate over biodiversity. The critical point I draw out of the taxonomy is that there are certain kinds of contemporary violence which are exceedingly difficult for political liberals to recognize. Institutional and systemic violence, as I call them, are distinct from individual, one-on-one violence in that there may be no *intention* of one person to harm another.

In the final two chapters of the book, I take up the second of my two questions, considering how institutional and systemic violence are particularly damaging to communities. Communities are partially constituted by sets of *internal goods,* interconnected sets of goods that structure valuable practices within a cultural context. These are the goods that are most threatened by institutional and systemic violence.

Thirty years ago, Newton Garver wrote an essay titled "What Violence Is." It begins, "Most people deplore violence, some people embrace violence (perhaps reluctantly), and a few people renounce violence. But through all these postures there runs a certain obscurity: it is never entirely clear just what violence is" (Garver 1968: 819). Violence, as Garver notes, is almost universally condemned, yet it is a pervasive feature of our lives. Despite our spirited condemnations, it is a key ingredient in how we entertain ourselves—in the stories we tell our children, in great literature as well as pulp fiction, and in television and the cinema. It is also an essential feature of many of our most hallowed social institutions: in family life, religious affairs, and political history. Yet despite its pervasiveness, violence evades definition.

Garver's essay provides the taxonomy of violence that is still useful. Violence, he says, "occurs in several markedly different forms, and can usefully be classified into four different kinds based on two criteria, whether the violence is personal or institutionalized, and whether the violence is overt or covert and quiet" (Garver 1968: 819). The easiest of these to recognize, particularly given the liberal individualist assumptions of Western societies, is overt personal violence. Mugging, murder—these are cases of one-on-one physical violence that are routine features of the evening news.

In recent years we have become more sensitive to the second form of violence: covert personal violence. Child abuse or spousal abuse can be overt, physical violence, but they may also be covert, as in quiet psychological abuse. Being concealed from view does not lessen its damage. In fact, because it is often difficult to discern it may be more problematic, both philosophically and practically. A teacher's suspicions may be aroused immediately by a child's bruised body, but it may take prolonged contact to begin to suspect the kind of psychological violence that damages a child's self-respect.

Garver's third and fourth forms of violence are perhaps the least widely recognized in our culture. Violence can be institutional as well as individual. The military, the police force, the church, and the educational system are cultural institutions that, most believe, may use force which can be justified as a public good. However, they may go beyond force to violence that undermines the public good.

Some institutional violence is overt. Although the justification for use of military force is widely debated, it seems possible to distinguish between force that is justified for self-defense and military violence that cannot be justified as legitimate force. The victorious army that rapes and pillages is committing overt institutionalized violence.

As with covert personal violence, covert institutional violence may be difficult to identify. Yet, its damage is no less real. If a pervasive assumption is made within a school district that boys, but not girls, should take additional years of science or mathematics, this is covert institutional violence. If a public examination for firefighters makes unjustified assumptions that only men can be firefighters, this is covert institutional violence. If a retail store hires only white clerks because it operates on the assumption that its customers will not feel comfortable being waited on by persons of color, this is covert institutional violence.

Individual and institutional violence may often shade into one another. Institutional prejudice within the police force may facilitate acts of individual violence, such as occurred with Rodney King in Los Angeles, California. Sexism within the military makes gendered violence against individual women more likely, as in the Tailhook Scandal in the U.S. military. A legitimate question is, "How can we decide precisely when spousal abuse is purely 'personal,' and when it is violence that is facilitated by sexism or the law?" The search for a single distinction may be futile, and this may be due to the tendency of pervasive societal institutions to establish conditions that facilitate violence on several levels.

Institutional violence not only *facilitates* certain kinds of violence, it also creates new *categories* of violence. It was not an accident, for example, that the violence in the Tailhook Scandal was directed only against women. Institutional violence, in this case sexism within the military, operates on *categories* of persons. It identifies women as suitable recipients of violence because they are women.

When institutional violence becomes the status quo it generally moves from overt to covert forms. As Garver noted in 1968, very little overt violence is needed to sustain a system of deprivation in the ghettos of American cities. The riots in Los Angeles and other large cities are rare occasions of overt violence. Most of the systematic exclusion from important life options occurs in much more subtle and covert ways: in inferior school systems, in pervasive suspicions about the intentions of police, and in exclusion from economic opportunities.

Colonialism often began with a period of overt military violence, but, as was the history of British colonialism in India, it triumphed when it could become covert. The military prepared the way, but it was Thomas Macauley's system of education for the colonies that won the minds and hearts of an indigenous elite. In the caustic words of Ranajit Guha, "Macauley . . . prescribed [education] as a nutritive for native minds that had subsisted far too long on a poor diet of indigenous superstitions" (Guha 1989: 291).

When institutional violence takes on the character of the status quo, as it did in colonial India, the institutions that create and facilitate violence become synonymous with "justice." Colonial laws define "justice," and yet are forms of institutionalized violence. Resistance to institutional violence is often defined, therefore, as "unjust." Before the elimination of apartheid in South Africa, racist legal institutions were so pervasive that "justice" was equated with racist oppression. Opposition to this exclusion was outlawed.

Perhaps the critical question for liberal individualism is the assignment of individual moral responsibility. Yet, when violence is institutional, and especially when it becomes the covert status quo, no single individual may be responsible. One of the common responses to affirmative action programs is, "Why should I suffer? I was not involved in past injustices, and I never individually willed any form of discrimination on the basis of race or gender." If the only question were individual responsibility for individual violence, arguments for affirmative action would be impossible to defend. Put another way, if we focus solely on individual violence, as (at least one, simple, version of) liberal individualism encourages us to do, we cannot understand what it means to be oppressed by an institution.

Garver makes a fundamental point in distinguishing individual and institutional violence. I suggest, however, that *institutional* violence should be distinguished further from *systemic* violence. Institutional violence is violence made possible and facilitated by social organizations having relatively explicit rules and formal status within a culture. Examples are the educational system, the military, the police force, and the judicial and legislative systems. When such institutions promote violence, however, they often do so within a broader social context of systemic violence. Here, the rules are more vague, and there may be no identifiable social institutions that facilitate violence.

Racism, sexism, and colonialism are systemic patterns of thinking and cultural organization that often result in the creation of institutionalized forms of violence. For example, colonialism as a systemic form of violence required the British to export a formal system of education designed to create a loyal elite among their subjects. Systemic violence necessitated institutional violence. Similarly, racism as a form of systemic violence may lead a legislature to create a racially biased legal system in the name of "justice." That is, systemic violence may create an atmosphere conducive to the creation of violent institutions.

The taxonomy of violence[14] suggested here can be schematized as follows:

Type:	Overt:	Covert:
Individual:	muggings	personal threats
	murder	character assassination
Institutional:	police brutality	slavery
	terrorism	apartheid
Systemic:	domestic violence	sexism
	genocidal violence	racism
	land disenfranchisement	colonialism

Granted, there are problems with naming in a taxonomy like this. "Colonialism," for example, may refer either to a systemic set of attitudes, or to an actual set of institutions created to support and foster the basic attitudes. By the same token, a murder may be simply an act of one-on-one violence, but it may also be a direct result of institutional violence. The fact that these verbal shifts are possible is philosophically interesting and important. We have clear and precise terms for what we have clearly and precisely identified. The lack of such firm ground in discussing violence suggests that we may still not understand very well what violence is.

The observation that institutional and systemic forms of violence are difficult to recognize, given liberal individualist assumptions about ethics, explains the profound shift in moral perception which often occurs between insiders and outsiders to an institution. Those included in a structure and an institution and benefited by them will likely define the structures and institutions as promoting social welfare, as just. Those excluded by these structures and institutions are likely to view them differently. What appears just from within may be experienced as unjust from without. And yet, given the structural and institutional forms that such violence takes, there is no individual to blame. Two features, then, of systemic and institutional violence are critical: the powerful divergence of inside and outside perspectives, and the fact that, unlike individual violence, no single individual is culpable.

The first world project to develop the third world is an example of such a shift in moral perception. Seen from within, what could be more morally justified than the attempt to improve the "less fortunate"? Since we are categorically different from "them," since we inhabit a different world, our efforts on their behalf amount to performing a supererogatory act, something we do only out of the goodness of our own hearts: charity. Viewed from the other side, however, such acts of charity are regarded as cultural violence, the attempt to supplant community values with the misguided assumption that cultural development is equivalent to Western liberalism.

NEGOTIATING BORDERS: NATURE AND CULTURE

According to Daly and Cobb, neoclassical economic theory is an example of "the fallacy of misplaced concreteness," the fallacy of thinking that the world must be the way one's theory says it is. Defining all ethical considerations, all non-quantifiable commitments, as externalities, as outside the reality projected by economic theory, means that ethics becomes unspeakable, unreal, "subjective." As a remedy for this intellectual hubris, Daly and Cobb propose a radical idea: a conception of economics in service to community should actually look to see the way the world is outside of economic theory. They propose an "economia" of concreteness, an economics of the household inhabited in the daily lives of real people.

At the borders between the first and third worlds, marginalizing constructions of labor often mean that men's labor counts since they engage in wage-labor jobs. Women typically work in the "informal sector." When they do not produce incomes, or their incomes are understood solely as a supplement to men's labor, women's labor does not count. Studies show that women almost always work longer hours than men, but since their labor is heavily dedicated to maintenance of the family, their labor does not count toward "development." Only men's typical labor in a cash economy counts toward per capita income and gross national product.[15]

Similarly, while most of the world's medical care is delivered by women with natural medicines derived from plants and minerals, this kind of labor is often regarded with disdain. A doctor, we are told, is a highly trained professional who uses medicines that are active agents synthesized in the laboratory. In contrast, to say that someone is a "midwife" suggests that the person lacks extensive, highly theoretical training. Midwives do not count as "experts." In agriculture, as well, men are regularly deemed the "experts" despite the fact that most agricultural labor, and therefore most agricultural knowledge, falls within the domain of women's traditional work.

As long as we continue to project biases that raise mind work over body work, that praise theory over practice—or, more precisely, that see theory and practice as categorically distinct—we will never be able to understand the ecological expertise of indigenous women. As long as women's expertise is not valued, we are unlikely to understand our own culturally specific negotiation of the culture/nature relationship.

To reconstruct the marginalizing tendencies of the culture/nature distinction, we need a pragmatic, empirical approach to material culture. Paying attention to women's actual practices suggests an alternative reading of the culture/nature distinction that cannot be described as exclusively theory or practice; it is neither exclusively mental nor bodily. Traditional women typically define the eco-self through ordinary, daily interactions: with children and others, with foods and with the land that produces them, and with homeopathic medicines culled from animals and the ground. These are interactions that are distorted by the exclusive dualism of culture/nature.

The emphasis on material culture leads me to focus on traditional agriculture and medicine as core ecological issues. This is highly unusual in a philosophy book, so it is worth asking why these subjects come as a surprise. Philosophy—political liberalism is an example—has understood itself as the most theoretical of activities. As such, human activities that are clearly not pure theorizing—agriculture, child-bearing and child rearing, traditional medicines, day-to-day caring for the environment—have been regarded as beneath philosophical notice. In giving serious philosophical attention to these human activities, I am curious to learn what would be required to understand them sympathetically.

A pragmatic philosophy of material culture also allows for a different approach to environmental philosophy than was common among first generation environmental philosophers. Although the defense of nature's intrinsic value was well-intended, this idea either ended up splitting human beings from nature in order to defend nature, or it ended up saying that *all* beings have intrinsic value, in which case nothing morally distinctive is said about nature.

I agree strongly with many of the goals of environmental philosophers in defending nature against the machinery of cost-benefit analysis, but I articulate the problems with environmental destruction, not through the standard philosophical category of intrinsic goodness, but through the categories of systemic and institutional violence and community expertise. There has been much doubt raised about whether traditional moral categories that were designed to apply exclusively to human beings—such categories as intrinsic value and rights—can be extended to non-human and non-sentient entities. It does sound strange to say that we can oppress a rock, an ecosystem, or a dog. There can be no doubt, however, that we can treat an ecosystem or a non-human animal violently. The taxonomy of violence provides a way of understanding the dynamics of environmental destruction, as well as an account of why we do not fully recognize the violence that is occurring. Furthermore, where environmental philosophy takes it as its task to defend the moral standing of nature, a pragmatic philosophy of material culture takes it for granted that there are cultures in which the boundaries of community extend beyond the human to include the sense in which a set of internal goods only exists within an ecological niche. There are ecocommunities; the question then becomes, what prevents other communities from recognizing—and acting upon—this truth as well?

INSIDERS/OUTSIDERS

I have used the terms "first world" and "third world" rather uncritically to this point. Before proceeding further I need to clarify how I use these terms. I agree with Ashis Nandy when he writes, "The concept of the third world is not a cultural category; it is a political and economic category born of poverty, exploitation, indignity and self-contempt" (Nandy 1987b: 21). With the apparent disappearance of the so-called second world, the former Soviet Union and its sphere of influence, it becomes all the more clear that the first and third worlds remain only as a conceptual polarity. They exist solely in relation to each other, the "first" marking the center from which all things draw their meaning, the "third" marking the periphery that must exist if the center is to hold.

If the first and third worlds are not what Nandy calls "cultural categories," neither are they geographical terms. This is important, since I often use the term "third world" to refer to countries that are geographically distant from the primary audience for this book. But to accept the geographical definition blocks the point that there is a third world in the first world. Much of what I will say about the marginalization of indigenous people in India and Mexico, for example, applies equally to the process through which the native people of the United States, people of color, and women have been marginalized.

Understanding the "first" and "third" worlds as a system of marginalization raises another question. I began with the story of the Terai not only to introduce the subject, but to mark from the beginning that I write as an outsider. I came to problems of environment and community in the third world as a resident of the first world. This book was written primarily for a first world audience. It is legitimate to ask, then, "What are the roles of first world theorists in defending the interests of third world people?" "What are the appropriate roles of men in defending the interests of women?" "What are the roles of whites in defending the interests of people of color?"

Of course, the concept of insider/outsider is contextual: a white woman may be an insider in defending some feminist interests, but an outsider to defending the interests of women of color. In chapter 9, I will take up this issue in detail and propose an ethic of responsible criticism that recognizes the authority (though not the infallibility) of insiders, but also allows for carefully circumscribed roles for outsiders. Generally, I believe outsiders do have roles to play in defending the interests of insiders. One way of marginalizing the interests of women, for example, is to say that defending women's interests is the exclusive domain of women. Men can hear this as implying that they can afford to ignore feminist theorizing. Nevertheless, the outsider does not become an insider. An outsider works transparently through the position from which one starts.

First world theorists who articulate and defend the interests of third world women's environmental practices need to work through their positions as (sympathetic) outsiders. An analogy is helpful. Third world theorists in the last two decades have formulated theoretical positions that grow from their particular positions, for example, liberation theology in Latin America, and Dalit theology (or Dalit ideology) in India.[16] First world theorists might work to achieve transparency about their positions as recipients of certain kinds of privileges, and resolve to work against those privileges, partly by formulating a first world theoretical orientation that plays a transformative role in the first world parallel to liberation theology or Dalit theology in the third world.

2

The British Utilitarians and the Invention of the "Third World"

[The ontology of the center] did not come from nowhere. It arose from a previous experience of domination over other persons, of cultural oppression over other worlds. Before the *ego cogito* there is an *ego conquiro:* "I conquer" is the practical foundation of "I think." The center has imposed itself on the periphery for more than five centuries. But for how much longer? Will the geopolitical preponderance of the center come to an end? Can we glimpse a process of liberation growing from the people of the periphery?

Dussel (1980) 1985: 3

CENTER AND PERIPHERY

We are fast approaching the day when 80 percent of the world's people will live on Enrique Dussel's periphery, in the so-called third world. In a world where MTV and Sylvester Stallone movies are broadcast daily into small agricultural villages that had no television at all within recent memory, the ideology of center and periphery is built on advertising for Western commercial goods, television programs, and American movies. They depict the lives of the small minority as "developed." The minority sets the standard. It is a paradox that the ordinary lives of the great majority of the world's people have come to seem "abnormal" and "peripheral," while the lives of the few have become "normal" and "standard."

The danger of this reversal is that the minority do not live ordinary lives. The planet cannot survive in anything like its present form if the consumption rates of the privileged few are accepted as the standard by which development is judged. Twenty-five percent of the world's population uses 75 percent of the world's energy, 85 percent of all forest products, and 72 percent of its steel, while producing 75 percent of its waste (Sagoff 1993: 8). How did this happen? How did an ecologically impossible lifestyle become the standard by which development is measured?

To answer these questions we need to begin by looking back to the historical context in which population and environmental policies were connected with the liberal "idiom of Improvement," as Ranajit Guha calls it. Contemporary visions of social progress are often informed by the visions of utilitarian social reformers of the nineteenth century. In the writings of Jeremy Bentham, James Mill, and John Stuart Mill, we witness the invention of modern, liberal attitudes toward the concept of progress that were at once progressive in Europe and colonizing in India.

The utilitarians were not just philosophers speculating idly about their own existence. Bentham wrote a system of laws for colonial rule in India, describing his role in that country as being reminiscent of the role of Solon, the ruler of ancient Athens. James Mill published *The History of British India* in 1817 hoping to secure a position with the East India Company. He succeeded, becoming assistant examiner in 1819, and chief examiner in 1830. His *History* was the standard text at the company's college at Haileybury, and deeply affected its policies for decades. The core of Mill's plan for liberal reform in India, the land rent system, was adapted from Thomas Malthus, who held the first chair in political economics, also at Haileybury College.

John Stuart Mill, now the most famous of the utilitarian reformers, worked for the East India Company for thirty-five years. Under the guidance of his father, Mill was trained to write the political correspondence with India, rising, finally, to the rank of examiner of Indian correspondence. Until his retirement in 1858, just after the Great Mutiny broke the hold of the East India Company on India, he effectively governed the economic, legal, and political affairs of the British Empire's most important colony.

Remarkably, John Stuart Mill regarded his lifelong employment as nothing more than a good job which had no bearing on his philosophical writing. Mill wrote of his duties: "While they precluded all uneasiness about the means of subsistence, they occupied fewer hours of the day than almost any business or profession, they had nothing in them to produce anxiety, or to keep the mind intent on them at any time but when engaged in them" (Mill 1990: vii).

How the author of *On Liberty* and *Representative Government* could have felt no anxiety about his Indian correspondence demands an explanation. In *Principles of Political Economy*, for example, Mill described the British Empire's colonies as:

> hardly to be looked upon as countries . . . but more properly as outlying agricultural or manufacturing estates belonging to a larger community. Our West Indian colonies, for example, cannot be regarded as countries with a productive capital of their own . . . [but are rather] the place where England finds it convenient to carry on the production of sugar, coffee and a few other tropical commodities. (Mill 1965: 693)

This passage is endlessly revealing as an example of systemic violence. There is a "larger community" for Mill comprising both England and its colonies. But the colonies are "outlying," distant from, dependent upon, and defined by, the center for its domestic purposes. The fact that the rules applying to proper "countries" do not apply to the colonies caused Mill to regard himself as a morally neutral technician in his writings on India. Relations with these dependencies are matters of "convenience," as he said. For Mill, colonies are not countries because they have no productive capital of their own. They must be given a productive capital, and defined in terms of their existing and producing for the center. What they produce is significant too. Foods produced for domestic consumption, peasant foods, are not mentioned. They are defined by production of export crops produced for the center: sugar, coffee, and other commodities.[1]

If we want to understand contemporary suspicions in the third world concerning neocolonial subtexts to international economic, population, and environmental policies, therefore, the legacies of Malthus, Bentham, and the Mills are key. Most important among these figures is James Mill. Despite John Stuart Mill's contemporary standing in the history of philosophy, the colonial game had already been won for the East India Company by the time he influenced its affairs. It was James Mill, influenced by Bentham and Malthus, who literally wrote the colonial agenda.

For James Mill, India was the great social experiment by which to test the success of utilitarian doctrines during the period that Britain worked to transform itself, again in Ranajit Guha's words, from "conquistador" to "legislator." Mill's *History* marks the transition in British colonial discourse from the idiom of Order to the idiom of Improvement, from overt military violence to the covert control of thought (Guha 1989: 287).

COLONIALSIM AND THE "IDIOM OF IMPROVEMENT"

"Improvement" became part of colonial discourse decades before Mill's *History*. The verb "improve" and its related constructions appears approximately nineteen times in two documents from September 1789 and February 1790 in which Lord Charles Cornwallis, governor-general of Bengal, sought to introduce his "Permanent Settlement" for land claims in Bengal. Nevertheless, Cornwallis's instincts were conservative. "A landholder, who is secured in the quiet enjoyment of a profitable estate," he said, "can have no motive for wishing for a change" (Philips 1977: 207).

The Permanent Settlement recognized the zamindars, a class of tax collectors who had not previously been land owners, as permanent holders of property rights. Cornwallis's goal in choosing the zamindars was to create a wealthy agricultural class who could modernize agricultural production. This was necessary not only to "restore this country to a state of prosperity," but, quite explicitly, to create a propertied class that would be loyal to Britain in case of foreign invasion. As Ranajit Guha describes it, "Improvement was a political strategy to persuade the indigenous elite to 'attach' themselves to the colonial regime" (Guha 1989: 242).

In the Permanent Settlement we can see the way ideological struggles in Britain played out in the colonies. Cornwallis's conservatism was a reflection of the views that culminate in Edmund Burke's response to the French Revolution in *Reflections on the Revolution in France* (1791). Burke defended common law as Britain's best defense against the revolutionary chaos that was sweeping Europe. What was a defense of the status quo in England became an argument for creating a new social class in colonial India, the zamindars transformed from tax collectors to landed elite.[2]

Cornwallis and the Permanent Settlement represent the older generation of colonial authority in India that responded to conservative forces in British society. As such, they are the principal targets of Mill's radical reformist spirit in the *History*. Mill and the utilitarians were ardent critics of Burke and the common law tradition. They advocated a system of statute law in England as the only fair basis for society, believing that common law gave sanction to traditional privileges that benefited the aristocratic minority over the interests of the greatest number.

Mill's solution to the land revenue problem was the ryotwari system. In this system we witness the joining of colonial policy on population and the environment with liberal ideas of progress. The ryots, small peasant farmers, best satisfied Mill's utilitarian desire to implement agricultural improvements that would benefit the greatest number.[3] The system differed from Cornwallis's, not only in terms of the economic class he sought to support, but, just as importantly, in terms of the role of the state. Cornwallis had attempted to make the zamindars a class of landowners functioning between the state and small peasant cultivators partly for the sake of simplifying revenue collection. According to Mill's plan, the state itself was to be the landlord with the ryots as tenants renting directly from the state. The system of land rent required this direct relationship between each peasant tenant and the omnipresent state. As Eric Stokes and others see it, this led Mill to a startling conclusion for a liberal: "He was prepared to accept the oriental role of the State as landlord of the soil, because this happened to coincide with his views on taxation" (Stokes 1989: 92).

The "law of rent" was discovered by Thomas Malthus in 1815 and first presented to students at Haileybury College as a system that could pay for a colonial administration without hindering the economic progress of tenant farmers (Malthus [1798] 1965; Malthus [1815] 1969; Malthus [1872] 1971). Malthus based his idea on the propensity of a population to outgrow its food resources, necessitating use of poorer soils as both population and wealth grew. In any society making economic progress there will be a disparity, he pointed out, between the output of good and poor soils. On poor soils, profit barely offsets the cost of production. Better quality soils yield a profit and a surplus. In the latter case, Malthus reasoned, the landlord can lay claim to this surplus as rent. Since rent is the return over and above profit, it presumably does not affect the ability of the cultivator to reinvest for future profit. Rent is not a tax, so Malthus argued, since it does not act as an economic disincentive. It therefore does not impede economic progress.

David Ricardo's version of land rent was more jaded. He viewed the private landlord as nothing but a parasite whose interests were "always opposed to every other class in the community" (Stokes 1989: 88). Mill's anti-aristocratic leanings caused him to side with Ricardo and to lobby for a direct state/tenant-farmer relationship in India, eliminating Malthus's leisure class.[4]

We should not, however, mistake Mill's support for the ryots with support for indigenous peasant traditions. Mill had no interest in preserving traditional Indian social structures since they were based on subsistence agriculture that did not produce rent. The land rent system sought to create new social relationships by exporting British ideas of progress to the colonies, ideas that consciously undermined traditional social and ecological relationships. The ryots were to be transformed from subsistence cultivators to a new class of small capitalist producers.

Mill defined progress as movement toward a utilitarian society, a society in which an economically rational capitalist middle class produces for its own individual good, and thereby produces a surplus in the form of rent that benefits society as a whole. As he said, "Exactly in proportion as *Utility* is the object of every pursuit, may we regard a nation as civilized" (Mill [1817] 1858: 2:105). In "backward" societies, where land is owned communally, according to Mill, the state must intervene as oriental despot to collect rent until peasants are transformed into capitalist producers (Majeed 1992: 160).

Mill's hostility to indigenous systems of knowledge emerges clearly in contrast to another of Mill's main targets of criticism in the *History*, Sir William Jones. Jones arrived in Bengal in 1783 as a Supreme Court judge. His influence, however, went far beyond judicial matters. As a linguist, Jones is credited with discovering that Indo-European languages are related. Knowledge of Sanskrit allowed him to compile a digest of Indian laws. He resisted efforts to impose British law on India. A poet, he wrote hymns to Hindu deities. In short, Jones sought to preserve traditional Indian cultures, although, we must remember, as part of a plan of colonial governance (Majeed 1992: chap. 1).

If Jones's colonial agenda depended upon preservation of Indian cultures, Mill's liberal program was "to emancipate India from its own culture" (Majeed 127). In the *History* he goes to great lengths to criticize Hindu culture as childish and backward: "It is allowed on all hands that no historical composition existed in the literature of the Hindus," since "they had not reached that point of intellectual maturity, at which a value of the record of the past for the guidance of the future begins to be understood" (Mill [1817] 1858: 2:67). Guha points out that Mill here creates an intellectual void which demands to be filled by a colonial presence. India has no history until it is given one by India's first true historian, Mill himself (Guha 1989: 286).

Mill accomplished this feat never having visited India, and without any knowledge of Indian languages. Far from a scholarly defect, Mill took this to be a mark of scientific objectivity. He criticized scholars such as Jones for being too close to Indian culture, and therefore for being too gullible in accepting local accounts of culture. Jones failed to write history because he failed to understand "the signs of social improvement" (Mill [1817] 1858: vol. II, 109–10).[5]

Mill's liberal imperialism diverged even from other supporters of the ryotwari system, such as Thomas Munro, who instituted the system in the Madras presidency. Munro "distrusted the chilly dogmatics of the reforming spirit," and was influenced by William Wordsworth and British romanticist ideas of the "noble peasant" as a citizen of nature (Stokes 1989: 13–14). Through his own poetry he expressed, perhaps longingly, the convergence of romantic ideas of nature with the sensibility of peasant farmers for the land.

Mill regarded poetry and the imagination as causes of unscientific superstition in backward societies. He had no need of Sanskrit to understand India because rationality was, for him, scientific, empirical, and universal. For Mill, to be civilized is to empirically weigh costs and benefits. The "instrumental rationality" of the new middle class makes a culture progressive (Majeed 1992: 137).[6]

This model of progress toward civilization applied as much to legislators as to economic individuals pursuing their rational self-interest. For Bentham, as for Mill, utilitarianism provided a universal legislative code. Bentham advocated a "censorial jurisprudence," "a common standard," "by which the several systems of law prevailing in every country may respectively be compared, and thereby their mutual agreements and disagreements represented, their comparative excellences and defects exhibited to view." Once the facts are known, he asserted, "all places are alike" (Bentham [1789] 1970: 274, 179–81).

In Mill's *History*, then, we have a narrative of progress from collectivist societies, without histories, governed by the imagination, to progressive societies having historical purpose, in which there is a capitalist middle class, governed by instrumental rationality. The movement from backward to modern is also the movement from cultural particularity, people deeply embedded in a place and in subsistence methods of production, to a universal capitalist culture of the future which is everywhere the same.

The paradox of liberal imperialism is clear. It arose out of historically particular conditions in Europe during the Industrial Revolution. It satisfied the needs of an emerging middle class for a more egalitarian society. It provided a radical social foundation for progressive movements that is still useful today, for example, in fights for equal treatment for women.[7] Nevertheless, liberal ideas of progress in one context became hegemonic policies in another. Liberal imperialism masks historically specific economic agendas in a narrative of progress that claims to speak in universal and trans-cultural terms.

When I say that liberal imperialism was hegemonic, I depend upon Ranajit Guha's precise definition of an overused term: *"hegemony stands for a condition of Dominance . . . , such that, Persuasion . . . outweighs Coercion"* (Guha 1989: 231). That is, in the transition from the idiom of Order, characterized by military power, to the idiom of Improvement, whose locus is Mill's new language for an emerging middle class of collaborators with the colonial regime, persuasion succeeded coercion as the instrument of control. Liberal policies concerning population and the environment were hegemonic in this sense.

RESISTING "DEVELOPMENT"

Despite their ideological and military power, liberal policies were resisted by indigenous populations. There were two distinct patterns of resistance. The first grew out of claims of liberalism, and depended upon the language of rights. It appealed to elite Indians who had benefited from British education. They used rights language to point out the contradiction between guarantees of the universal scope of rights in British moral theory, and its failure to be applied universally in India.

The second form of dissent, called "Dharmic Protest," arose from indigenous sources. Entirely apart from of any transcendental notion of rights, it emerged from the shastras and customs of the caste system. During the period of the raj, various forms of indigenous protest occurred among miners, tea plantation workers, and other sectors based on the failure of traditional dharmic responsibilities (Guha 1989: 264–69). It was this kind of indigenous protest that the British least understood.[8]

Dharmic Protest is notable because it contradicts the universalist, individualist tendencies of the liberal mind. Where the liberal demands the right to an abortion for all women in every context, despite the fact that this is sometimes used to further undercut the social positions of third world women, Dharmic Protest is localized. It gains its strength from the fact that it speaks from a cultural and economic location; it does not pretend to speak in a universal voice.

To see how such indigenous protest connects to issues of the environment and population, consider the work of Indian ecologist Madhav Gadgil and sociologist Ramachandra Guha who present an ecological reading of the caste system in their book *This Fissured Land: An Ecological History of India.* On their reading, diversification and territorial exclusion helped minimize inter- and intra-caste competition over living resources. We believe that this unique system of cultural adaptation to the natural environment was devised by Indian society in response to the resource crunch which it faced in the Gupta and post-Gupta periods, i.e., between the fourth and ninth centuries A.D. It was then that social organization crystallized in the form of caste society, defined by its hereditarily prescribed modes of subsistence. (Gadgil and Guha 1992: 103)

Gadgil and Guha report that the basic unit of social organization, the village, often included several endogamous caste groups. They were governed by a council of leaders representing the different castes, and most had procedures for reassigning cultivable land to families according to need. Villages had a hereditary caste whose occupation was to serve as village guards. Their duties included keeping records on property held by families in the village. One of the duties of the Mahar caste in pre-British Maharashtra, for example, was to prevent any unauthorized wood cutting on the village commons; since their caste position depended upon maintaining adequate wood supply, the Mahars took a keen interest in maintaining the village commons.

In other cases, scarce resources and high population density result in an elaborate system of ecological diversification along caste lines. Gadgil and Guha also studied the caste breakdown in a set of villages in Karnataka (Gadgil and Guha 1992: 103ff). They found thirteen endogamous groups that break down into seven occupation categories: fishing communities, agriculturists, horticulturists, entertainers, service castes (barbers and washermen), artisans, and traders. One caste does not eat meat or fish. Of the other twelve, three trade for meat and fish. The remaining nine that do hunt or fish have developed a complex system of ecological diversification. They employ thirty-three different methods, each of which is adapted to a different habitat and prey. Deepwater fishing from boats using elaborate nets is the monopoly of the Ambigas. Larger animals, such as deer, are hunted exclusively by the Halakkis. Trapping fruit bats is restricted to the Patgars and Madivals. The Naiks trap bandicoot rats. Gadgil and Guha report similar kinds of diversification in caste access to plant materials.

The universalist, anti-Hindu temperament of liberal imperialism, which sought to replace stable subsistence modes of production with expansive capitalist modes, was a direct attack on indigenous systems of population and environmental management. In the minds of many Indians, this attack has continued with the policies of the green revolution, which also sought to implement capitalist modes of agricultural production that benefited wealthy farmers (chapter 3; Curtin 1995; Shiva 1988; Shiva 1991). Recent wide-scale protests against intellectual property rights regimes that the new GATT agreement required are also regarded by peasant farmers as a defense of traditional village-based forms of knowledge and the biological commons upon which village life depends. The attack on Cargill factories in Bangalore by peasant farmers protesting the GATT was the most widely reported example of such unrest (chapter 4; Shiva 1993; Shiva and Holla-Bhar 1993).

My point is not to defend the moral abominations of the caste system as it has been distorted by centuries of colonial intrigue. Nevertheless, a sympathetic appraisal of the traditional methods by which caste society minimizes conflict over and access to the environment in contexts of high population density can still inform contemporary policies. The problem is not primarily one of population density. India's average population density today (3,016/1,000 hectares) is less than in Japan (3,319), the Netherlands (4,502), and Belgium (3,311) (Institute 1994: 284–85). India has always had indigenous methods for managing access to the environment. The issue, still, is social and environmental justice. Culturally insensitive farm policies continue to drive subsistence producers off their land and into the cities. The rate of population growth in cities far outpaces that of rural areas in India. Between 1965 and 1995, average annual population change in cities has been 3.3 percent in contrast to 1.8 percent in rural areas (Institute 1994: 286). Often, the patterns of job migration affect women and children most disadvantageously since it is typically only the males who migrate. The family is divided, women are left with children, and, deprived of land, they are often without the means to provide food.

The Western narrative of progress depicts communalism as backward. But the story of progress defined as movement toward a world utilitarian, scientific, capitalist culture still lacks an answer to the basic question: "How can capitalist modes of production continue to expand in areas of great population density without causing massive social and environmental injustice?" In such areas, staying alive must take precedence over production of the contemporary equivalent of rent.

The ecological account of caste society reveals how disastrous certain first world formulations of the population/environment problem have been. Most notable is Garrett Hardin's "tragedy of the commons" (Hardin 1968). His Malthusian vision of population expansion begins from the mistaken assumption that the biological commons connected to traditional villages are not managed in any way. Individual producers will steadily increase their take of the commons until disaster strikes, thus the image of third world hordes scrambling to climb into first world lifeboats. This is the legacy of Haileybury College, and it is far more the reflection of first world capitalist producers' attitudes toward common "unowned" ecological resources than anything one might find in most villages.

3

War and Peace
The Politics of Agricultural "Modernization"

DEVELOPMENT AS THE IDEOLOGY OF POLITICAL LIBERALISM

Chapter 2 raised the possibility that nineteenth century liberal attitudes created what we now call the third world, defined as a dependency, a place needing development by the first world. Far from providing genuine development, these attitudes are implicated, conceptually and politically, in causing the destruction of ecocommunities. In turn, this has led to dangerous rates of population growth as subsistence farmers have been dislocated from the land, their traditional source of security. To further substantiate this idea that the "center" created the periphery, in this chapter I connect this nineteenth century legacy with the parent of all development programs in the twentieth century, the green revolution. In the next chapter, I will connect it with its contemporary descendent, the gene revolution.

It is often said that the modern developmentalist project began precisely on Thursday, January 20, 1949, when President Harry S. Truman announced in his inaugural address a new American vision for the postwar world. America was being called to bring about "a major turning point in the long history of the human race." The first half of the century had been marked by unprecedented attacks on "the rights of man" in two world wars. "The supreme need of our time," Truman assessed, "is for men to learn to live together in peace and harmony." Based on a conception of inalienable human rights granted by God, the new American vision offered peace and justice originating in "genuine agreement freely arrived at by equals." Truman asserted, "We have sought no territory and we have imposed our will on none." The chief threat to Truman's vision was communism, which opposed inalienable human dignity, and was based "on the belief that man is so weak and inadequate that he is unable to govern himself, and therefore requires the rule of strong masters (U.S. Government Printing Office 1989: 286–87).

Announcing the birth of the contemporary developmentalist project, Truman continued:

> We must embark on a bold new program for making the benefits of our scientific advances and industrial progress available for the improvement and growth of underdeveloped areas.
>
> More than half the people of the world are living in conditions approaching misery. Their food is inadequate. They are victims of disease. Their economic life is primitive and stagnant. Their poverty is a handicap and a threat both to them and to more prosperous areas.
>
> For the first time in history, humanity possesses the knowledge and the skill to relieve the suffering of these people. (U.S. Government Printing Office 1989: 289)

This peace agenda was to be realized through increased world trade. Truman envisioned a collaboration of "business, private capital, agriculture, and labor in this country" that will increase the standard of living of half the world's people. This was not the "old imperialism—exploitation for foreign profit," he reassured his audience, but a new, ethical "program of development based on the concepts of democratic fair-dealing" (U.S. Government Printing Office 1989: 290).

Truman's vision is a pure statement of modern American political liberalism. There are three "worlds": the first world is the United States followed by its recovering allies in Europe. The second world is the communist USSR along with its satellite countries. The third world is that heterogeneous 50 percent of the world's population that is targeted for "development" to block the expansion of communism. The third world is "primitive," "underdeveloped," and a threat to more prosperous areas. Political liberalism had two cornerstones in its agenda for this new world, two commitments that were often treated as one. It was not simply another form of economic colonialism of the kind that had failed in (the newly independent) India. The developmentalist project was *ethical,* although it defined ethics in terms of Western individualism. This conception of the ethical individual was compatible with the economic cornerstone: the global expansion of capital and transfer of American technological expertise.

Truman's moral and economic hierarchy was a case of systemic violence committed to all five of the general features of Western ethics that misrepresent social patterns in the third world: universalism, individualism, the autonomy of the moral will, the priority of the right, and progress (see chapter 1). It did not countenance alternative modes of economic production. The patterns of production Mahatma Gandhi had recently called for based on his ideal of village "swaraj"—small-scale, decentralized, village-based development using technologies appropriate to the village and communalistic lifestyles—are labeled "primitive."

It is notable that Truman represents his agenda as an *alternative* to economic colonialism, given how remarkably similar it is to the Mill's agenda for colonial India. Neither James Mill nor Harry Truman were interested in preserving traditional village life and its methods of ecological preservation. Both were espousing the creation of a new economic middle class of producers geared to produce export crops.

The destruction of village life in the name of a Western conception of social justice is not surprising. It is a feature of systemic violence: what appears to be just from within is experienced as unjust from without. We go wrong, that is, if we think of Truman's developmentalist project as a case of individual violence. Truman probably did not consciously intend to violate the lives of subsistence farmers in the third world. This was not a case of willful, one-on-one violence. Systemic violence is no less violent, however, and it is more pervasive since it requires the creation of institutions to facilitate its world view. The green revolution was the primary institutional tool for the advancement of Truman's vision.

THE VIOLENCE OF THE GREEN REVOLUTION

In 1970 Norman Borlaug won the Nobel Prize, which recognized his role as father of the green revolution. While Borlaug's work was on plant genetics, he did not win for biology. He won the prize for *peace.* Thus culminated the effort of more than two decades to represent the green revolution as a peace program. According to narrowly defined criteria, the green revolution has been proclaimed a success: yields on all the major seeds it produced have at least doubled in annual production since World War II. Yet, the assertion that it was a peace program, and, underlying this, its explicit claim to a moral justification, demand a broader assessment. In its own terms, it calls to be judged by its social, political, and environmental impact.

Borlaug's Nobel acceptance speech was titled "The Green Revolution, Peace, and Humanity." Part of his introduction reads:

> In the misty, hazy past, as the Mesolithic Age gave way to the Neolithic, there suddenly appeared in widely separated geographic areas the most highly successful group of inventors and revolutionaries that the world has ever known. This group of Neolithic men and women, and *in all probability largely the latter,* domesticated all the major cereals, legumes, and root crops, as well as all of the most important animals that to this day remain man's principal source of food. (Borlaug 1971: 226, emphasis added)

I do not doubt Borlaug's sincerity in honoring women's agricultural knowledge, nor his moral sincerity in believing that green revolution techniques would bring peace to the world.[1] Nevertheless, no well laid plan could have been more successful than the green revolution in marginalizing what women came to know through centuries of agricultural practice, nor more successful in causing their impoverishment through erosion of the political control women have had over their own lives.

Since women have been the third world's principal food producers, the green revolution displaced women's agriculture—although perhaps unintentionally. This is all the more ironic since women's agricultural practices tend to be forms of ecological peacemaking, akin to pacifism. Such practices are relatively nonviolent in their treatment of communities and the land.[2]

Given its explicit peace agenda, the most curious feature of the green revolution is its systemic and institutional violence. Like nineteenth century colonialism, the green revolution's violence operates through Enrique Dussel's dynamic of center and margin. It puts the first world at the center ethically and conceptually, spinning out other "worlds" from that center to ethical and conceptual margins. This system of marginalization—developmentalism—is a system of violence that connects with, and benefits from, other systemic forms of domination such as racism and sexism.

This chapter focuses on the effects of the green revolution in India because, as one of the two original test sites for the new technologies, its effects can be seen most clearly there. Even within India, however, generalization can be difficult. The state of Kerala, for example, has a matrilineal social structure, high literacy rates, and a stable system of small subsistence farms that make it an exception to developmental change that occurred elsewhere in India. Nevertheless, from the very fact that the green revolution was a *global* plan whose purpose was to effect a revolutionary change in traditional relationships to land, a plan far more comprehensive in scope than nineteenth-century colonial ambitions, it is a powerful vehicle for understanding global change despite otherwise culturally diverse contexts.

The green revolution began in 1944, when the Rockefeller Foundation invited Borlaug to leave his wartime job in a Dupont laboratory to direct the wheat breeding program at the International Maize and Wheat Improvement Center in Mexico. Under Borlaug's direction, the Center produced the so-called High Yielding Variety (HYV) of wheat that was initially targeted for two areas, northwest Mexico, and the Punjab region of what is today India and Pakistan.

In principal, Borlaug's accomplishment was simple. Inorganic nitrogen fertilizer, when applied to traditional varieties of wheat, made the whole plant grow larger. Tall varieties, top-heavy with grain, had the tendency to topple over (called lodging), thus reducing the yield. Borlaug genetically engineered a dwarf variety of wheat to concentrate fertilizer in the grain (and profit) producing part of the plant. The green revolution was possible because HYVs can accept very high doses of fertilizer.

While the core of the green revolution is simple, the broader impact is complex. As Borlaug explained, a whole package of technologies was transferred to the Punjab, including "seeds, fertilizers, insecticides, weed killers, and machinery—and the credit with which to buy them" (Borlaug 1971: 231). High doses of fertilizer require much greater reserves of water to be effective; green revolution crops therefore require massive irrigation.[3] In contrast to traditional agriculture, which is based on crop rotation, the green revolution depends upon plant monoculture. This makes HYVs especially susceptible to pests and diseases, thus the dependence upon pesticides (Chabousson 1986). In contrast to agriculture based on the principle of recycling organic inputs, the green revolution depends upon external sources for seeds, chemicals, and machinery. Green revolution hybrid seeds are often not self-pollinating, so they must be purchased each year from a seed company. The biotechnology revolution now occurring in agriculture carries plant monoculture further, to the level of individual brand names. Agrochemical companies are now engineering seeds to respond (or not respond) only to their particular commercial brand of fertilizer, herbicide, or pesticide.[4]

The systemic violence of the green revolution presupposed the invention of new institutions. The two principal institutions predated Truman's inaugural address by five years. The Bretton Woods Conference, held in New Hampshire in 1944, created the International Monetary Fund (IMF) and the International Bank for Reconstruction and Development, commonly called the World Bank. These institutions are funded by wealthy nations and provide development loans to poor countries for the purpose of converting to export economies.[5]

Although brief, this summary of green revolution technology is sufficient to illustrate the impact it has had on indigenous agriculture. The green revolution does not depend upon replenishing the soil, the peasant's traditional source of security, but upon forcing fertility through use of inorganic fertilizers. It does not depend upon conserving water, but upon the assumption that access to water is unlimited. It demands political and economic dependence upon a small number of seed and agrochemical companies rather than building on local self-reliance. Since its economy of scale holds to the notion that bigger is better, it depends upon loans—and the ability to repay loans—from such Western dominated international agencies as the World Bank.

It is tragic, furthermore, that much of the impetus to "develop" the third world was based on a misunderstanding of the causes of famine in the third world. Amartya Sen has examined the causes of the Great Bengal Famine, which took 1.5 million lives in the early 1940s, and concludes that it was not due to the inability of Indian agriculture to produce sufficient food (Sen 1981: chap. 6, "The Great Bengal Famine").

Richard Levins captures the dynamic of center and margin through which the green revolution operates by what he terms "seven developmentalist myths in agriculture":

(1) Backward is labor-intensive, modern is capital intensive agriculture.
(2) Diversity is backward, uniform monoculture is modern.
(3) Small scale is backward, large scale is modern.
(4) Backward is subjection to nature, modern implies increasingly complete control over everything that happens in the field or orchard or pasture.
(5) Folk knowledge is backward, scientific knowledge is modern.
(6) Specialists are modern, generalists backward.
(7) The smaller the object of study, the more modern. (Levins 1986: 13–20)

Developmentalism encompasses a complex set of attitudes. It includes issues of economic scale, epistemic reductionism (including the epistemic status of the outside expert as against the insider to a practice), and views about the relationships of the person and community to the land.

WARISM AND INDIGENOUS PEOPLE

Before the green revolution, there were important research programs in both Mexico and India on a wide variety of self-pollinating seeds traditionally cultivated by peasants. These programs were forcibly terminated by the politics of the green revolution.[6] In India, the Cuttack Institute was investigating techniques to increase yields on traditional varieties of rice based on the knowledge of tribal people. The institute had collected and preserved 20,000 indigenous varieties of rice, a storehouse of genetic information patiently developed over centuries by village women. Unlike the genetically uniform rice the International Rice Research Institute (IRRI) developed in the Philippines—another Rockefeller/Ford food for peace program—these indigenous species were genetically diverse, having been bred across the entire Indian subcontinent. Nevertheless, for political reasons, the Indian minister of agriculture, who had been trained in Mexico, demanded to have the Cuttack Institute's wheat-germ plasm turned over to IRRI. When the director resisted, he was fired (Shiva 1991: 43–44).[7]

There were elements in Mexico and India that resisted the green revolution as an assault against national autonomy. They were often silenced when food was used as a political weapon. In 1966, for example, President Lyndon Johnson refused to commit food aid to India until it adopted the green revolution as national agricultural policy (Shiva 1991: 31). The U.S.-led Agency for International Development (AID) was also involved in subverting the Salvador Allende administration in Chile by withholding food aid (Lappé and Collins 1978: 357–60).

There was no scientific reason for directing research exclusively toward improving seeds that undercut the political control of the world's poor. Such programs already existed, as I have noted. Harvard scientist Richard Lewontin has argued that open-pollinated varieties of seeds could have been as productive as HYV hybrids (Lewontin 1982: 16). In fact, under less than ideal conditions, traditional seeds are often *more* productive than HYVs. Since most third world farmers work small plots of marginal land with irregular access to water, less than ideal conditions are the norm, not the exception. The fact that HYVs were chosen for development, therefore, while programs on open-pollinated varieties were forcibly shut down, reflects the class and gender interests of the green revolution. HYVs are genetically engineered to be a privately owned commodity.

Most of the world's sources of genetic diversity, upon which first world research depends, are in the third world. Colonialism has always relied on exploitation of this diversity to produce commodities that are sold back to the third world on credit provided by the first world. As early as 1848, for example, the East India Company was collecting plant species in India. In 1853, when Admiral Perry colonized Japan, he collected plant species, including rice (Kloppenburg 1988: 14, 55).

The effects of this "top-down" ideology on indigenous people are both predictable and tragic. Vandana Shiva and Maria Mies have challenged the claim that so-called ethnic violence is responsible for increasing violence in India's Punjab region (Mies 1986; Mies 1988; Shiva 1991). Religious conflict, they argue, is the effect. The cause was the green revolution. The same system of irrigation that caused the Punjab to be chosen in the first place as the test site for green revolution techniques is now causing violence over water rights. Farmers who had the means to mechanize and repay foreign loans have benefited, their acreages increasing rapidly as small farmers are driven out of business. Small farmers—women and men—have been displaced, cut off from their traditional source of security. Men who are displaced by this process seek wage-labor jobs on the large farms, or they migrate to the cities leaving their families behind. Women who are displaced often are expected to work as an unpaid adjunct to their husband's wage labor. In many cultures, the same women who grow and prepare the food are the last to eat, even in the best of times.

As is almost always the case in such situations, violence against women has increased in the form of sati, "kitchen accidents," and female infanticide. Sati is the practice of burning the widow on the husband's funeral pyre. The euphemism "kitchen accident" refers to situations in which women are doused with kerosene in the family kitchen and burned to death, typically by the husband's relatives. The cause is often disappointment over a dowry. Female infanticide has become a subject of national debate in India with the advent of genetic testing for gender before birth.

WARISM AND THE FATE OF NATURE

The green revolution's vision of agriculture is the violent conquest of nature. This begins with a reductionist, non-contextual conception of science. A Harvard botanist observes, "We now operationally have a kind of world gene pool . . . Darwin aside, speciation aside, we can now envision moving any gene, in principal at least, out of any organism and into any organism." Nobel laureate David Baltimore puts it even more succinctly. He said, "We can outdo evolution" (Kloppenburg 1988: 3). The desire to outdo evolution in the control of nature reveals the dualism of green revolution ideology. Science is not a romance *with* nature, it is a race *against* nature, and science is winning.

Most revealing are the conceptual and empirical connections between green revolution techniques and the technology of war. Vandana Shiva points out that, "Violence was part of the very context of discovery of pesticides during World War I. The manufacture of explosives had a direct spin-off on the development of synthetic insecticides. The tear gas, chloropicrin, was found to be insecticidal in 1916 and thus changed from a wartime product to a peacetime one" (Shiva 1988: 156).[8] Organophosphates, such as malathion, are designed to destroy the central nervous system. Insecticides and herbicides are tested by their "kill ratios." Broad spectrum herbicides kill all vegetation, leaving the earth biologically neutral. Agent Orange, used as a defoliant during the war in Vietnam, is one such product.

The infamous 1984 disaster in Bhopal, India, summarizes the impact of developmentalism. It was caused by a leak of methylisocyanate from a Union Carbide plant that produced nitrogen fertilizer. More than 3,000 people died; roughly 500,000 were injured. A 1989 survey found that 50 percent of women in the affected area were experiencing menstrual problems, and there had been a marked increase in stillbirths, spontaneous abortions, and genetic defects in infants. Fifty-seven percent of those examined suffered from post-traumatic stress disorder, the same disorder that affects many veterans of war. Union Carbide has refused to admit any liability, claiming it was a terrorist act by a disgruntled employee (Crump 1991: 32).

It is often claimed that science and technology are morally neutral, and that only political judgments about the applications of science are open to moral scrutiny. The green revolution makes this distinction between technology and gender bias difficult to sustain. Class, race, and gender biases have been genetically engineered into the "miracle seeds" of the green revolution. Research such as the Cuttack Institute's that is sensitive to local traditions shows that women's agriculture is not at all opposed, in principle, to culturally sensitive development or scientific research. It is opposed to the political genetics of the green revolution.

WOMEN'S AGRICULTURE AS ECOLOGICAL PACIFISM

Given the urgency of this need to change the third world, one might ask what these traditional practices were that so urgently needed development. Anthropological research helps explain the gendered roles of traditional farmers. The hunter/gatherer paradigm, according to which the hunters provide most of the food, has been dismissed as a sexist myth. In such societies, up to 80 percent of food is gathered by women. Women's roles as gatherers, in turn, led to the invention of agriculture as predominantly a women's practice. On the assumption that "the workers invented their tools" (Stanley 1982), most anthropologists now agree that women invented the important agricultural tools. Because women have also been the traditional plant breeders, they bred most of the world's grains, including wheat, rice, maize, barely, oats, sorghum, millet, and rye. These cereals still supply 75 percent of all human food energy (Stanley 1982: 293–94).

In Africa and many parts of Asia, agriculture is still disproportionately women's work. According to a Worldwatch Institute paper, "Gender Bias: Roadblock to Sustainable Development," women in sub-Saharan Africa grow 80 percent of household food. Women's labor produces 70 to 80 percent of food on the Indian subcontinent, and 50 percent of food consumed in Latin America and the Caribbean (Jacobson 1993: 19).

This is much the situation Sir Albert Howard encountered in the late 1800s when the British government dispatched him to India to investigate methods of improving Indian agriculture. He found, much to his surprise, that their crops were free of pests, and that insecticides and fungicides were not used in their system of agriculture. Impressed, he decided, "I could not do better than watch the operations of these peasants, and acquire their traditional knowledge as rapidly as possible. For the time being, therefore, I regarded them as my professor of agriculture. Another group of instructors were obviously the insects and fungi themselves" (Howard 1943: 160). It is clear from the history of Indian agriculture that Howard had placed his education primarily in the hands of Indian peasant women.

The best agriculture, Howard later wrote, is modeled on "nature's agriculture":

The main characteristic of Nature's farming can therefore be summed up in a few words. Mother earth never attempts to farm without live stock: she always raises mixed crops; great pains are taken to preserve the soil and to prevent erosion; the mixed vegetable and animal wastes are converted into humus; there is no waste; the processes of growth and the processes of decay balance one another; ample provision is made to maintain large reserves of fertility; the greatest care is taken to store the rainfall; both plants and animals are left to protect themselves against disease. (Howard 1943: 23, 14)

The cyclical principle made Howard's book, *An Agricultural Testament*, a classic in the organic, sustainable agriculture movement. It is not often recognized that this movement owes a great debt to third world women's agricultural knowledge. The Rodale system of organic gardening is a direct result of peasant women's farming. J. I. Rodale was a student of Howard's.

The foremost commitment of cyclical agriculture is to biological diversity. In a healthy ecosystem, decay balances growth. Soil regenerates through recycling plant and animal matter. Plant agriculture, therefore, requires animals for fertilizer. Crops that use nitrogen, such as wheat and rice, must rotate with plants that return nitrogen to the soil, such as pulses (beans, peas, and lentils).

The cyclical principle also embraces water conservation, which begins with healthy soil that retains moisture. Water depends upon mixed land use as well. Agricultural land must be mixed with forested land. Trees prevent flooding, and are a self-regenerating resource for fodder that retains water. Forests are also necessary for food, building materials, and traditional medicines.

Traditional agriculture does not depend upon pesticides. It lets biological diversity do the work. As any agriculturalist knows, it is not true that everything is connected in nature. If that were the case, Dutch elm disease would have wiped out oak and other species. Traditional agriculture takes advantage of the disjunctions in nature to control pests. Corn rootworms will not eat soybean roots, for example, so crop rotation removes the rootworms' source of food.

Also, traditional agriculture is localized in the genetics of its seeds. It is typical for each family to maintain its own stock of seeds from year to year. Women usually are responsible for selecting the best seeds for cultivation the next season. Village-based genetic breeding means that seeds are developed to meet the needs of widely diverse growing conditions. Seeds are bred to "meet the expectations of the land" (Jackson 1987); land is not altered to meet the demands of the seed. The genetic diversity of traditional agriculture is a safeguard against widespread devastation of crops due to climatic change or pests. Village plant breeding is also a political issue. When women control plant breeding, they are at the nexus of activities that most determine family and community survival. It is this sense of what is appropriate to a place, the refusal to dominate a place, that developmentalism reads as backward. In stark contrast to the ideology of the green revolution, third world women's agriculture is akin to pacifism in its commitment to ecological peacemaking. Its mode is "collaboration with" nature. Unlike the universalism of the developmentalist, which regards everything that is different as needing "development" in its own image, women's cyclical practices reveal a sense of what is appropriate to and sustainable in a particular place. Nature is not on the far side of the moral divide. The community includes the land as much as its people. Treatment of the land, therefore, reveals the moral self.

Pacifism is not passivism. Characterizing typically women's farming as pacifist does not mean that women must simply accept the violence perpetrated against them and their communities. On the contrary, pacifism is a form of resistance. The Green Belt Movement in Africa, the Chipko Movement in India, and countless other small-scale women's movements the world over testify to the fact that women are not passive in defending the integrity of their communities and environments.

Founded by Wangari Maathi, the Green Belt Movement in Kenya is run by women. It provides tree seedlings for planting in green belts in rural and urban areas. The women who plant the trees receive twenty-five cents for each tree that survives for at least three months. This generates income for women, who are generally excluded from the wage labor market. It also generates self-esteem: these plantings have a success rate of over 80 percent. Fifty thousand women and children have planted over 10 million trees since the movement began. Maathi recently won the alternative Nobel Prize.

The Chipko Movement is a movement of indigenous women in the Himalayan foothills which began when they hugged trees to prevent deforestation at the hands of lumber companies. The movement has grown into a comprehensive development program that addresses the environment, health, education, and political justice.

The sense of the deep relation of person and place is often expressed in moral or mythological terms. Consider, for example, the arrogant perception in the following passage from the *Journal of the Indian Pesticide Industry* as the author struggles to explain the peasant's relationship to the land:

[A] more important [difficulty in marketing products in India] is the mental attitude of the agriculturalist about killing. Pesticides spell killing, maybe small and perhaps invisible insects. But it is killing that they are used for. This killing is anathema to the majority of the agriculturalists, be they Hindu, Jain or others. By nature, the agriculturalist is generous, wanting to bestow on others what he reaps out of Mother Earth. He [*sic*] does not think that he alone should enjoy the fruits of his labour . . . to kill those unseen and unknown lives, though they were thriving on what Mother Earth yields, is foreign to his nature. . . . It takes some time for the simple folk to

get acclimatised to the very conception of killing tiny helpless and un-
armed creatures. (Lappé and Collins 1978: 61)

The Indian idea of "ahimsa," or nonharming, puts the violence of the
green revolution, and its cultural specificity, into sharp relief. Ahimsa
requires a moral universe that includes insects in the moral cycle of
life and death. Nature is seen in moral relationship to human beings.
We are defined morally by our conduct with nature.

It is telling how often, in practice, development experts fail to perceive this deep relationship among women, indigenous cultures, and
place. Third world women, for example, have long depended upon
grasses that grow along the borders of fields to make baskets and mats.
When development experts decide that these grasses have no market
value and plan programs which kill them with herbicide, this is arrogant perception. When these same experts decide that public, forested
land is "undeveloped," and only has value when it is privatized and
"developed" for profit, this too is arrogant perception.

Of Richard Levins's seven developmentalist myths, one seems
most powerful in explaining the developmentalist's inability to appreciate place: "Backward is subjection to nature, modern implies increasingly complete control over everything that happens in the field or orchard or pasture." In the developmentalist's moral pecking order, one
is either dominant over nature or subject to it, either master or slave.
The sense of living with nature in a particular place, which is neither
subjugation nor dominance, is misread by the developmentalist as
backwardness, as a life fit for a slave.

Far from defending the world's poor, the green revolution sought
to defeat communism by destroying the world's peasant class. It did
this by dividing the peasant economically, politically, and spiritually
from the sense of place. Conversely, one could understand much about
peasant resistance movements by considering them to be localized defenses of the connection between person and place (Guha 1990). It is
no accident that liberation theology in Latin America or Dalit theology in India are perspectives which express the particular conditions
of people. They reject the universalizing tendencies of traditional theology.

PACIFICATION IS NOT PEACE

Having seen the effects of the attempt to "develop" the third
world, we are now in a better position to sort out the various ethical
claims that are made for development. It is important, first, to recall

the distinction between institutional violence and individual violence. Liberalism, underpinned as it is by individualism, has no trouble recognizing individual, one-on-one violence. Since, however, it tends to think of society as nothing more than a "fictitious *body*," in Jeremy Bentham's words, an entity that is nothing more than a collection of individuals and their individual intentions, liberalism has trouble recognizing deeper, more pervasive, forms of violence that operate primarily through cultural systems and institutions. Institutions are complex social structures that have "lives of their own" beyond what individuals intend. They shape what will count as actually available choices for a person in a social context, not just an abstract range of theoretically available options.

Often, individuals—particularly individuals who have been raised under the extreme ideology of "corrosive individualism"—are not even aware of the institutions within which they operate, and through which they gain, or are denied, social powers. In a sexist society, for example, men tend to possess certain kinds of social powers that they never asked for, and are unaware of even possessing. We have seen, for example, that men are much more easily accorded standing as "experts" in such a culture. In a liberal individualist culture it is easy to think that this status is solely due to individual merit, rather than merit functioning within a system of social preferences.

An important implication of the distinction between individual and institutional violence is that responsibility accrues to individuals in two very different ways. There are cases in which we are solely responsible for the violence we commit, and must bear individual responsibility. In many cases, though, we bear responsibility indirectly for institutional arrangements that allow us to function in society. Granted, our responsibility is more indirect—an individual cannot will to end sexism in the same way one can decide to stop abusing one's spouse. We do not control institutions in the same way we control our own actions. Nevertheless, because social institutions provide possibilities to some that are systematically denied to others, we do bear responsibility for those institutions, particularly when we consciously take advantage of them.

Within the context of liberal individualism, the intuitive method for determining responsibility is to introspect and ask whether one consciously intended to commit an act of violence against another individual. When such an act of introspective analysis fails to turn up an admission of guilt, we are relieved of responsibility. There are cases where this method works. If the question is whether I am responsible for robbing a bank, and I know I did not, then such an introspective survey settles the matter.

This method fails, however, when we are dealing with broader, institutional issues, such as the institutional relations between the first and third worlds, or relations based on gender or race. Here it may be true that an introspective survey fails to turn up evidence of conscious ill will. Nevertheless, I may still gain social and economic powers as a result of institutional arrangements. The fact that they are institutional makes them exceedingly difficult to see, especially when such concepts as first and third are understood geographically. We often do not know how our morning cup of coffee was produced; often we do not want to know.

The institutional/individual distinction means there is an important difference in the ways we accrue responsibility. In characterizing developmentalism and the green revolution as forms of institutional violence, I am granting that most residents of the first world never intended to oppress the third world. Nevertheless, not intending to oppress is not the same as not oppressing someone. Institutional relations bring institutional responsibility.

If the first world is responsible for the institutions it has created, the question remains, "How should we describe these relations?" Given that they are difficult to recognize, just because they are institutional, it is especially important to develop a language that makes them visible. Duane Cady coined the useful term "warism" as a parallel term to "pacifism." Warism is the view "that war is both morally justifiable in principle and often morally justified in fact." Pacifism holds that, "war, by its very nature, is morally wrong and . . . humans should work for peaceful resolution of conflict." Cady was thinking in terms of explicit military violence rather than the covert political violence of the green revolution. Recently, however, he has connected warism with other forms of domination: sexism, racism, and classism (Cady 1989; Cady 1991). As a reminder that I am stretching Cady's meaning beyond military violence, I say that the ideology of the green revolution is *akin* to warism, that developmentalism is warist.

Since Cady describes warism as making a moral claim—war is morally justifiable in principle and often in fact—I add a third term to this discussion. "War realism" claims that war has nothing to do with ethics. It is simply a fact of life in the "real world." Perhaps Garrett Hardin comes closest to this view with his call to dispense with ethics for the sake of survival.

Warism, which, of course, comes in various shades according to how it justifies the morality of war, says that war is morally justifiable under some circumstances. The utilitarians' justification for colonialism approaches this view. That is, they understood colonialism as a morally justified attempt to supplant indigenous traditions through institutional change. An important part of their rationale, for example, was that "the Hindus" had not yet reached the point in cultural history where they needed history (or ethics). Cultural traditions, given the utilitarians' commitment to universalism, are not yet ethical principles.

Pacifism, when applied to institutional violence, is the view that such institutionally justified violence is morally wrong, and that we should work toward peaceful resolution of conflicts. Notice, it is not naive about violence, as its critics often claim. It recognizes that violence may be difficult to avoid in certain circumstances, as when institutions tell us it is justified. Pacifism differs from warism, however, when it denies that pervasiveness implies moral justification. Violence, even if pervasive, is a morally regrettable outcome. To the extent that warism attempts to provide a moral justification for violence, it makes violence more likely.

War realism, while a popular view these days, particularly in first world attitudes toward the third world, seems exceedingly difficult to justify. Denying moral responsibility does not make it so. Institutional relations are difficult to see and easy to deny. It may be that we often deny responsibility in good faith. But ignorance of these relations does not dissolve responsibility.

The force of war realism comes from its connection to a defense of capitalism as a morally neutral set of relations of production. Niccolò Machiavelli wrote, after all, at the time when capitalism was invented as a substitute for medieval relations of production out of the need for Italian city-states to defend themselves against economic and military threats. The most powerful version of this argument, however, derives from the language of economists. The moral and cultural impacts of "development" on traditional communities are regarded as an "externality." Externalities, as described in chapter 1, are "ad hoc corrections introduced as needed to save appearances, like the epicycles of Ptolemaic astronomy. Externalities do represent a recognition of neglected aspects of concrete experience, but in such a way as to minimize restructuring the basic theory" (Daly and Cobb, Jr. 1989: 37). Like the language of "collateral damage," "externalities" are merely linguistic devices designed to "save appearances." Nothing prevents us from saying that "collateral damage" is actually a term for innocent civilians, usually women and children, who are killed by military violence. Similarly, the language of externalities is nothing more than a circular argument within an academic discipline designed to hold together their Ptolemaic universe.

Warism and pacifism at least have the advantage over war realism of admitting that institutional relations are irreducibly moral. In saying this I do not mean "moral" in the sense that utilitarians give the term: reduction of obligations to a set of universal rules. I mean simply that institutional relations are irreducibly a dimension of life in which we must make qualitative distinctions. Such distinctions shape our conceptions of what social powers are necessary for a valuable and fulfilling human life. These distinctions, as I shall argue in chapter 8, are not reducible to quantities, as the utilitarians would have us believe. They mark deep commitments to distinctions between what is qualitatively better or worse.

If we grant that institutional violence raises irreducibly moral issues, then the question becomes whether it can be justified. Again, this is a difficult case to make out. In connecting warism with other forms of domination, for example, Cady draws on Marilyn Frye's insight that arrogant perception underlies the structures of oppression. According to Frye, Western civilization's answer to the question of man's place in nature is, "everything that is is resource for man's exploitation. With this world view, men see with arrogant eyes which organize everything seen with reference to themselves and their own interests" (Frye 1983: 67). Developmentalism and warism both perceive the world arrogantly. Like racism, sexism, classism, and naturism, they construct a moral pecking order. Those at the top "know," "act," "develop," and "enjoy" the moral prerogative. Those at the bottom are ignorant, passive (and deserving) recipients of the actions of others.

If the green revolution is a peace program, as it claims to be, then, it must defend the claims that violence, at least in this case, was a moral good, and that peace comes through violence. But this confuses peace with pacification. We, like the British utilitarians, are then back to a moral agenda which created the third world for the purpose of "developing" it. Partisans of the green revolution should come clean and admit that its goal is pacification of the world's poor, not positive peace. Historically, this was the case. The first world designed the green revolution to block the expansion of communism among third world peasants after World War II by converting subsistence agriculture to export agriculture that depended upon first world loans and technology for its survival (Shiva 1991).

This policy of pacification is murderous for the third world and suicidal for the first world. It is murderous because it is causing the cultural and ecological dislocation that is linked to unsustainable population increases and unjust treatment of people and their communities, particularly for women and children. While institutional in origin, its impact on real people is all too real. This policy is suicidal for the first world because the exploitation is not only unethical, but unsustainable. The first world self-image as "normal" depends upon Edward Luttwack's scenario of more effective forms of exploitation. When the 20 percent insists on consuming 80 percent of the resources, this creates billions of environmental refugees who can only be pacified by force.

There are optimists who think that new forms of technology will allow for continued first world economic growth (Simon 1981). As will become clear in the next chapter, the problem is that these new forms of technology largely depend upon access to biological diversity, most of which is in a narrow ring around the center of the earth—in the third world. Far from proposing something new that deals with the causes of our present situation, the optimists propose more of the same.

4

Gandhian Legacies

*Indigenous Resistance to "Development" in
Contemporary India and Mexico*

GANDHIAN IDEALS

India recently celebrated the 125th anniversary of Mahatma Gandhi's birth. It is worth asking: "What remains of Gandhi's legacy?" Two Gandhian principles seem particularly relevant to struggles of the poor in the late twentieth century: swadeshi and swaraj. Gandhi believed in swadeshi, or home production of goods, as a part of his goal of village swaraj, or small-scale, decentralized, village-based development. In the half century since these principles helped to win India's freedom, there have been new, institutionalized threats to the Gandhian ideal of self-sufficiency at the village level. We have witnessed the effects of the green revolution. Indian farmers are now warning of a new, related threat: the gene revolution.

In this chapter I turn my attention to two contemporary cases of spontaneous, indigenous protest to "development," the Seed Satyagraha Movement among peasant farmers in India, and the rebellion of Mayan people in Chiapas, Mexico. These two protests arise from dramatically different cultural conditions. Yet, this cultural diversity is precisely what demands our attention. For despite these vast cultural differences, indigenous protests against development have demonstrated a remarkable level of agreement. It may be that the very nature of development as a *global* threat to indigenous autonomy, traditional forms of knowledge, and preservation of biological diversity, reaching down to the level of microbiology, and to places so remote that they have been spared in previous waves of colonial appropriation, is something new. Far from being historically outmoded echoes from pre-industrial societies, I believe indigenous protests against development mark the cutting edge of contemporary conflict over the environment.

INDIGENOUS PROTEST AGAINST
THE GATT AND THE NAFTA

The Seed Satyagraha Movement

To understand the response of Indian farmers to the GATT, we must first understand the ways in which the GATT both advances the agenda of the green revolution, and also the ways it marks something new. We have seen that the wheat of the green revolution was based on a Japanese variety whose short, compact stalk resisted wind damage. It was then engineered to profit from huge doses of inorganic nitrogen fertilizer which increased grain production without increasing the size of the stalk. Effective use of inorganic fertilizer requires a vast increase in water usage, so green revolution crops require irrigation and dams. Further, since these seeds are genetically uniform, they require chemical pesticides and herbicides to deal with threats that could quickly wipe out an entire crop.

The green revolution was as much a social as a genetic revolution. It usually eliminated indigenous systems of agriculture that were finely tuned to a particular ecological niche, replacing them with chemicals, and bank loans, from outside the village. It was first implemented in India's wealthiest region, the Punjab, and was targeted to farmers who could most afford to take on loans from the newly created World Bank and Ford Foundation. The wealthy did benefit for a time, but poor farmers suffered massive dislocation from the beginning. Worldwatch estimated that fifteen million indigenous people in India have been displaced by dams alone since the beginning of the green revolution. While outsiders continue to depict the savage fighting in the Punjab as "ethnic," meaning religious, it is the legacy of the green revolution. The conflict began with disputes over water rights required by irrigation.

Despite this tendency to dislocate the poor, however, it is important to understand that the revolution's official agenda was stated in terms of the public good. The research institutions that produced the new form of agriculture were public and supported by foundations, particularly the Ford and Rockefeller foundations, not private corporations. Furthermore, while the effect of the green revolution was to make farmers dependent upon seed and chemical companies for inputs, the seeds of the green revolution can sometimes be reused for two to four years, and they can be used in combination with herbicides and pesticides from a variety of companies.

Recognizing that seed genetics is a matter of the public good, Indian law long prevented companies from patenting seeds. This has been a major impediment to the privatization of the green revolution. The principal effect of the new GATT is that it will remove whatever indigenous autonomy remained after the green revolution. India has been pressured by the World Bank and the Bush and Clinton presidential administrations to change its laws regarding seeds and pharmaceuticals. The new element in the GATT is the attempt to gain internationally recognized rights to patent intellectual property, thus insuring that multinational corporations, such as Cargill, Sandoz, Monsanto, and Merck, can profit from their seed and chemical research. Furthermore, seeds that are the product of recombinant DNA research are sterile, so they cannot be reused as green revolution seeds often are. These new seeds will also work only with a package of fertilizers, pesticides, and herbicides marketed by a single company. In a period of two generations, then, Indian farmers have gone from seeds that are biologically diverse and controlled at the village level to seeds that must be bought yearly from multi-nationals and which are impossible to genetically manipulate outside the laboratory.

At one level, the conflict is economic. The GATT agreements are a set of international trade agreements going back to 1948 (Raghavan 1990: 49). The Uruguay round of negotiations failed to reach consensus between first and third world countries, principally the United States, India, and Brazil. Then chairman of the GATT Commission, Arthur Dunkel, subsequently drafted a comprehensive document called the Dunkel Draft. Its most controversial section is a set of provisions on Trade Related Intellectual Property Rights (TRIPS). Cargill and other multi-nationals want enforcement procedures for intellectual property so they can privatize seed genetics and guarantee a profit on their research (Public Interest Research Group 1993).

At a deeper level, however, the conflict is social and ethical. India has a rich history of peasant rebellion against colonialism. A new chapter was written on December 29, 1992, when five hundred Indian farmers stormed the office of Cargill's seed subsidiary in Bangalore, Cargill Seeds India Pvt. Ltd., ransacking and destroying the company's financial plans. This action was led by the Karnataka Rajya

Sangha, an organization of small peasant farmers. Although their principal target was Cargill, the protest in a larger sense was against the intellectual property rights provisions of the GATT.

This action was the beginning of the Seed Satyagraha Movement among Indian peasant farmers. Following Gandhi's use of satyagraha, "holding fast to the truth," as a force to confront colonialism, the farmers regarded their actions in burning the factory as following from Gandhi's burning British cloth. In another carefully chosen symbol, after U.S. trade representative Carla Hills had recently called on India's elite to "pry open new markets with a crowbar," the farmers chose crowbars as the instrument of choice for ransacking the factory.

Cargill, the protesters point out, does not invent seeds. Its research begins with the genetic results of centuries of breeding by peasant farmers, for which it pays nothing. Furthermore, Cargill cannot mass-produce seeds for the market. It depends upon middlemen to contract with Indian peasant farmers to produce mass quantities of seeds for public sale. Under these contracts, farmers produce seeds for 1/20th the market price. They do not own the seeds or the genetic material, and are legally prevented from replanting seeds in future years. They must also sign away their rights to sue Cargill in the case of crop failure. Despite the fact that Cargill does not own the fields, its contracts prevent farmers from even walking through each others' fields when they have been planted with Cargill seeds, a difficult proposition in India. Despite the impressive video productions promising quick riches for all that Cargill's middle-men show to entice village farmers into signing contracts, typical incomes have dropped from Rs.3,000 to Rs.300/hectare.

Cargill has also resisted attempts to comply with Indian law that requires all seeds be placed in a national, public seed bank, on the grounds that their seeds are private intellectual property. Recently the World Bank stirred controversy by appearing to initiate actions that would take control of the gene banks created during the green revolution, supposedly for the public good. If they succeed, the genetic resources of centuries of peasant farming will be turned over to private corporations without reimbursement to farmers (Shiva 1993; Shiva and Holla-Bhar 1993).[1]

It is important to understand that the GATT defines only *trade related* inventions as intellectual property. When indigenous cultivators breed seeds or harvest medicines for their own use outside the market economy, these forms of knowledge are not protected by the GATT. The debate over TRIPS is, therefore, biased in favor of multi-nationals. The only debate is over how to profit from technology transfer from "developed" to "undeveloped" areas; the question of appropriation of indigenous knowledge and biodiversity without compensation cannot be raised (Shiva 1993: 555).

One of the concrete responses of the Seed Satyagraha Movement has been to encourage peasant farmers to create their own seed banks, which will allow for an organized system of seed exchanges. M. D. Nanjudaswamy, president of the Karnataka Rajya Sangha, declares: "Our goal is self-reliance in seeds." This means rejection, not only of all seeds promoted by multi-nationals, but also High Yielding Varieties developed in Indian laboratories. Any HYV depends upon fertilizers and pesticides that are not available locally. Nanjudaswamy observes that "these so-called 'miracle seeds' have been introduced with the sole objective of enslaving farmers" (Nanjudaswamy 1993a; Nanjundaswamy 1993b).

From the perspective of Cargill, the peasant attack on its factory was a case of individual violence: when its plant and documents were ransacked, this was a violation of individual property rights. They treated the attack as entirely unprovoked and unjustified. From the perspective of the farmers, however, they had been subject to institutional violence, in the form of one of the world's largest privately owned companies the GATT supported, and systemic violence in the form of a pervasive way of literally silencing—making unspeakable in the public arena—community concerns for cultural and ecological transformations of place.

The Chiapas Rebellion

My primary concern is with the response to cultural and ecological change in India. Nevertheless, if the green and gene revolutions are framed in the universalistic individualism of political liberalism, we ought to be able to witness similar concerns elsewhere, despite vast cultural differences. This is certainly true of the Zapatista Rebellion in Mexico. The rebellion of descendants of the Mayan people began on New Year's Eve 1993, just as the NAFTA went into effect. The indigenous autonomy issues centering on land, food, and biodiversity that were evident in the Seed Satyagraha Movement were also central in Chiapas. The famous Declaration of the Lacandon Jungle summarizes these concerns. It begins:

> We have nothing to lose, absolutely nothing, no decent roof over our heads, no land, no work, poor health, no food, no education, no right to freely and democratically choose our leaders, no independence from foreign interests, and no justice for ourselves and our children. But we say enough is enough!

We are the descendants of those who truly built this nation, we are the millions of dispossessed, and we call upon all of our brethren to join our crusade, the only option to avoid dying of starvation! (Quoted in Rosset with Cunningham 1994)

At issue was Article 27 of the Mexican constitution, a hard-won product of the 1910–1917 revolution which guarantees peasant farmers title to the land they work, as well as traditional forms of communal ownership of property. President Carlos Salinas de Gortari had forced changes in Article 27 in preparation for the NAFTA, just as the GATT required changes to Indian law to allow for patenting intellectual property. As with the green revolution, the NAFTA favors large, corporate farms that can compete without trade barriers. The Zapatistas were concerned that the maize they produce would not be economically viable under the NAFTA and the process of disenfranchisement would accelerate.

The concern to maintain traditional forms of agriculture is part of a larger ecological agenda. Land disenfranchisement has resulted in an ecological cost to the Lacondon Jungle. Some international environmental organizations have proposed setting up ecological reserves in the jungle to prevent further depletion of natural resources. But Subcomandante Marcos has been resolute in linking environmental preservation with social justice:

> We say, we don't want to cut the trees. Because the mountain is very important for Indian people. It is part of their tradition and their history. So we agree, we say, "No, there should be no more cutting of trees—but give me the life conditions for another way, so I will no longer have the necessity to cut the trees." (Quoted in Rosset with Cunningham 1994)

Biodiversity depletion due to poverty and displacement of indigenous people is common. But it is ironic that this process is blamed on indigenous people, given their close relationship to biodiversity preservation.

THE CONNECTION BETWEEN
BIODIVERSITY AND CULTURAL DIVERSITY

A recent Worldwatch Institute report shows that of the nine most culturally diverse countries, as measured by number of spoken languages and dialects, six are biological "megadiversity" nations, with high numbers of unique species.

Country*	Languages/Dialects
Papua New Guinea	850
Indonesia	670
Nigeria	410
India	380
Cameroon	270
Australia	250
Mexico	240
Zaire	210
Brazil	210

*Countries in italics are biological megadiversity countries. (Brown 1993; Durning 1992)

Several important international documents recognize this connection between cultural and biological diversity. Agenda 21, for example, the official document of the Rio Summit of 1992, recognizes the roles of indigenous people in preserving biological diversity. It commits signees to:

Recognize and foster the traditional methods and knowledge of indigenous people and their communities, emphasizing the particular role of women, relevant to the conservation of biological diversity and the sustainable use of biological resources, and ensure the opportunity for the participation of those groups in the economic and commercial benefits derived from the use of such traditional methods and knowledge. (Quarrie 1992: 129)

There is evident tension between such guarantees to indigenous people in Agenda 21 and the effects of GATT and NAFTA. Respect for indigenous autonomy means limited access for multi-nationals to biological diversity, most of which is in the third world. President Clinton has therefore attempted to attach memoranda of interpretation to international agreements that reduce them from the status of a legal requirement to an "understanding." He does this at the same time that he strongly supports the successor to the GATT, the World Trade Organization (WTO), which will have the power to make legally binding trans-national judgments abridging control of biological diversity when it conflicts with free trade. Despite the fact that this will have a devastating effect on indigenous autonomy, the U.S. trade representative's office issued a memorandum (June 30, 1994) saying that "Indian Tribes" are sub-federal governments that would be subject to the rulings of the WTO.[2]

Logging, mining, prospecting for new chemical compounds, diversion of water, and fishing disputes can all come under the authority of the WTO. The organization is empowered to make legally binding rulings in cases where it determines free trade has been abridged, and indigenous people cannot be heard as parties to any dispute. In short, the GATT, NAFTA, and WTO represent a new form of colonization on a world scale. Unlike earlier forms of colonization, the WTO represents no national government, since it has the legal authority to overrule national law when judged to be in conflict with free trade. And, unlike the green revolution, it does not even pretend to represent the public good. It defends only the autonomy of multinational corporations.

INDIGENOUS AUTONOMY AND THE POLITICAL LEFT

This is a bleak picture; it is bleak not only in the sense that the odds of resisting global centralization of capital are great, but because we in the first world lack any alternative program. There is no international labor movement, for example, positioned to confront the organized multinational interests represented in the WTO. Moreover, even if these traditional alliances of the political Left did still exist, they would not be well suited to speak to the contemporary concerns of indigenous farmers. There are several clear reasons for this.

First, the Left has tended to speak in universalistic terms that are not sympathetic to the particularistic claims of indigenous people. Both the Seed Satyagraha Movement and the Zapatistas have emphasized that they are *indigenous* movements. Although they welcome international alliances, they do not serve foreign interests, and they consciously speak from, and for, the conditions of people in a particular place.

One of the reasons Chiapas gained so much international recognition is that it is a post–Cold War event requiring a new kind of explanation. When President Salinas tried to undermine the Zapatistas by raising the issue of "foreign influence"—the same charge that had been effective in Nicaragua and El Salvador—no one listened. The fall of the Soviet Union dispenses with the representation of these spontaneous, indigenous rebellions as inspired by international forces. In a post–Cold War era, that is, we have the possibility of understanding indigenous claims as *indigenous,* as non-repeatable claims of *these* people to *this* place.

Second, despite their vast differences, the Left in industrialized countries has traditionally shared an industrial model of development with the political right. One of the principal lessons I take from both movements discussed here is their uncompromising resistance to "development." Neither the classical Marxist model of industrial development, nor the capitalist model, needless to say, is positioned to respond to the "enough is enough" declaration from the Lacandon Jungle, nor the indigenous seed banks of the Seed Satyagraha Movement. These rebellions challenge one of the great orthodoxies that has dominated since World War II: the global model of industrial development.

Third, the common industrial and nationalist agendas of the Left and Right led to outright hostility to indigenous movements in the nineteenth century. Will Kymlicka, for example, has noticed the striking similarity between John Stuart Mill and Friedrich Engels in their antipathy to indigenous cultures. Mill argued that it would be better to "absorb" the Basque into French national culture—"a highly civilized and cultivated people"—"than to sulk on his own rocks, the half-savage relic of past times, revolving in his own little mental orbit, without participation or interest in the general movement of the world."

Apart from the references to Georg Wilhelm Hegel and revolution, Engels would be hard to distinguish from Mill: "These relics of nations, mercilessly trampled down by the passage of history, as Hegel expressed it, this ethnic trash always become fanatical standard bearers of counterrevolution and remain so until their complete extirpation or loss of their national character, just as their whole existence in general is itself a protest against a great historical revolution" (Kymlicka 1995a: 5). Still today, the inept response of European and American governments to the resurgence of ethnic identities after the fall of the Soviet Union shows how little such movements are understood.

This brings me to the fourth and final point. What has been lacking in traditional political analyses of the Left and Right is an adequate environmental analysis. Reinforcing the model of industrial development has been the attitude that nature is simply a resource for economic development. In saying "enough" to development, indigenous communities force recognition of the inseparability of social and ecological justice.

Viewed from the first world, it may be easy to see indigenous resistance to new forms of capitalism—capitalism without national boundaries—as the last gasp of a historically outmoded peasantry. Given the inability of organized labor to defeat the efforts of a Democratic president to pass the NAFTA and the GATT, what hope could there be for the non-industrial, agrarian forms of life that have arisen over centuries in response to a unique ecological niche?

If we set aside these first world expectations about the inevitable advance of capitalism, however, and listen to the voices of indigenous resistance movements, we may reach a different conclusion. It may be that, as Ramachandra Guha writes, in its conquest of the last people of the earth, "the ship of capitalism has finally run aground" (Guha 1990: 195). And the reason for this, according to Guha, lies at the nexus of environmental and social justice. The Zapatista warning, "We have nothing to lose, absolutely nothing" reveals their clear understanding that they will never gain from capitalism. Legacies of land appropriation, food scarcity, disease (AIDS), ethnic conflict, and war mean that the world's indigenous people no longer can retreat. Urban decay and rapid population growth mean that the cities, such as Mexico City and Bombay, are no longer alternatives when rural economies fail.

There is a cynical remark often heard among the poor in India: "In America, the poor have cars." While we may wish to quarrel with the details, we should not disregard the larger point: in the third world the poor have nowhere to go. Their resolute defense of small cultures occupying unique ecological niches is also a critique of the homogenizing effects of urban industrial culture.

There is a Gandhian legacy in the protests of indigenous resistance groups. They function as the leading edge of resistance to development. There will be broad-scale resistance to development among the poor of the third world because survival depends upon it. The only question is whether such resistance movements will be committed to a further Gandhian principle: ahimsa, nonviolence.

5

Recognizing Women's Environmental Expertise

INSTITUTIONS AND MATERIAL CULTURE

A frequent theme of this book has been the importance of recognizing the roles that women traditionally play in mediating between nature and human culture. They do this in many ways, but their roles as farmers, or traditional cultivators, are particularly critical to an accurate rendering of the environmental crisis we face. In chapter 3, I contrasted traditional agriculture, often the primary responsibility of women, with the agriculture of the green revolution, which is almost always thought of as men's work. The contrast is stark. Traditional agriculture tends to be small in scale. It depends upon adapting seed genetics to local conditions. It is diverse, requiring a mixture of crops with livestock. In turn, agriculture is only part of a larger system that includes biological commons which provide building materials and medicines.

Green revolution agriculture is massive in scale, therefore commanding major investment in farm machinery. Its seed genetics come from the multinational corporation, and the entire package of inputs is designed to make the land adapt to the requirements of the inputs. This necessitates massive irrigation. It is a system of plant monoculture, and thus defines everything that does not contribute to the production of this single crop as waste. The biological commons become wasteland in need of development.

Given that, despite fifty years of the green revolution, most food is still produced by women's labor in the traditional way, it is surprising that women's agriculture continues to be defined as needing "development." Modernization is still synonymous with the process of dislodging the poor from their land, which, in turn, causes migration to the urban slums. The GATT and NAFTA agreements, including their new instruments for privatizing the biological commons, clearly indicate that we have not learned to work with the land, or with indigenous cultures. Nothing, really, has changed since the days of the utilitarians.

In this chapter I ask why women's critical contributions to food production are often overlooked. Drawing on the distinction between individual and institutional violence, I suggest, again, that neglect of traditional women's perspectives is best understood as a form of institutional violence. That is, while there are certainly individuals who consciously want to marginalize traditional women's perspectives, a much more powerful analysis is to admit that certain features of the developmentalist story make it exceedingly difficult to recognize and value women's agricultural labor.

Yet, this is exactly the problem: How *can* we generalize about women's ecological practices, their material cultures, to the point that their roles become recognizable, without thereby losing sight of the enormous diversity of their lives? In India alone, for example, Dalit (Untouchable) women suffer the worst effects of the caste system, while tribal (Adivasi) women come from cultures that have traditionally been outside the caste system, and often fare better. Even among tribal groups, however, some have matrilineal social structures, others patrilineal. This means that social arrangements differ considerably, even among neighboring villages.

Western feminists have learned how difficult it is to generalize about "women." It is easy for race and class biases to slip into generalizations about the conditions of Western women. The attempt to generalize across such a deeply contentious and artificial category as "third world women" is surely more risky. Not to enter into this hazardous territory, however, risks something even greater: that the lives of women will continue to occupy conceptually marginal places.

It is often charged that feminism is a first world phenomenon that is inappropriately projected onto the third world. Fortunately, the attempt to represent the diversity of third world women's lives, as well as their common themes, is quickly becoming an international project. While the so-called Second Wave of feminism was originally a predominantly white, middle-class phenomenon, international feminism is evolving toward pluralistic perspectives that include relations between the first and third worlds, as well as relations among race, class, caste, and gender. Moreover, there are development perspectives that arise from the lives of third world women. In India, for example, these include the famed Chipko Movement, the feminist journal *Manushi*, and Kali for Women, which publishes important feminist development books in association with Zed Books. To dismiss feminism as a first world perspective denies that there are self-identified third world feminists.

This is not to suggest that third world feminists do not complain of being marginalized by first world liberal feminists. We saw this in the Shivas' objections to the International Conference on Population and Development in Cairo (chapter 1). The source of tension is often the perception that first world liberal feminism is corrosively individualistic. It attempts to put the needs of individual women ahead of, and in opposition to, the needs of their communities. If there is a common theme among Indian feminists, it is that they will not define feminist aspirations in terms abdicating responsibility for roles that hold together traditional societies.

Partly because of the problems of generalization, the approach I employ here is empirical and nonessentialist. It does not resort to abstractions about the supposed inherent natures of women and the environment. Such depictions of "women's nature" are often self-defeating. A famous bumper sticker that pictures the earth viewed from outer space reads "Love Your Mother." Read in a sexist culture, however, it has an unintended double meaning if we think it is our mother's job to pick up after us. Such images only tend to reinforce stereotypes of "man" as the builder of culture out of nature. "Woman" is left with the dirty work (Murphy 1988).

While women are not *essentially* more "natural," closer to nature, than men, while nature is no more female than male, the *actual practices* typically demanded of women by institutional structures involve direct mediation between culture and nature. This is particularly evident in the material lives of third world women farmers. We begin to remedy this situation when we stress the need for a philosophy of material culture. We need to attend to what women *do*, given their self-explanations. Most important, we need to set aside comfortable assumptions about what counts as expertise.

LITTLE IS KNOWN OF THEIR CONDITION

An Indian woman and scholar gave this description of the daily lives of village women in her country:

> While they work on an average many more hours than their men, they eat much less. When there is little food, it is the woman who has to go without. ... She works in the fields, looks after the children, comes home and prepares the family meal and then has to be available for her man whenever she is required. ... rural women endure childbirth after childbirth which drains them of physical energy and destroys their health. They have little or no access to health care and such facilities as there are are pitifully inadequate. In any militant struggle that they, or their men, have been involved in, they are the ones who are most vulnerable to police and state repression. They suffer violence and abuse within their own homes. Yet little is known of their condition. (Butalia 1985: 132–33)

Reading this, one could easily conclude that there is little hope for rural women's development in the third world, much less for an approach to ecodevelopment based on their distinctive practices.

As deeply troubling as these acts of gendered violence are, I suggest that this passage raises a deeper question: "What are the institutionalized ways of thinking that allow both developmentalist and local cultures to put women last?" Even attempts to help women often go disastrously wrong. It made good sense to well-intended development experts, for example, that women in a sunny continent such as Africa could benefit from solar stoves.[1] Experts' ignorance of what women know, however, caused them to ignore the fact that women are not likely to cook in the heat of the day, nor are they often able to cook during the valuable daylight hours, given the other demands that claim their time. In a first world culture in which women are expected to do most of the cooking, it would not be a very bright business policy to have men design stoves for use by women without consulting their needs. Yet, this happens all the time in the attempt to "develop" third world women.

Much of this tendency to look past third world women derives from our thinking about what counts as expertise. In characterizing developmentalism, I referred to Richard Levins's "seven developmentalist myths in agriculture." Since women are at the bottom of the developmentalist pecking order, they often experience the force of these myths most directly. Women are regarded as backward because what they do is often labor intensive rather than capital intensive; their labors are committed to maintaining diversity on a small scale, and this is surely an indication of subjection to nature rather than complete control over it; since their knowledge is the accumulation of centuries of village-based genetic experimentation, what they know is dismissed as superstition, folk knowledge (Levins 1986).

Vandana Shiva is particularly effective in challenging such assumptions about what counts as expertise. Describing traditional agricultural production, she says, "The backyard of each rural home was a nursery, and each peasant woman the sylviculturalist. The invisible, decentred agroforestry model was significant because the humblest of species and the smallest of people could participate in it." This plant diversity, and the mixture of private and public treestands, provides "food and fodder, fertilizer and pesticide, fuel and small timber."

In masculinist development projects, this kind of agricultural production and the knowledge it requires is replaced, Shiva says, by the "reductionist mind" of outside experts who do not understand the multiple uses of traditional plantings, nor their uses in traditional culture.

> The experts decided that indigenous knowledge was worthless and "unscientific", and proceeded to destroy the diversity of indigenous species by replacing them with row after row of eucalyptus seedlings in polythene bags, in government nurseries. Nature's locally available seeds were laid waste; people's locally available knowledge and energies were laid waste. With imported seeds and expertise came the import of loans and debt and the export of wood, soils—and people. Trees, as a living resource, maintaining the life of the soil and water and of local people, were replaced by trees whose dead wood went straight to a pulp factory hundreds of miles away. (Shiva 1988: 79)

The eucalyptus is valuable as a cash crop because it grows fast and straight, putting most of its energy into wood pulp instead of into branches and leafy matter. But it is also an ecological disaster whose impact is felt particularly by women. Its scarcity of leaves and small branches mean there is very little to return to the land to conserve moisture and fertility. It also does not provide wood for housing. The fact that it grows quickly means that it places a heavy demand upon water supplies. In arid regions the demand on water and its lack of contribution to humus, which maintains soil moisture, have contributed directly to the oppression of women who must walk further and further each year to obtain drinking water.

The eucalyptus has become a symbol for the many ways in which women's ecological knowledge is marginalized. Today in India, one cannot drive far along a major road without seeing advertisements calling for investments in new eucalyptus plantations. When such cash crops drive out traditional crops that return nitrogen to the soil without expensive inorganic fertilizers (crops such as pulses), this is gender bias. When herbicides kill grasses that are used to make baskets and mats, grasses that are defined by outside experts as worthless, this is gender bias. When plants are genetically engineered to produce only cash value, thereby reducing by-products that go to fuel and fodder, this is gender bias. When so-called undeveloped lands to which everyone has access are privatized and dedicated to plant monoculture, this is gender bias.

Technological innovations, such as hydro-electric dams to support large-scale irrigation and plant monoculture, are typical of men's agriculture. The impact of these and other green revolution techniques has often been devastating for women. The scarcity of water in the third world, for example, reveals much. Although 73 percent of the world's water use is dedicated to irrigation, only 20–30 percent gets to its destination. Such waste has a tragic impact on women's lives. Women are still overwhelmingly responsible for collecting water for drinking and cooking. Yet in India, 23,000 villages are without drinking water due to deforestation and irrigation. Seventy percent of the available ground water is polluted (Dankelman and Davidson 1988: 21, 33). Water collection increasingly demands women's time. The need to carry water over greater distances affects women's health, particularly the health of girls, whose bodies are still developing.

Despite misguided attempts at development, many third world women and their communities have not stood aside as their communities have been destroyed. The experiences of Chipko women in the Himalayan foothills are justly celebrated. The modern Chipko Movement began as a response to flooding due to deforestation in the mountains above Chipko villages. The response to deforestation varied by gender. Men were drawn to wage-labor jobs in the forestry industry. Women were drawn to reforestation since their concerns were different. These include the entire cycle of concerns that depend upon forests, from adequate water supplies to fuel and fodder and sources of traditional medicines. A healthy ecosystem is a necessity for the safety of children and the possibility of future generations. When villagers were asked about which trees should be planted as part of a reforestation plan, the men immediately chose fruit trees, a cash crop. The women responded, however, "The men would take the fruits and sell them by the roadside. The cash will only go to buy liquor and tobacco.

We women prefer fuel and fodder trees" (Dankelman and Davidson 1988: 50–51). The demonstrated effectiveness of women's projects that involve caring labor cannot be doubted. In a ten year study of trees planted and cared for by Chipko women, it was found that their survival rate had increased from 10 percent to the 80–90 percent range (Dankelman and Davidson 1988: 50). Similar statistics on women's reforestation projects can be found for other locations in India and in the Green Belt Movement in Africa.

Social forestry is a feminist issue. Tree hugging by Chipko women is more than the simple attempt to save trees from logging companies. It is a political act growing out of women's local knowledge of the forest. Tree hugging represents the broad circle of concerns that women understand. Trees mean water for Chipko women. Trees mean safety from flooding. Forests, not simply plant monoculture, mean food, fodder, building materials, and medicines. Tree hugging is as much a defense of culture and future generations as it is a defense of nature.

Development theory has progressed from what can only be described as racist and sexist beginnings. Ester Boserup, for instance, has documented the impact of colonial attitudes on development practices in Africa. Her work serves as an example of how sexist (and racist) categories have affected the concept of development historically. Prior to the arrival of European culture, men's traditional activities in Africa were tree-felling, hunting, and war. All were curbed by Europeans. Forcibly deprived of their traditional roles, African males were left with little to do, thus the Western stereotype of the "lazy African male." African women were responsible for most agricultural work and food gathering. Development might have begun, therefore, with women's traditional knowledge. However, because of the European bias that farming is men's work, most European efforts were addressed solely to men (Boserup 1970: 19, 55). Such biases certify masculine knowledge as official—they also certify indigenous men as ignorant—while challenging and marginalizing traditionally women's knowledge.

Nevertheless, contemporary programs that are advertised as pro-family often remain anti-woman. Masculinity and the culture of high technology are connected through the division of labor. Men's cultural status tends to increase under the influence of technology, while women's status tends to decrease. Young men, in particular, can insist on becoming "modern," often wearing Western clothes and sporting Western electronic goods. Women are expected to maintain traditional values and dress (Mies 1988: 138).

Many international agents—even the World Bank—now include

women's issues in their programs. Yet programs directed at the male "head of household" are conceptually flawed when they assume equity and identity of interests within the family. Because equity is rare, these programs pull the family apart. The effort to involve third world communities in international markets through introduction of technologies to produce cash crops is one example. This tends to cause dual economies with men working in the for-profit sector, while women continue with traditional agriculture to meet the needs of the family. Such programs rarely improve the lives of women and children.

TAKING WOMEN'S PRACTICES SERIOUSLY

This tendency of traditional development schemes to elevate men while further marginalizing women depends upon a familiar set of normative categories. Expertise requires the mind, not bodily labor; it requires reason, not feeling; it requires theorizing out of any social context, not concrete practice within a historied community. The masculine bias in these dualisms favors the "modern," scientific, rational, global, and the high-tech over the traditional, small-scale, and the low-tech. Developmentalism constructs masculinity as independent, autonomous, rational; it constructs women as dependent or interdependent. Men's agriculture, which can hardly be understood as anything but a practical activity, is, nevertheless, represented as a "theoretical practice," that is, as an applied *science*. Women's expert knowledge of soil, climate, and seeds is marginalized as anecdotal; it is often dismissed as mere "wives' tales."

The patriarchal story of development is based on a linear narrative according to which culture emerged out of, and then decisively departed from, nature. Practices that involve caring for others—mothering, cooking, traditional health care, and certain kinds of simple, traditional agricultural labor that are low-paid or unpaid, such as weeding and tending to livestock—are the spots at which nature is nurtured into culture. As with James Mill's "gift" of history to India, such nurturing practices have no meaning until they are given one by the developmentalist myth. In this process, self-explanations are erased. Women's labor is what the developmentalist says it is.

This creates a dilemma: the "public face" of women's labor is a systematic distortion. Yet, most third world women are emphatic that they will not define authentic development in terms of what they regard as the first world feminist narrative of liberal individualism.

They will not abdicate responsibility for traditional roles that hold communities together. Children's health and safety depend upon regular access to clean water. Traditional medicine and agriculture depend upon the biodiversity of an environment that can supply medicines as well as fuel, fodder, and food. Caring labor holds together the family and the environment, and is inherently interested in future generations. As with liberation and Dalit theologies, third world women are calling for a localized expression of their aspirations.

The issue, then, is how an epistemology can be constructed that is faithful to *what* third world women know, as well as to the *ways* in which they know. First, some clarifications. In emphasizing gender bias in the construction of what is counted as knowledge, I am speaking about the construction of gender categories, not about particular individuals. While gender does have a powerful hold on individuals, there are other forces that intersect in the individual as well, including race, caste, class, and religion. This means that some men are nonsexist, despite sexist constructions of gender; some women are implicated in the destruction of the environment even though traditional women's praxis involves caring. Consequently, my argument is that recognition of gender is a *necessary* condition—not a sufficient condition—for sustainable development.

Yet, gender is not the same as sex. If we take sex to be a matter of chromosomes, a biological distinction between males and females, gender—like race, caste, or class—is a social construction. It is a set of institutional signals that shapes what can and cannot be done in a particular social context. Constructions of gender shape the ways in which social powers are granted or withheld.

It would be a mistake, furthermore, to look to the traditional philosophical distinction between propositional (the belief that a proposition is true) and nonpropositional attitudes to clarify the distinction between men's and women's ways of knowing. I would say, rather, that such forms of knowledge are *constructed* by gendered categories as propositional or nonpropositional to the disadvantage of both. As medicine has been masculinized, for example, it has been important to construct medical knowledge as propositional (abstract, theoretical), despite the evident hands-on expertise required by the skilled surgeon. Cooking, a clear case of a hands-on epistemic practice, is diminished if it is reduced simply to knowing-how.

This brief overview of the construction of gendered agricultural knowledge leads me, instead, to focus on *practices* as a way of getting at a reconstructed conception of women's agricultural labor. Practices, as I understand them, are much more than sets of individual actions. They are fundamental ways of categorizing, experiencing, and valuing the world. In turn, the requirements of a practice generate distinctive forms of *knowledge*. Mothering, for example, is a practice that generates its own epistemology (Ruddick 1989).[2] There are also epistemologies of cooking (Curtin and Heldke 1992: section 3) and land cultivation. Epistemic attitudes derive from doings. If women have been assigned agricultural tasks throughout history, and knowledge derives from the requirements of a particular kind of practice, should we not expect to find that women have been responsible for the advances that practice has required? If women have been located at the intersection of the environment and those practices that sustain the community, such as mothering, health care, and care for the land, would we not expect them to be sources of traditional knowledge on these matters? Simply put, attention to practices has a better chance of capturing "thoughtful actions" such as traditional farming than philosophical distinctions between propositional and nonpropositional attitudes.

A sympathetic and accurate portrayal of women's actual involvement in agricultural production might begin with some revisionist history. In a review of anthropological and mythological sources, Autumn Stanley says, "From the earliest times until at least the horticultural period . . . women were largely responsible for the gathering, processing, storing, and eventually for the cultivation of plant foods." In contrast to the hunter/gatherer myth, according to which man-the-hunter provides most of the food, anthropological evidence indicates that until recent times 60–80 percent of food was provided by women. While both women and men must have been involved in food gathering, "female's gathering would be different from males'—more highly motivated, and more of a 'social role' from the start in that females were usually gathering for one or more offspring as well as for themselves. Females . . . would thus be more likely to innovate and improve" (Stanley 1982: 290).

Women have been farmers for more than forty centuries. Given the assumption that *"the workers invented their tools,"* it makes sense to assume that women were responsible for:

> (1) food-gathering inventions such as the digging stick, the carrying sling or bag, the reaping knife or sickle, and other knives; (2) food processing inventions such as the mortar and pestle or pounder, winnowing methods, grain-roasting tray, querns . . . washing to remove grit, detoxification . . .

and some forms of cooking . . . and (3) food-storage inventions such as baskets, clay-lined storage pits, drying and smoking of food, and preservation with honey.

Stanley also argues that women were responsible for domestication of wheat, rice, maize, barley, oats, sorghum, millet, and rye. These cereals still provide 75 percent of all human food energy (Stanley 1982: 293–94). The same pattern can be found in the development of traditional medicines. Still today, women are responsible for 80 percent of the world's medical care (Kheel 1989).

We should not expect to find women's expert knowledge at work everywhere in the contemporary world. The ancient patterns of women's knowledge have been distorted and disrupted. Women struggle to invent and reinvent forms of knowledge that are appropriate to their complex situations as mothers, wives, traditional farmers, health care workers, and last line of environmental defense. If their indigenous knowledge of the sustainable ecological community has often been destroyed by maldevelopment, women are still invested by their daily practices in the reinvention of such knowledge. That women are dedicated to saving and restoring their knowledge is shown in the many organizations worldwide that are doing just this, organizations such as Chipko in India, Development Alternatives with Women for a New Era (DAWN) based in Brazil, the Third World Network in Malaysia, the Green Belt Movement in Kenya, and Women of All Red Nations (WARN) in Chicago, Illinois.

The work of these organizations demonstrates it would be a mistake to think that women's knowledge is backward-looking, that it is anti-technology, or anti-progress. In fact, if Stanley is correct, women have been responsible for most technological innovation. Women can hardly afford to be against progress if it is genuinely life-nurturing. It is simply that genuine progress for women and their communities is always judged by its relevance to a context.

This historical account of women's agricultural labor undercuts the typical reductionist accounts of the relation between nature and culture. Women are often pressed in two ways by this distinction. The first claims that nature ought to be preserved museum-like, free from human interaction. As we have seen, this mistake has caused some third world countries to remove indigenous people from their traditional lands to create American-style national parks. The second version claims that nature is only here for human manipulation and consumption, one cause of the tragedy of development. Both are forms of the myth that "man" lives apart from nature. Because of their traditional practices, women are typically well positioned to know that eco-development inevitably changes nature, and that changes which constitute real progress must be measured against the welfare of whole communities and future generations.

What, then, is distinctive about women's ecological knowledge? Based on the cases previously considered, I offer several generalizations. Since we are talking of constructions of gender, we need to keep in mind that these are, indeed, generalizations, not universal rules. No set of generalizations can capture the complexity of women's lives.

- Because women have been charged with many kinds of caring labor, *traditional women's knowledge tends to be relational.* Women tend to locate knowledge in the concrete, relational space between individuals and their communities, not in the abstraction of isolated, autonomous individuals. The relations that define community are broader than the human community. They include the entire ecological community, *this* place.
- *Traditional women's knowledge tends to be collaborative.* It is the project of the whole ecological *community* that is engaged by caring practices. A familiar example of this is home cooking. We tend not to even think of cooking as an epistemic practice that has its own rules and procedures. Yet, sharing family and community culinary traditions is a perfect example of a collaborative epistemic community. A less familiar example is sharing seeds over generations of women farmers. Such patient development of ecological knowledge reflects the complexity of local ecosystems. Within a single valley, women often plant dozens of genetically different strains of a single crop to take advantage of subtle changes in growing conditions.
- *Traditional women's knowledge tends to be transparently situated,* not abstract and rule-bound. To form an opinion, women need to know the life histories of the people and contexts they are speaking about. Concretely, we have seen this often means that what the outsider dismisses as waste has value within a context, for example, grasses at the edges of a field, or commons areas used by an entire village.
- *Traditional women's knowledge tends to be temporal,* if it grows out of actual contexts and histories. It is also future-directed. As those who have been defined in terms of their responsibility for children and future generations, women cannot help but test their knowledge against a criterion of sustainability. Women's knowledge is not only knowledge that operates in the spaces between individuals, but in the times between generations.
- Finally, *traditional women's knowledge tends to be bodily knowledge.* Because

cultural dualisms have defined women in terms of the body and nature, women tend to cultivate knowledge that integrates head and hand. Their knowledge consists more in "thoughtful ways of doing" than in "ways of thinking about."

Given these ways of characterizing traditional women's knowledge, we can understand why it is easy to miss women's knowledge, and thereby to abuse it. To those who look for knowledge as a decisive intervention from above, a self-confident declaration, women's relational knowledge can appear indecisive. It appears to the outsider as what Plato would have called "accidentally true belief" rather than knowledge. Women often have difficulty saying what they know about *all* situations just because they know how complex *this* situation is. Growing out of practices that cannot escape their temporality, women's knowledge has the appearance to outsiders of being qualified or tentative. One task required by the revaluation of caring labor is to value this apparent tentativeness as a positive quality. Since women's knowledge is marked by its group collaboration, for example, we should expect that third world women's knowledge is expressed through the group rather than through the individual.

Because knowledge varies in relation to different forms of practice, moving between forms of knowledge involves what María Lugones calls "world-travelling" (Lugones 1987). Her term is useful because it emphasizes that entire worlds must be traversed for communication to occur. If we assume, for example, that the epistemic world of the outsider, the (male) scientific expert, is the standard against which all others are measured, it is impossible to cross over into the world of hands-on expertise that is characteristic of women's ecological knowledge.

Since we are talking about different worlds of discourse, each having its own standards for knowledge and success, there is an important distinction between those who function as insiders to the practice and those who come to it as outsiders. The rules of the practice are, by definition, known to the insiders, those who engage in the practice. To outsiders, it may appear there is no knowledge at all. The outsider, particularly when motivated by institutional biases, can easily dismiss as mere superstition the real inside knowledge that motivates and sustains the practice. Gender-biased development programs, therefore, are not always reducible to simple malice. It may well be that, from the perspective of another "world," the insider's knowledge is not, or cannot be, revealed as knowledge. The work of those concerned with the lives of third world women is a matter of devising strategies for making these forms of practice and knowledge visible.

While insiders' knowledge may be initially invisible to the outsider, that does not mean it lacks power. If it is true that "real knowledge is history that comes from below" (Rose 1986: 162), then we must learn to recognize the intersection of forces in tribal or Dalit women that makes their forms of knowledge conceptually central to the task of reconstructing caring labor. In the "lowest of the low," in those who must care for others without being cared for themselves, there is a praxis that is the key to sustainable development. Those who are marginalized and charged with responsibility for caring labor cannot fail to know the lives of those who marginalize them. The converse is not true. The master need not know the servant. Simply stated, because of their caring practices, third world women of low caste and class know things that others—including outside development experts—do not know.

Poor third world women cannot even pretend to escape the temporal reality of life that is demanded by caring labor. They do not have secretaries to reschedule appointments; they do not have servants to whom work can be delegated when they are tired or busy. Meals must come with predictable regularity, therefore food and fuel must be gathered *now*. Need for medical care is unpredictable; the need is immediate and cannot wait.

Women cannot afford the illusion that it is possible to escape time and place. This is one reason for calling typically women's knowledge expert knowledge. Caring labor produces transparent knowledge; such knowledge is superior just because it is transparent that it is situated between nature and culture. Survival depends upon it.

In contrast, there is delusion in constructions of life that claim to be free of time and place. While men are inevitably dependent upon many forms of caring labor, they have the power to construct the self-serving myth of themselves as independent, autonomous, and atemporal. Patriarchal constructions work to bolster this delusive self-construction.

Liberated from patriarchal distortions, caring contexts are potentially those in which women and men can experience themselves as citizens in a broadly ecological community. This space, which is normally an ambiguous borderland, neither fully culture, nor fully nature, can become a context in which the dualistic opposition between culture and nature is transformed. While caring contexts are defined oppressively, that is, they can be reconstructed as small-scale contexts in which citizenship for women and men is defined in relation to an environment that can produce safe food and water, sustainable fuels, and health care that works toward the well-being of this and future generations.

It does make sense, therefore, to say that traditional women's knowledge of the environment is privileged. It is privileged, not in the sense that women "know nature by nature." Rather, engagement in a practice requires development of localized expertise. Of course, this does not mean that such localized expertise is infallible, or that it would not benefit from context-sensitive change. Women do not often think of themselves as infallible, and they often have no choice but to recognize localized change that makes sense. When I describe traditional women's environmental knowledge as privileged, I mean that they are the primary experts, the people whose opinions must come first.

Although many things can be said about the practical consequences of the practice-oriented approach I have developed here, I will mention only one. There is the tendency to assume that one aspect of development must come first. It has been argued, for example, that the development of the head of household should come first, or that race or class must take precedence. A nonreductionist perspective indicates that race, caste, class, and other issues are intricately woven into a quilt whose patterns vary subtly. Women's issues within the community should not be delayed for the sake of solidarity with another group. From the beginning, women need the resource of other women in groups whose purpose is to articulate their distinctive concerns. This is required not only because the character of women's knowledge tends to be collaborative, but simply for the safety of women who risk much by speaking out alone. If development is to be truly dialogical, then all aspects of development must move together. Dialogue can only take place among dialogical equals.

A STORY: UJAL KHILLO AND THE BANKER

Several years ago I visited a group of tribal villages in a remote section of Orissa state in India.[3] The area had been logged-off twenty years ago. People face all too typical problems of bonded labor, access to land, alcohol abuse among the men, and illiteracy, which makes it difficult to communicate with those outside experts who have an impact on their lives.

I was invited to meet with people of one village to hear their concerns. For the first hour I listened to a confident young man, dressed in Western clothing, talk about how much his leadership had accomplished for the village. The faces of others in the room made it clear that they, too, were tired of this man's self-advertisements. Then, a middle-aged woman, dressed traditionally, was asked to speak. Her name is Ujal Khillo. She began tentatively, saying she had become tired of her life and decided to do something to help herself and her village. The local development office offered a carpentry training program, and she decided to enroll. This overt act of independence embarrassed her husband, and he appeared the next day threatening to beat her. She would not be deterred, telling him that if he beat her again, she would report him to the police. The shock of her defiance was enough to send him back down the road to his village.

Training complete, she went to the local bank to apply for a small loan the government makes available to tradespeople for tools. The banker noted that she is a woman; women are not carpenters, so she was not eligible for a loan. She refused to leave his office until he agreed to visit her village to observe her skills for himself. He came, saw, and agreed to authorize the loan.

Told to mark the loan forms with an X, she refused, saying she knew how to sign her name. That was impossible, he said. Tribals are illiterate. After a further standoff, the banker relented and she finally signed her name. She is now the first certified woman carpenter in her area. Her husband, by the way, has accepted his wife's accomplishments and appears to be proud of her.

I tell the story of this courageous woman because, as a carpenter making wooden furniture and children's toys for her village in an area that has been decimated by deforestation, she works in that ambiguous borderland between injured nature and a dysfunctional society. With her caring labor, and her refusal to be dismissed, rest hope for a genuinely ecological community.

Part 2
Radical First World Environmental Philosophy

A New Colonialism?

6

Callicott's Land Ethic

DID WE LEARN ANYTHING FROM THE UTILITARIANS?

In 1989 an article appeared in the principal journal of Western environmental ethics titled "Radical American Environmentalism and Wilderness Preservation: A Third World Critique." Its author, Indian sociologist Ramachandra Guha, summarized his intentions thus: "I examine the cultural rootedness of a philosophy [deep ecology] that likes to present itself in universalistic terms. I make two main arguments: first, that deep ecology is uniquely American . . . ; second, that the social consequences of putting deep ecology into practice on a worldwide basis (what its practitioners are aiming for) are very grave indeed" (Guha 1989: 72).

Guha identified and criticized four commitments of deep ecology: the shift from an anthropocentric to a biocentric ethical perspective as the "litmus test of deep ecology"; the exclusive focus on the preservation of unspoiled wilderness at the expense of questions of human justice; invocation of Eastern spiritual traditions as forerunners of deep ecology; and the self-perception among deep ecologists that they represent the "leading edge" of the environmental movement, the "spiritual, philosophical, and political vanguard of American and world environmentalism" (Guha 1989: 73–74).

Describing himself as a "sympathetic outsider," Guha nevertheless took strong exception to all four of these commitments. The biocentrism/anthropocentrism distinction does nothing to address the two fundamental environmental problems we face according to Guha: "overconsumption by the industrialized world and by urban elites in the Third World" and growing militarization. Far from threatening the environment for the benefit of human beings, overconsumption and militarization threaten human beings *as well as* the environment. Guha concluded that "invoking the bogy of anthropocentrism is at best irrelevant and at worst a dangerous obfuscation" (Guha 1989: 74).

The focus on the value of wilderness to the exclusion of human interests follows from the misguided focus on biocentrism and has already had disastrous consequences for the third world. Project Tiger, which set aside "wilderness" to preserve tigers in India and a project widely supported by international conservation groups, further disenfranchised the poor and benefited India's feudal elite and the ecotourism industry.

Guha charged, further, that deep ecology indiscriminately invokes a variety of Eastern religious and spiritual traditions as biocentric precursors of deep ecology. Such positing of "The East" as a repository of spiritual oneness with nature is the mirror image of the pejorative Western view of the East as backward and pre-scientific. Both objectify "The East." Both are "monolithic, simplistic, and have the characteristic effect . . . of denying agency and reason to the East and making it the privileged orbit of Western thinkers" (Guha 1989: 77).

Finally, Guha questioned whether deep ecology is, after all, a radical environmental movement. If it is, it is only radical within a narrowly American understanding of the environment inspired by such American thinkers as John Muir and Aldo Leopold, who were responding to distinctively American problems.

In short, Guha challenges radical American environmental philosophy with advancing a neocolonial agenda. Deep ecology dresses itself up in a deceptive cloak of universalism, subsuming other cultural traditions within it. The anthropocentric/biocentric distinction, represented as a universal diagnosis of environmental wrongdoing, obscures an accurate understanding of the diverse ways that non-Western people engage the environment. It patronizes "The East" by depicting it as an intuitive rest stop on the way to a full-blown, clearly articulated philosophical defense of biocentrism.

It is easy to sympathize with Guha's charge of neocolonialism, having already examined the role of utilitarianism, an earlier "radical" universalism come to save the pre-scientific "East," whose colonial agenda was cloaked in the garb of universal justice. Guha's is not the only voice from the third world to question the universalism of Western moral categories. We have also encountered Vandana Shiva and Mira Shiva's objections to first world liberal feminist prescriptions for "the population problem" as espoused at the International Conference on Population and Development in Cairo, where first world liberal individualism actually made the lives of third world women more precarious.

In this chapter and the next, I devote extensive consideration to two pioneering Western environmental philosophers whose work appears to represent the sort of neocolonialism that Guha detects. This chapter examines J. Baird Callicott's defense of the "land ethic," an ecocentric environmental ethic he claims to derive from Aldo Leopold's masterpiece, *A Sand County Almanac*. Although Guha does not directly challenge Callicott, he does see his essay as leading to a critical reassessment of Leopold's legacy. Like John Muir, Leopold "makes sense only in an American context; he has very little to say to other cultures" (Guha 1989: 83). Furthermore, Callicott has made a career arguing for environmental ethics as the defense of a theory of intrinsic value for nature (biocentrism), universalism in moral theory (more precisely, moral monism), and he has argued extensively that many of the world's indigenous cultures espouse some version of Leopold's land ethic.

In the following chapter I take up the work of Norwegian Arne Naess, the founder of deep ecology. Naess has defended the intrinsic value of nature as one of the core commitments of deep ecology. He has often had recourse to ideas and thinkers outside the Western intellectual tradition, particularly Mahatma Gandhi, and elements of Hinduism and Buddhism. Naess has inspired many environmentalists around the world, and some of them have espoused alarming positions on issues of human social justice in the name of biocentrism.

Whereas Guha's charge of neocolonialism fairly applies to Callicott's land ethic, I offer at least one reading of Naess's version of deep ecology (as distinct from the many versions he has encouraged others to develop themselves) that at least partially deflects Guha's criticisms. Taken together, these two chapters may be seen as pointing the way through American forms of environmental ethics to a more global and culturally sensitive understanding of environmental problems. In chapter 8, I begin to consider explicitly pluralistic approaches to environmental ethics.

"THE CENTRAL PROBLEM FOR ANY
FUTURE ENVIRONMENTAL ETHICS"

Guha and Callicott agree that American environmental attitudes have evolved from two competing paradigms. The first emerges from the Transcendentalist writings of Ralph Waldo Emerson and Henry David Thoreau, and through the stirring defenses of wilderness found in the writings of John Muir and Robinson Jeffers. According to this tradition, nature's value does not equate with utility; it does not exist for the exclusive economic benefit of human beings. Nature has its own intrinsic worth.

In the culture of expansive capitalism, a culture that tends to reduce all value to the common denominator of cost-benefit analysis, we would expect to find such a non-instrumentalist response. Henry David Thoreau's "In Wildness Is the Preservation of the World" and Robinson Jeffers' "Not Man Apart" were adopted as rallying crys in defense of wilderness. In the 1960s, David Brower brought unprecedented notice to the Sierra Club, which was founded by John Muir in 1892, when he orchestrated publication of a series of books combining photographs by Eliot Porter, Ansel Adams, and a new generation of nature photographers with writings from the American naturalist tradition (Brower 1965; Porter 1967). The non-instrumentalist response was critical to the establishment and defense of the American national park system. Although overuse by human beings and decreasing federal funding make this difficult to remember, the national park system marks a distinctively American commitment to the value of wilderness.

The other position that weighs heavily on the American mind is associated with President Theodore Roosevelt's preservation program. Gifford Pinchot, Roosevelt's chief architect for environmental management, put it succinctly: "There are just two things on this material earth—people and natural resources" (Pinchot 1947: 326). Pinchot was a utilitarian who sought to defend the wise use of natural resources for "the greatest good of the greatest number for the longest time" (Pinchot 1947: 325–26). Like John Stuart Mill and the earlier generation of utilitarians, Pinchot wanted to transfer title of natural resources from the wealthy elite, determined to plunder the environment *now,* and for their exclusive benefit, to the democratic majority. We see Pinchot's legacy today in the United States Forest Service, whose first director was Pinchot himself. Trees, like corn or wheat, are to be managed for maximum sustainable yield.

Muir and Pinchot, once friends and allies, engaged in an increasingly rancorous debate over the environment that continues to have a profound effect on American environmental attitudes. Muir's camp became the "preservationists" while Pinchot's became the "conservationists." Still today, debates over environmental policy quickly break down into these two camps.[1]

Given this intellectual climate, more importantly, given what has happened in the United States to first-growth forests, its wetlands and rivers, and its rich ecological heritage of fertile topsoil, it made sense for environmental philosophers to draw the line in defense of the environment. They thought that a utilitarian environmental policy only allows discussion of how quickly "resources" can be exploited.

It should be noted that a significant extension of utilitarianism may help us to understand how non-human sentient beings can possess moral standing. According to one standard version of the theory, any being that is capable of suffering pain has moral standing. Since human beings are not alone in their ability to experience pain and pleasure, they are not alone in receiving moral standing. It may even be that this argument commits us to vegetarianism.

However, this argument applies only to individual moral beings. As long as the idea persists that natural ecosystems *themselves* have no integrity, the radical environmental philosophers thought, environmental destruction will not stop. An environmental ethic, as distinct from an animal welfare ethic, needs to demonstrate the moral considerability of whole ecosystems.

Considering the utilitarian underpinnings of the resource management approach, it is not surprising that the pioneering first generation of environmental philosophers was inspired by the other great alternative in modern Western moral theory: a Kantian ethic of principles. Following a Kantian distinction between things that have value "in themselves" and things that can justifiably be used for the benefit of another, these philosophers granted that nature may have instrumental value, as when lumber is "harvested" to build homes, but they claimed nature also has intrinsic value, value in itself, apart from human needs and desires.

Callicott was not the only environmental philosopher to resort to the concept of intrinsic value. Other major figures, such as Paul W. Taylor and Holmes Rolston III, have also made intrinsic value, or inherent value, the core commitment of their work and have thus collaborated in establishing this concept as the Holy Grail of Western environmental philosophy. To understand how variable the application of the idea of intrinsic value is, and to locate Callicott's view within a larger spectrum of positions, consider, briefly, these alternative accounts.

Paul W. Taylor has offered the most detailed and sophisticated account of the concept in his book *Respect for Nature*. For Taylor, each "teleological center of life, pursuing its own good in its own unique way" (Taylor 1986: 45) has "inherent worth." Such goal-oriented activity need not involve a conscious purpose; even a sunflower, which follows the course of the sun through the day, may be regarded as a teleological center of life. For Taylor, though, only living individuals, not species, can possess inherent worth, since only individuals can be said to be goal oriented.

Taylor is the most Kantian of the philosophers considered here. His view is best described as a form of individualistic biocentric egalitarianism: it is committed to equal treatment of all *biological* entities. Where Immanuel Kant posited rationality as the criterion for moral considerability, thus limiting it exclusively to human beings, Taylor posits the broader criterion: being a teleological center of life. I do not consider him more extensively because he is not offering a philosophy for the moral standing of the *environment*. Sunflowers may have moral standing, but the whole ecosystem that supports sunflowers instead of yellow swamp lilies is not a teleological center of life.

Holmes Rolston III is the most inclusive of all the ecocentric ethicists. He agrees with Taylor that individual non-human beings are intrinsically valuable. Unlike Taylor, he believes that species and ecosystems also possess such value. He attempts to block potential conflicts among obligations to these diverse entities by granting extra moral standing to more complex systems. Thus, while humans are integral parts of ecosystems, they also retain many of their moral prerogatives. Where Taylor advocates vegetarianism, for example, because of his commitment to individual sentient beings, Rolston regards meat eating as a prerogative of more complex forms of life.

Clearly, while there has been widespread agreement among the first generation environmental philosophers on the need for a theory of intrinsic value, there has also been substantial disagreement over which entities are candidates for such standing. From an ecological standpoint it would certainly be attractive to say, unlike Taylor, that species and ecosystems are candidates for such value. But it is questionable whether a concept designed to account for the moral autonomy of *individuals,* can be extended to complex, interrelated *systems.* We see this struggle most plainly in the evolution of Callicott's attempt to map out a position between Taylor and Rolston.

When J. Baird Callicott began to defend the land ethic in the late

1970s, he presented it as an ecocentric (nature-centered) position in contrast to the common anthropocentric (human-centered), utilitarian position of reform environmentalism going back to Pinchot. Of all the pioneering environmental philosophers, Callicott remains the most assertive in claiming a single origination story for the discipline. Environmental philosophy *is* the defense of the intrinsic value of nature. Underpinning this is a monistic metaphysics of morals that led him to argue against pluralistic options for environmental ethics.

Callicott's early conception of the task of environmental philosophy drew upon a Kantian moral language. "There are, in general," he said, "two kinds of value: (1) intrinsic value and (2) instrumental value" (Callicott 1989d: 130). He identified instrumental value with utilitarianism. In contrast, "Something is intrinsically valuable if it is valuable *in* and *for* itself—if its value is not derived from its utility, but is independent of any use or function it may have in relation to something or someone else. In classical philosophical terminology, an intrinsically valuable entity is said to be an "end-in-itself," not just a "means to another's ends" (Callicott 1989d: 131).

In a renowned early paper which he has partially recanted, "Animal Liberation: A Triangular Affair," Callicott emphasized that biotic communities "own" (to use a term Callicott resorts to only in a later essay [Callicott 1989c: 163]) their value. Value is not conferred on biotic communities, it is possessed by them. He wrote, "An environmental ethic which takes as its *summmum bonum* the integrity, stability, and beauty of the biotic community is not conferring moral standing on something *else* besides plants, animals, soils, and waters. Rather, the former, the good of the community as a whole, serves as a standard for the assessment of the relative value and relative ordering of its constitutive parts and therefore provides a means of adjudicating the often mutually competing demands of the part considered separately for *equal* consideration" (Callicott 1989b: 25).

In this passage we meet with an enduring theme in Callicott's land ethic, that a theory of natural intrinsic value "provides a means of adjudicating" competing moral claims. As with Kant, the function of a land ethic was to dictate morals to a culture. It was to "speak from the mountaintop," pronouncing moral truths that may be abhorrent to the anthropocentric biases of human culture. Thus, as Callicott asserted in "Animal Liberation," "The extent of misanthropy in modern environmentalism . . . may be taken as a measure of the degree to which it is biocentric" (Callicott 1989b: 27).

Environmental ethics, he stressed, is not an animal liberation ethic. Where "humane moralists" such as Peter Singer and Tom Regan defend the moral integrity of individual animals, an environmental ethic, according to Callicott, throws the value of individual lives into question. He provocatively quoted Edward Abbey, saying "he would rather shoot a man than a snake" as a way of putting human over-population into stark relief. Garrett Hardin's lifeboat ethic passed Callicott's biocentric test because it shocked philosophers "schooled in the preciousness of human life" (Callicott 1989b: 27). On these grounds, Callicott rejected Singer's and Regan's vegetarianism, say-ing an animal's worth decreased with the populousness of its species. Callicott saw nothing wrong in hunting deer, but would have acted to protect rare Bengal tigers.

Callicott's inherentist ethical theory led him to meta-ethical mo-nism, the idea that there is a single, internally consistent, set of prin-ciples from which environmental duties can be deduced. We get a sense of Callicott's meta-ethical agenda for environmental philosophy in passages such as this:

> In a programmatic paper published in 1973 Richard Routley dramatically delineated, but did not attempt to solve, the central theoretical problem for any future environmental ethics. What Routley called "dominant Western ethical traditions," or what might better be labeled "normal Western eth-ics," provide, he claimed in effect, only instrumental, not intrinsic, value for nonhuman natural entities and nature as a whole. . . . Routley, thus, sug-gested that a genuinely *environmental* ethic would be both "new" and in-volve as a central or "core" feature an axiology that vested intrinsic value in nature. (Callicott 1989c: 157)

Callicott's "origination story" for environmental ethics contains sev-eral features that the rest of the world might find curious. "[T]he cen-tral theoretical problem for *any* future environmental ethics" (empha-sis added), Callicott said, originates in a rejection of one option in the "'dominant Western ethical traditions,'" but it sides with the other op-tion. What is "new" in environmental ethics turns out to be anything but a fundamental rethinking of the categories of Western moral phi-losophy, categories implicated in environmental destruction. The new project requires the acceptance of the oldest distinction in Western moral theory as the language in which environmental ethics must be framed, the distinction between intrinsic and extrinsic value.

Along with assumptions about the kind of value required for the defense of the environment, Callicott also took on old assumptions about the function and powers of philosophy itself. As with Kant, en-vironmental philosophers sought a universal, monistic theory of value that could then be applied cross-culturally. The model was deductive: given a theory of intrinsic value, we can deduce obligations that determine our actual behavior. For Callicott, environmental philosophy had to be universal in scope, and its universality had to be grounded in a commitment to a single kind of value, and a single metaphysic of morals.

Guha and the Shivas would not quarrel with the claim that the task of Western environmental philosophy is to analyze and deconstruct the moral categories in *Western* culture that have led to the destruction of the environment. But Callicott's origination story is more ambitious than that. It is universalistic in claiming one question and one answer for "any" environmental ethics.

We should also take careful note of distinctively individualist assumptions in Callicott's early terminology, despite his concern for the moral standing of species. For him, as for the Kantian tradition from which he draws, intrinsic value is "independent." It does not depend upon any "relation to something or someone else." Despite the fact that ecosystems are systems of integrated, dynamic *relationships,* Callicott explicitly expressed this in moral language designed to account for the autonomy of *individuals.* In short, the moral tradition from which Callicott began is the ethical individualism of first world liberalism.

A critical issue that faced Callicott's first position, then, was how to graft the tradition of liberal individualism onto a view that allows him to defend the moral standing of *non*-individuals: species and whole ecosystems. He did this by defending the moral considerability of what he called, following Leopold, the "biotic *community*" (Callicott 1989b: 21). The land ethic, as Callicott announced early on, is based on a single moral "categorical imperative" first issued by Aldo Leopold: "A thing is right when it tends to preserve the integrity, stability, and beauty of the biotic community. It is wrong when it tends otherwise" (Callicott 1989b: 21). Biotic communities are "wholes" that have "integrity." They are, in effect, super-individuals. So, natural entities, whether "the blue whale" or the "Bridger Wilderness," "may . . . be said in a quite definite, straightforward sense to own inherent value, that is to be valued *for themselves*" (Callicott 1989c: 163).

Callicott's early biocentric holism, and the diminished standing of individuals that holism implies, provoked a powerful response from animal rights theorist Tom Regan. Pressing his defense of the moral standing of *individual* animals against Callicott's holism, Regan charged that "Individual rights are not to be outweighed" by considerations of the biotic integrity of species and ecosystems. "Environmental fascism and the rights view are like oil and water: they don't mix" (Regan 1983: 362).

Regan hit on the central paradox of Callicott's early theory: despite its Kantian language, language Kant expressly designed to defend the moral inviolability of human beings, in Callicott's hands it raises doubts about "the preciousness of human life." The land ethic challenges the utilitarian principle that it is bad for individuals to suffer pain.

Despite the fact that Callicott partially recanted his early position, saying he was exaggerating to make a point, one cannot also help noticing the implicit privilege that the early Callicott, Abbey, and Hardin assume: they all imagine themselves doing the "shooting." They never imagine themselves being shot at in the war over the environment. The third world's poor, the unspoken recipients of morally justified violence, are depicted as the targets of biocentrism—just to make the rhetorical point.

If the intrinsic value of nature is the core of justice for the environment, what does this imply for human justice? Does radical environmental philosophy require radical "solutions" to problems of overpopulation? American poet Gary Snyder, who has long shown concern for the world's primal cultures, has, nevertheless, called for a 90 percent reduction in human population to allow restoration of wilderness. Dave Foreman of Earth First!, a radical environmental action group often associated with deep ecology, has presented what he calls "A Modest Proposal for a Wilderness System" which would cordon off large regions of the globe from human access. Hardin, a prophet of certain self-styled radical environmental groups, proposed the lifeboat ethic which advocates letting the third world "drown," not only so first world occupants of the lifeboats can survive, but also because our lower population density will allow us to preserve "our" wilderness, wilderness that is threatened by the influx of third world immigrants.

Episodes such as these raise serious questions about the agenda of first world environmental philosophy. Should it be understood as the pursuit of intrinsic value for nature if this leads to violation of the moral autonomy of humans? What consequences would a universalized theory of natural intrinsic value have for the third world? Can these positions, which claim to be deep and radical, presume to speak for everyone, labeling those who are concerned for human justice as shallow reformists? Are the universalist assumptions of radical American environmental philosophy racist, classist, and sexist? Bluntly, does commitment to radical first world environmental philosophy entail genocide for the poor of the third world?

These are difficult questions, difficult not only theoretically, but practically. One hopes that there is room for solidarity among all those who work for environmental and social justice. The urgency of the world's problems would cast a shameful reflection on those who engage in intellectual infighting at the same time they claim to work in common for a better world. Yet, given the dismal legacy of first world utilitarian philosophers who *created* colonial environmental policy, who, in fact, created the "third world," it is important to address these contentious questions honestly.

CALLICOTT'S COMMUNITARIANISM

Following his first statement of the land ethic, Callicott was faced with the need to address two connected problems: the charge that his view was fascist because it neglected the moral standing of individuals, and the need to defend the moral standing of ecosystems which are non-individuals. The goal of his second position, as I will call it, was to reconcile human and environmental justice. He does this through a new reading of Leopold's "biotic community."

Where the first position was characterized by a Kantian language of moral autonomy, the second position goes over to the tradition that Kant consciously rejected, a form of communitarianism deriving loosely from David Hume, Adam Smith, Charles Darwin, and Aldo Leopold. Here is a summary of Callicott's second position:

> [T]he proto-moral sentiments of affection and sympathy (upon which David Hume and Adam Smith erected their moral philosophies) were naturally selected in mammals as a device to ensure reproductive success. The mammal mother in whom these sentiments were strong more successfully reared her offspring to maturity. For those species in which larger and more complex social organization led to even greater reproductive success, the filial affections and sympathies spilled over to other family members—fathers, siblings, grandparents and grandchildren, uncles and aunts, nephews and nieces, cousins, and so on. Human beings evolved from highly social primates in a complex social matrix, and inherited highly refined and tender social sentiments and sympathies. With the acquisition of the power of speech and some capacity for abstraction, our ancestors began to codify the kinds of behavior concordant and discordant with their inherited communal-emotional bonds. They dubbed the former good and the latter evil. Ethics, thus, came into being. (Callicott 1990: 121)

To solve "the central theoretical problem for any future environmental ethics" (as we have seen Callicott boldly said in recalling Immanuel

Kant's language in the *Prolegomena to Any Future Metaphysics*), Callicott crosses over to a Humean theory based on the culturally contingent evolution of moral sentiments within a community.

Callicott calls this second position a "truncated" theory of inherent worth. Whereas *intrinsic* value is value "in and for itself"—it objectively "owns" its value, and its value is "independent of all valuing consciousness"—something has *inherent* worth when it is valued for itself, but not independently of valuing consciousness (Callicott 1989c: 161–62). Callicott's second position follows Hume's "subjectivist axiology," based on sympathy, which dictates that nature has inherent worth, but not intrinsic value. According to Callicott's second position narrative, ethics "came into being" with the evolution of sympathetic beings. While the "source" of all value is human consciousness, it does not follow that the "locus" of all value is human consciousness. Nature's value is not just instrumental. In its new truncated version, ecosystems are valuable *for* themselves, but not *in* themselves. When the dust settles, Callicott's second position is really an extended evolutionary argument for the possibility of altruism. He is arguing (correctly) that when I value something I need not value it only for its use to *me*.[2]

The test for the new, truncated position is whether Hume's communitarian leanings allow Callicott to respond to the problem that blocked his first position: the charge of fascism. According to Callicott's communitarian ethic, "we are members of nested communities each of which has a different structure and therefore different moral requirements. At the center is the immediate family. I have a duty not only to feed, clothe, and shelter my own children, I also have a duty to bestow affection on them. But to bestow a similar affection on the neighbors' kids is not only not my duty, it would be considered anything from odd to criminal were I to behave so." Similarly, he admits that he has obligations to neighbors that he does not have to "less proximate fellow citizens," and to "human beings in general which I do not have toward animals in general" (Callicott 1989b: 55–56).

Put in terms of an environmental ethic, the truncated second position says that altruism concerning non-human beings is possible. We can value other animals and ecosystems inherently when we extend the boundaries of moral sympathy to the biotic community. Conflicts between human and environmental justice are resolved in the second position not by "letting them drown," but by reference to the evolutionary precedence of nested moral communities. As Callicott asserts, human concerns generally trump the concerns of other animals and ecosystems; concern for friends trumps concern for remote acquaintances; concern for family trumps concerns for friends.

Callicott's claim for the second position is that he had arrived at a theoretical position that is univocal, but that can also account for the multiplicity of moral relationships which have developed over time. It is univocal "because it involves one metaphysics of morals: one concept of the nature of morality (as rooted in moral sentiments), one concept of human nature (that we are social animals voyaging with fellow creatures in the odyssey of evolution), one moral psychology (that we respond in subtly shaded ways to the fellow members of our multiple, diverse, tiered communities and to those communities per se) (Callicott 1990: 123–24). Since the origin of ethics is subjective, however, there will be multiple "hierarchically ordered and variously 'textured' moral relationships (and thus duties, responsibilities, and so on), each corresponding to and supporting our multiple, varied, and hierarchically ordered social relationships" (Callicott 1990: 123). Callicott resorts to the idea of hierarchies as a way of sorting out competing demands upon our moral allegiance. As a monist, Callicott is committed to the view that there is, ultimately, a mutually consistent and complete set of principles that will exhaustively specify our duties and obligations (Wenz 1993).

In fact, Callicott's second position does not achieve a consistent axiological framework. When he wants to address the specter of moral pluralism, he turns to a universal metaphysics of morals reminiscent of the first position. In Kantian fashion, Callicott distinguishes between culture and ethics, prudence and moral judgment. He still holds out the possibility of an algorithm for solving any moral dilemma. As a moral monist, he still looks to ethics to dictate issues of moral standing to cultures.

When faced with the need to truncate his theory in order to establish moral standing for non-individuals—when he devises an environmental ethic—Callicott argues for a Humean communitarianism which says we should solve moral dilemmas by reference to whatever the moral evolution of one's own culture happened to have been. Callicott's culture tells him that human concerns trump non-human animals. It tells him it would be considered "odd to criminal" were he to extend the same concern to his neighbors' children as to his own. But this fails to connect with his Kantian metaphysics of morals. Callicott's hierarchy of nested communities is utterly contingent. It is possible that there are (and certain that there could be) communities which require the same care for the children of neighbors as for one's own. It seems possible to imagine cultures evolving first through concern for animals and natural forces, placing care for humans only within that broader context as a secondary responsibility. The moral sympathies Callicott claims to be deducible from a universal metaphysics of morals are firmly rooted in the moral intuitions of Western liberal culture.

Far from resolving Regan's charge of fascism, Callicott's second position replicates the unsavory results of the first position. In the first position, Callicott sided (rhetorically) with Hardin's prescriptions for the third world: let the overpopulated "drown" for the sake of "our" environment. Does the second position prescribe anything different? The idea of nested communities implies that obligations decrease with distance. Callicott said that we have greater obligations to our family and neighbors than to "less proximate fellow citizens." If we understand "third world" as a geographical term, this means that Callicott's view justifies, in the style of Richard Luttwack and Garrett Hardin, the exploitation of remote communities for the sake of local communities. When we ask Callicott what to do about the fact that 20 percent of the world's people consume 80 percent of the natural resources, does his theory imply anything different than Hardin's or Luttwack's? Surely, if I should prefer my children to my neighbors' children, then I should also prefer the interests of neighbors in the first world to distant acquaintances in the third world.

Callicott's response is that ecological literacy will reshape our commitments. In some circumstances we should not prefer the interests of neighbors to distant acquaintances. We may learn that the sympathies of our community are wrong. It is not difficult to find passages in which Callicott still speaks with the reshaped assurance of a Kantian monist: "We have before us then the bare bones of a *univocal* ethical theory embedded in a coherent world view" (Callicott 1990: 123). This coherent worldview is not that of "The primitive family, clan, and tribal communities" (Callicott 1990: 122), however, that were at the aboriginal origin of Callicott's narrative of moral progress These views are trumped by Darwinian science, and, in some accounts as we shall see, by Heisenberg's Indeterminacy Principle, which provides the basis for quantum mechanics.

Against the charge that Callicott's land ethic colonizes other views (Cheney 1989a; Cheney 1989b), Callicott responded by saying that philosophers must be willing "to come up to speed on our growing body of knowledge and rationally think through how that knowledge might be integrated into a single coherent world view" (Callicott 1990: 119). "Our growing body of knowledge comes from science" and science is an "international activity, the hallmark of which is the falsifiable hypothesis and repeatable experiment" (Callicott 1990: 119–20).

It appears what we have here is a narrative of moral progress that allows the "Primitive family, clan, and tribal communities" their moral prerogatives until conflicts arise. Then we will all need to "get up to speed" with the current state of modern rationality and discover that something new has happened in ethics which trumps the "primitive."

Unlike some of Callicott's critics,[3] I am not arguing that science is inherently colonizing. Let me be emphatic: We need the best knowledge that ecologists can provide if we are to return the planet's complex ecosystems to health. What I find astonishing in Callicott's narrative of moral progress is its almost Spencerian acceptance of the sequence from "lower animals" (Callicott 1990: 122, quoting Darwin) to "primitive" or "savage" man to modern scientific man. I am not calling for the displacement of scientific knowledge, but for a far more pluralistic, multi-dimensional account of moral and ecological knowledge.

Consider the case Guha raised in which tribal people were displaced by Project Tiger for the sake of preserving natural biodiversity. Whose knowledge counts here, the knowledge of people indigenous to the place, or outside experts whose training tells them that large mammals often survive only in the absence of human populations? Callicott may say that ecologists are coming to incorporate local knowledge of the environment, but this is just another ("culturally sensitive") way of saying that the natives need to "get up to speed."[4]

A more strictly philosophical way to put this point is in terms of the work of John Rawls, the most distinguished liberal philosopher of the last thirty years. As we have seen, Rawls emphasized the tension in modern moral theory between the substantive goods that communities may commit to, and "the priority of right" (Rawls 1971; Rawls 1985; Rawls 1987; Rawls 1988; Rawls 1993a; Rawls 1993b). This is really a modern version of the dispute between Hume and Kant: Is ethics a matter of the moral sentiments of communities, or is it a pre-cultural imperative issuing from rationality per se (the Truth with a capital T, as Callicott likes to say [Callicott 1990: 119]), which issues from a single coherent view of the world?

Just *because* diverse cultures, and subcultures within a culture, may endorse conflicting views concerning deep, substantive conceptions of a good life, Rawlsian political liberalism requires that justice is pre-cultural. "Justice is fairness" according to the celebrated formulation of Rawls. To judge fairly we must bracket off and systematically disallow any appeal to goods that are particular to a culture or an individual. Fairness requires that we operate from behind a "veil of ignorance." We cannot know our gender, our race, our location in an economic system, or anything else that might lead us to unjustly favor one person or group over another. This is the Kantian element in Rawls's theory of justice: justice is prior to culture.[5]

Callicott simply never decides on this great issue of modern moral theory. He wants us to believe that there is a univocal moral voice, but that it is consistent with culturally plural expressions of this voice. Unlike Rawls, with Callicott, we are to accept the coincidence of right with culturally variant conceptions of the good as nothing more than an article of faith.

In fact, Callicott endorses two inconsistent moral systems. One, still rigorously Kantian and biocentric, is designed precisely to set aside our normal human prejudices about what kinds of entities get moral standing. According to this view we should set aside mere human prejudice to judge moral standing in an unbiased, impartial way. This will lead us to accept the inherent value of nature. The second view contradicts the first. It says, "when the going gets tough, resort to your old cultural prejudices about who gets moral standing." The closer something stands to the "subjective" affections of the one who parcels out moral standing, the more value it receives. Callicott endorses both an ethic of principles, applied universally to situations prior to the judgments of a community, and a communitarian ethic which says that the substantive goods of communities come before the right.

This contradiction can be traced back to Callicott's emphasis on two distinct ideas that he claims to derive from Leopold's "categorical imperative": "A thing is right when it tends to preserve the integrity, stability, and beauty of the biotic community. It is wrong when it tends otherwise." The first position focuses on what makes a thing "right" and leads to Callicott's early conclusion that a biocentric ethic must be misanthropic. The second position begins with the idea of a "biotic community" and leads to the idea of a hierarchy of nested moral communities. If the substantive goods of nested communities precede the right, then, Callicott has failed in his goal of providing a single categorical imperative. If the right precedes the substantive goods of communities, Callicott's reference to the evolution of morals is vacuous.

QUANTUM THEORY AS A CRITIQUE OF SELF

Like his first position, Callicott's second position is unstable. Perhaps in recognition of this he has gone on to intimate a third position. No longer a truncated theory of inherent worth, Callicott now begins to question the very assumptions that led him to define environmental ethics in terms of a search for intrinsic value in the first place. The first half of Callicott's essay "Intrinsic Value, Quantum Theory, and Environmental Ethics" is a restatement of his second position. But halfway through the paper he begins to question the assumptions that make the second position possible: the Cartesian separation of subject and object that is required for the "problem" of altruism to arise. In words that may be read as a critique of his second position, he says:

> One of the cornerstones constituting the metaphysical foundations of classical modern science is the firm distinction, first clearly drawn by Descartes, between object and subject, between the *res extensa* and the *res cogitans*. The famous distinction of Hume between fact and value and Hume's development of a subjectivist axiology may be historically interpreted as an application or extension to ethics of Descartes' more general metaphysical and epistemic distinction. (Callicott 1989c: 165)

The Cartesian/Newtonian distinction between subject and object was cast into doubt, however, by "revolutionary developments in twentieth-century science, especially in quantum theory . . . [which] have forced the abandonment of the simple, sharp distinction between object and subject. . . . Hence, . . . Hume's classical subjectivist axiology . . . is not consistent with a contemporary or post-revolutionary scientific world view" (Callicott 1989c: 165–66).[6]

Influenced by the idea that the properties of light quanta are relative to the viewer, Callicott is led to question the more general assumption that subject and object, Self and Other, are categorically distinct. Quantum theory teaches us that nature and self can only be defined in relation to one another. Summing up his new position, Callicott says, "Since nature is the self fully extended and diffused, and the self, complementarily, is nature concentrated and focused in one of the intersections, the 'knots,' of the web of life . . . , nature is intrinsically valuable, *to the extent* that the self is intrinsically valuable" (Callicott 1989c: 174). The new "principle of axiological complementarity" holds that "*If* it is rational for me to act in my own interest, and I and nature are one, then it is rational for me to act in the best interest of nature" (Callicott 1989c: 173).

If Self and Other are no longer categorically distinct, human beings are no longer separate from nature. Callicott disavows the definition of "wilderness" found in the Wilderness Act of 1964: "'A wilderness, in contrast with those areas where man and his works dominate the landscape, is hereby recognized as an area where the earth and its community of life are untrammeled by man, where man himself is a visitor who does not remain'" (quoted in Callicott 1994b: 259).

Partly in response to Guha's charge of neocolonialism and partly in response to the work of biologist Daniel Botkin and historian William Cronon who have challenged the view that nature is a stable state which exists independently of human intervention (Botkin 1990; Cronon 1995), Callicott has come full circle from the original "misanthropic" defense of nature against human interference. Admitting that the concept of nature is affected by human intentions, and that little or nothing in nature remains unaffected by human actions, Callicott has given up the defense of wilderness in favor of the idea of "biodiversity preserves."

I do see the third position as an advance over the two earlier positions. For the first time, Callicott questions the Western, liberal assumptions about the moral self that have generated the problem of altruism, and, in turn, the problem of how we can value nature intrinsically. The problem with the third view is that he still describes it as an answer to "the central axiological problem of environmental ethics." He still sees himself as solving the old Western philosophical problem rather than dissolving the need to ask the question in the first place. "[T]he central theoretical problem for *any* future environmental ethics" still originates in the "dominant Western ethical traditions."

Furthermore, Callicott's new principle of complementarity, "nature is intrinsically valuable, *to the extent* that the self is intrinsically valuable," cannot function as an *environmental* categorical imperative. It says, in effect, that *anything* can be valued inherently. If so, the new axiology continues to say nothing about the difficult cases. It still fails to provide a decision procedure of the kind Callicott requires from ethics for deciding on conflicts that arise from valuing nature and human beings inherently.

Callicott alters his view in response to Guha, but he never recants on the basic themes of his origination story for environmental ethics. He glances off Guha's concern for the effects of ecocentrism in the third world, but never faces Guha's view head-on that Leopold "makes sense only in an American context; he has very little to say to other cultures." To do so would require Callicott to abandon *the* land ethic.

Viewed in retrospect, it is ironic that the very critical rigor which Callicott brings to environmental philosophy reveals the contradictions in his three attempts to establish an environmental ethic. The misanthropic overtones of the first position, combined with his rejection of animal welfare ethics for not being sufficiently radical, mask the fact that Callicott's own philosophical resources are hardly radical. He resorted to the oldest philosophical distinction in the Western tradition, the distinction between intrinsic and extrinsic value. We can now see that these terms are supremely unsuited to express the *relational* values required of a true environmental ethic. The point of a claim to intrinsic value is to cut off moral relations among entities, to make them morally autonomous. Claims to intrinsic value function in the same way as claims to having a right. As Joel Feinberg has said, "To have a right is to have a claim *to* something *against* someone" (Feinberg 1980: 139).

The second position recognizes the need to express a relational sense of value through the idea of an ecocommunity. But it falls into contradiction because of Callicott's claim that the second position simply clarifies the first, that he is engaged in a single, coherent project which is both Kantian in its universality and Humean in its contextuality. The second position thus fails to answer the dilemma of how to reconcile environmental and social justice.

The third position claims to transcend the subject/object distinction that underpins the work of both Kant and Hume. But, again, out of a concern to claim a coherent origination narrative, Callicott does not grant that the third position is a rejection of the land ethic. The philosophical arguments for a universal ethic that is culturally sensitive fail. This requires Callicott to turn from philosophy to a more anthropological argument for the same conclusion: Native American cultures have an implicit, or partially articulated, environmental ethic that implies the land ethic.

CALLICOTT'S "SAVAGE"

Parallel to his attempt to ground environmental philosophy firmly in a theory of intrinsic/inherent value, Callicott has also argued that the pre-Columbian "savages" (Callicott 1989e: 187) of North America had an environmental ethic—*a* land ethic, as he puts it—that is logically consistent with his defense of Leopold and *the* land ethic. Callicott is explicit about his intentions: If "some American Indian peoples portrayed their relationship with nature as essentially social and thus, by implication, as essentially moral, then their rich narrative heritage could provide, ready-made, the myths and parables missing from abstract articulations of biosocial environmental ethics like Aldo Leopold's" (Callicott 1989a: 219). That is, if American Indians had a social relationship with nature, this implies that they had ethics; thus they had the possibility of an environmental ethic. Their environmental ethic, in turn, can be used to fill a gap in Western, analytical, "biosocial environmental ethics" which is precise and conceptually defensible, but lacks a rich narrative heritage. Native American ethics comes "ready-made" to serve this need of Western philosophy.

A second role American Indian environmental ethics plays is to stand as a pure contrast to "Western European civilization": "I argue that the world view typical of American Indian peoples has included and supported an environmental ethic, while that of Europeans has encouraged human alienation from the natural environment and an exploitative practical relationship to it" (Callicott 1989e: 177). Callicott has no interest, therefore, in indigenous people after they have been "contaminated" by the arrival of European culture. Neither their ideas nor the material conditions of the lives of post-Columbian Indians are relevant to the construction of the land ethic.

When Callicott surveys Indian myths, his constant point is that they reveal a sense of community which includes nature:

> The implicit overall metaphysic of American Indian cultures locates human beings in a larger *social,* as well as physical, environment. People belong not only to a human community, but to a community of all nature as well. Existence in this larger society, just as existence in a family and tribal context, places people in an environment in which reciprocal responsibilities and mutual obligations are taken for granted and assumed without question or reflection. (Callicott 1989e: 189–90)

The boundaries of the community are also the boundaries of the moral for Callicott. He says, "Following Hume, I am willing to label behavior toward nature 'ethical' or 'moral' which is motivated by esteem, respect, regard, kinship, affection, and sympathy" (Callicott 1989e: 196).

So, too, with the land ethic: "the primary feature of the land ethic is the representation of nature as a congeries of societies and of human-nonhuman relationships as essentially social: 'The land ethic simply enlarges the boundary of the community to include soils, waters, plants, and animals, or collectively: the land'" (Callicott 1989e: 197).

I am sympathetic to the idea of environmental ethics as a form of communitarianism. The goal of chapters 9 and 10 is to work out such a view. My problem with Callicott, then, is not the communitarian element in his theory, nor with the Humean idea that the boundaries of the ethical are the boundaries of the community. I see nothing at all incoherent in the idea of a more-than-human community. The problem with Callicott's communitarianism is that he finds the need to provide a philosophical grounding for such a theory in non-communitarian arguments. Communities only "count" for Callicott if they espouse a version of *the* land ethic.

Callicott explains, for example, how the views expressed in an American Indian text such as *Black Elk Speaks*, while displaying a certain "environmental wisdom," do not qualify as an environmental ethic. The Lakota view found here "pictured nature as more like a vast extended family than a congeries of societies." There is a categorical difference, apparently, between families and societies: "One's familial duties, it seems to me, go beyond ethics. Ethics suggests, at least to me, a formality inappropriate to intimate family relationships" (Callicott 1989a: 216). And why does ethics "suggest" this to Callicott? Apparently because he assumes with Kant that there is a categorical distinction between the "public" and "private" spheres of life, and that the public (formal) sphere coincides with the ethical. Although the critical question is whether Callicott is importing ideas from "Western European civilization" into his description, he never pushes his argument beyond what ethics "suggests" to him.

Again and again Callicott draws upon deep Kantian and Cartesian assumptions about ethics in his description of American Indian environmental ethics. At one point, he considers Regan's concern that Indian attitudes toward the environment were motivated more by fear (read, "self-interest") than for an "appreciation of nature's inherent values" (Callicott 1989e: 199). In his response, Callicott simply accepts the terms of Regan's Kantian approach: either Indians are egoists, and only appear to be concerned about the environment, or they are altruists, either in the fashion of Kantian respect, or Humean sympathy for something categorically different from themselves. Regan and Callicott, then, both accept the Western idea of self as separate and autonomous. Only on this assumption does the question of egoism versus altruism become critical: either one acts to benefit what is on one side of the line, the self, or one transcends the border of self to self-lessly benefit something else.

The issue of correct interpretation of Native American ethics turns out to be the perennial problem of Western moral philosophy.

Regan quite fairly points out that "the ambiguity of Amerind behavior is the ambiguity of human behavior, the ancient puzzle over whether, as humans, we are capable of acting out of disinterested respect for what we believe has value in its own right or whether, beneath all manner of ceremony, ritual, and verbal glorification of the objects of our attention, there resides, in Kant's memorable words, 'the dear self,' the true, the universal sovereign of our wills." (Callicott 1989e: 200, quoting from Regan 1982)

Regan (a consistent Kantian) and Callicott (an inconsistent Humean) unreflectively apply the categories of Western moral theory to Native American Indian ethics and find them puzzling, their behavior "ambiguous." Despite Callicott's earlier gesture in the direction of cultural pluralism, to make sense of this passage we have to assume that underlying cultural difference is a universal sovereign will. Pluralism is allowed only if it can be rescued by the sovereign will, a categorical moral law underlying "all manner of ceremony."

This is the paradox of J. Baird Callicott's recent book *Earth's Insights: A Multicultural Survey of Ecological Ethics from the Mediterranean Basin to the Australian Outback*. Callicott's exhaustive survey is really an extended empirical argument for the existence of a transcendental categorical imperative. One can question, in Humean fashion, whether empirical evidence, no matter how extensive, can ever prove a universal. The paradox, however, is that this "multicultural" book gives the clearest indication possible that Callicott does colonize other views. In searching for the "Rosetta stone of environmental philosophy" required to "translate one indigenous environmental ethic into another" (Callicott 1994a: 186), Callicott simply wipes entire continents off the map of environmental ethics. We read, "Africa looms as a big blank spot on the world map of indigenous environmental ethics" (Callicott 1994a: 158). Africa is still the "heart of darkness" for Callicott. Why? Because African communitarianism is too anthropocentric to qualify as a biocentric ethic in the fashion of Wisconsin's Leopold.

African environmentalist Jimoh Omo-Fadaka writes that the distinctive feature of an African environmental ethic is its commitment to community:

> *Communalism*, then, is the basis of the traditions of African countries. This has fundamental ethical and philosophical implications. The communal organization in Africa is not just a matter of individuals clinging together to eke out an existence: nor is it comparable, except superficially, to the organization of rural communities in Europe: nor does it trace its evolution from an urban cultural centre. It is a form of communal organization which has evolved its own philosophical system and its own way of interpreting and projecting reality. In brief, it is a communal structure which has affirmed its particularity through forms of religion and thought arising directly out of its own organization. (Omo-Fadaka 1990: 178)

Such indigenous systems by which local communities divide access to the environment and preserve it for future generations do not register with Callicott's theory. When he writes off such views, depicting Africa as the philosophical equivalent of the "Dark Continent," how is this different from James Mill's criterion for the moral considerability of a civilization: "Exactly in proportion as *Utility* is the object of every pursuit, may we regard a nation as civilized"? (Majeed 1992: 136).

DOES THE DEFENSE OF NATURE REQUIRE MORAL MONISM?

Despite Callicott's monolingual account of moral truth, it is necessary, nevertheless, to acknowledge some of the concerns that motivated his monism. Environmental philosophy is motivated by the deep conviction that something is wrong. It exists because individual beliefs and public policies need to change. Callicott's conviction is that only moral monism is up to this task of radical reform. Is this true? Does defense of the environment require moral monism?

Much of Callicott's enthusiasm for monism is revealed, negatively, in his "case against moral pluralism" (Callicott 1990). There, Callicott responds to a form of ethical pluralism defended by Christopher D. Stone (Stone 1988). Stone holds that no single ethical theory can capture all dimensions of our lives. A legislator may want to adopt a utilitarian lens in formulating social policy, in citing a toxic waste facility, for example, but at home among family it would be inappropriate to "legislate" according to a principle of the greatest good for the greatest number. Here a Kantian ethic of the inviolability of individuals may be preferable. Again, when we treat non-human animals or the environment, still other approaches may be required.

What concerns Callicott, quite rightly I think, is that *this* version of moral pluralism "implies metaphysical musical chairs." The idea of putting on one theory for one purpose, only to be replaced by another for another purpose, fails as a description of the way our moral lives function: "we human beings deeply need and mightily strive for consistency, coherency, and closure in our personal and shared outlook on the world" (Callicott 1990: 115). Callicott worries, further, that pluralism will slide into a deconstructive postmodern relativism of the sort that seems to be advocated by Jacques Derrida, Richard Rorty, and (according to Callicott) Jim Cheney.

What motivates Callicott is important even if, as I believe, his response to these concerns is misguided. Ethical standpoints are not like a collection of differently tinted glasses to be replaced when they no longer improve vision. Any possible narrative of moral life must include an account of the pursuit of coherence and meaning. Stone thinks of morals as the individual trying on various (Western) moral theories as the need arises. This is typical of Western liberalism: the autonomous individual exists prior to the ethical system he or she "adopts." If one does not work, we simply try another. The sort of communalism described by Omo-Fadaka in which we are partially *constituted* by the moral horizon of our community is not expressible in these terms. Given Callicott's conception of pluralism, he is correct to warn of the slide to relativism.

Where Callicott begins to go wrong is in his insistence in the above passage that coherence requires "closure." The antidote to relativism is not metaphysical monism. Coherence is a deep, pragmatic human *project.* As such, it requires not closure in a metaphysic of morals, but openness to new moral horizons that challenge and extend the deep set of moral meanings which constitute one as a member of a moral community. Pluralism, in short, needs not be relativistic.

Where Callicott sees it as the role of philosophy to establish a theory of intrinsic value that adjudicates between cultures on the basis of whether or not they have yet discovered such a concept, as a communitarian I am content to point out that many communities, many indigenous communities, do, in fact, have a sense of community that includes the non-human world. I take this to be consistent with Omo-Fadaka's point. The idea that community is limited to human beings seems to be an unfortunate invention of the West. The idea of the more-than-human community is not, therefore, something that requires a philosophical demonstration.

Given the monist's expectations about what will count as an adequate theory, namely that it provides "unity and closure," the sort of pluralism I advocate may not even look like it should count as a theory. Pragmatic pluralism does not attempt to provide necessary and sufficient conditions for moral standing. As Bryan Norton points out, "There are no important positive positions or tenets that unify pluralists" (Norton 1995: 345). Granted, then, pragmatic pluralism does not give the monist a "theory." Perhaps we were mistaken in expecting philosophy to produce such theories.

Norton has distinguished between applied ethics and practical ethics. Where applied ethics produces full-blown theories that can be applied, after the fact, to the world, practical ethics begins in the world: "Practical philosophy, in contrast to applied philosophy, is problem-oriented: it treats theories as tools of the understanding, tools that are developed in the process of addressing specific policy controversies" (Norton 1995: 344). For practical ethics, the ultimate question is, "How can we foster democratic resolutions of public policy issues starting from the actual context in which the issue arises?" The role is not to adjudicate issues of moral standing, but to listen for the possibility of nonviolent resolution of conflict.[7]

Thinking of Callicott, Norton observes that, "Monism and the role it offers philosophers is therefore attractive to those who hope to maintain a separation between philosophy and the messy details of everyday environmental management practice. As applied philosophers, they hope to resolve environmental problems by throwing fully formed theories and principles over the edge of the ivory tower, to be used as intellectual armaments by the currently outgunned environmental activists" (Norton 1995: 345). Callicott has himself endorsed this image of the ivory tower philosopher. He admits that when we begin with a metaphysics of morals, "The specific ethical norms of environmental conduct remain for the most part implicit—a project postponed to the future or something left for ecologically informed people to work out for themselves" (Callicott 1995: 21–22). We have seen that this project has not simply been "postponed." No concrete policy results can come from Callicott's evolved moral theory because it is inconsistent.

Indigenous communities do provide a radical challenge to the Western prejudice that the limits of a human community are the limits of the moral domain. What we need is not a categorical imperative, a moral Esperanto that will translate all moral languages into one, but an account of why some moral communities act to prevent honest, deeply ethical exchange over the dimensions of the moral community. Practical philosophy seeks to understand the actual causes of systemic moral miscommunication.

Practical philosophy begins from the observation that many communities *are* ecocommunities. No philosophical demonstration in Western philosophical categories will make this more certain. The real question is why powerful Western institutions act, in the name of justice, to subvert such communities. The distinction between intrinsic and extrinsic value does nothing to answer this question. Development is *defended*, after all, as a just system motivated by respect for human moral autonomy. The analysis of systemic and institutional violence, to the contrary, does provide at least a part of the answer. Indigenous communities show that it is possible to care for the environment without distinguishing categorically between nature and human culture. The function of practical philosophy is to mediate the causes of moral conflict, not to legislate moral standing.

7

A State of Mind like Water
Ecosophy T and the Buddhist Traditions

[T]o see mountains and rivers is to see Buddha-nature. To see Buddha-nature is to see a donkey's jaw or a horse's mouth.

"This" is Buddha-nature. . . . We can find this in everyday life, eating a meal or drinking green tea.

(Dogen 1975: 12, 13–14)

REMOVING THE ARROW

When the Buddha's followers pressed him for answers to abstract, theoretical questions, he refused to respond. To speculate about mere theories when there is suffering in the world, he said, is like speculating about the origin of a poison arrow while it is still lodged in one's flesh. First remove the arrow! Questions about origins can come later. This story is typical of many in the early Buddhist writings that depict the Buddha's teachings as rigorously phenomenological, constantly returning his students' attention to the concrete reality of suffering.

The Buddha was probably not concerned about "the environment." Nevertheless, in the same phenomenological vein, he once counseled his son,

[O]n the earth men throw clean and unclean things, dung and urine, spittle, pus, and blood, and the earth is not repelled or disgusted. . . . Similarly you should develop a state of mind like water, for men throw all manner of clean and unclean things into water and it is not troubled or repelled or disgusted. (De Bary 1972: 27, from Majjhima Nikaya)

Abuse of the earth reflects our own suffering; suffering issues from ignorance of our true nature. An environmental philosophy, then, must begin with a rigorous phenomenology of self.

Arne Naess, hailed as the founder of deep ecology, has come under many influences. Some—most notably Mahatma Gandhi and Benedict de Spinoza—are more pervasive in Naess's work than the influence of Buddhism. Gandhi, for example, inspired Naess's political philosophy of nonviolence. Yet, the Gandhian influence does little to explain such key deep ecological concepts as Self-realization. Gandhi's "Self," the Hindu atman, is explicitly rejected by Naess in favor of a Buddhist conception of no-self (Naess Unpublished: 4). Similarly, while Spinoza's influence is profound, it is the Spinoza of Paul Weinpahl's *The Radical Spinoza,* a Spinoza of Becoming rather than Being (Weinpahl 1979). Weinpahl's Spinoza finds its true nature in the Zen monastery.

The Buddhist influence, although less pervasive, provides the most explicit account of key deep ecological concepts such as Self-realization and intrinsic value. I read Ecosophy T, Naess's personal vision of deep ecology, as a rigorously phenomenological branch of deep ecology. Like early Buddhism, Naess constantly responds to the human suffering that causes environmental destruction by summoning us to return to the reality of lived experience. This is not only a response to suffering, but, at a deeper level, to "the suspicion of reason." Like certain strains of Mahayana Buddhism, Naess believes that reason can become opaque to itself and mischievously lead us away from direct experience of the real relational processes he calls "gestalts." Naess rejects "any kind of established system of thought" and counsels that "in every moment you must choose your life, again and again. 'To hell with everything'—start anew, as if this moment were your first and last." When he explains what goes wrong with the bureaucrat's (shallow) thinking about the environment Naess says, "all his education is to forget about spontaneous experience!" "The language they use is what I don't like. It is a quantitative language, which does not go into the particulars, such as the heart of the forest" (Rothenberg 1993: 55–56, 161, 162–63).

This Buddhist reading clarifies, but it also complicates. It reaffirms Naess's essential vision, but it challenges him at two points to push further. It challenges him to affirm that Self-realization is a process of co-realization with *all* beings, not just with sentient beings. And, while this reading accepts that humans do not create the value of nature, it questions whether Naess's insights are best expressed through the concept of intrinsic value. Finally, this reading puts us in a position to reassess Ramachandra Guha's questions: "Does deep ecology, does Ecosophy-T in particular, misappropriate Oriental traditions?" "Does its commitment to nature's value block a commitment to social justice in the third world?"

My interpretation depends upon drawing out connections between an important unpublished paper, "Gestalt Thinking and Buddhism,"[1] and Naess's published works. I focus very selectively on three aspects of the Buddhist traditions that seem to influence him the most: the oldest Buddhist texts, found in the Pali Canon; the great Indian Buddhist philosopher Nagarjuna (ca. 150–250 A.D.); and the Soto Zen monk, Dogen (1200–1253). Naess explicitly traces his understanding of Self-realization to Dogen, and Dogen, in turn, traces his lineage to Nagarjuna and the Pali texts.

THE SUSPICION OF REASON

"Gestalt Thinking" begins, "In the oldest forms of Buddhism, monks were reluctant to answer metaphysical questions. And if answers were offered, they were expressed undogmatically. 'Take it or leave it.' Even if true, a philosophical opinion might be of meager help, or even a hindrance on the eightfold path" (Naess Unpublished: 2). One reason for the meager help one might expect from philosophy in the process of Self-realization has to do with the Buddhist account of suffering. We have already seen that ancient Buddhist texts report that the Buddha refused to answer metaphysical questions, comparing such talk in the face of suffering to the person who just talks after having been struck by a poisoned arrow. Suffering calls for action; we can see this sentiment reflected in Naess's reaction to the suffering of nature, and to the modern tendency to "just talk."

This gives an existential urgency to Naess's thought, and pushes him toward the need for deeper ecological thinking. Still, we must ask, what is deeper thinking in Ecosophy T? Beyond the well-known, very general platforms that distinguish the shallow from the deep (Devall and Sessions 1985: chap. 5), Naess's personal branch of ecosophy is distinguished by its "suspicion of reason." Reason and precision have their place in Naess's thinking, as in Buddhism; yet, reason can also obscure and distort the reality of immediate experience. This is delusion, not clarity; it produces the suffering that degrades our relations with human beings and the environment.

Since his early experience with the Logical Positivists of the Vienna Circle, Naess has been concerned with precision in thinking. This concern still exists in his work, but it stands alongside the suspicion of reason. Naess says, "there may be important things that are very difficult to make more precise. . . . If you leave out nonprecise things, you are lost in accuracy. One must go back and forth, from precision to ambiguity" (Rothenberg 1993: 29). To say that "nature is one," for example, is not precise. It is what Naess terms "an *entia rationis.*" But it is a highly useful distortion if it points people to the spontaneous gestalt experience of connection in nature. Even "Self-realization" is dangerous if it becomes an abstraction that does not constantly return us to the "concrete contents" of experience.

In "Gestalt Thinking," Naess draws on a connection between what he calls "gestalt ontology" and a Buddhist account of experience to elucidate these ideas. "Reason," he says, "works out abstract constructions" to facilitate its work: when permanence and eternal being are asserted of substance, as in René Descartes and Spinoza, these entities are considered to be mental constructions by gestalt ontology (Naess Unpublished: 2). They are, at most, helpful fictions. Helpful, but dangerous: if we forget they are fictions, we become deluded about ourselves and our place in the world.

In contrast to these fictions of reason, Naess speaks of "concrete reality" as having a "gestalt character, that is to say, no part and no wholes but subordinate and superordinate gestalts" (Rothenberg 1993: 155). Gestalts are concrete, relational processes. Naess insists that he is speaking of ontology here, the way the world *is,* not simply of psychology. When we rigorously examine the gestalt we commonly call "self," we find not the substance of Descartes and Spinoza but "no-(permanent) Self." "Selves are frequently recurring items, or knots, in the structure of contents" (Naess Unpublished: 2).

Reason is inevitable, perhaps, but we go wrong when we fail to note that its entities are merely constructions invented to do a particular job. We can be seduced by reason, never directly experiencing the world as it really is, the world in its concreteness. Reason, when we do not suspect its efficacy, obscures reality. The realized Self that exists in concrete, relational processes is transformed and distorted by reason into the permanent, non-relational self of Western philosophy and the Christian religion.

When asked why this form of self-delusion is so common in human life, Naess resorts to talk about spontaneity. Shallow ecological thinkers, he says, "forget about spontaneous experience!" (Rothenberg 1993: 161). Their education actually *trains* them to be so caught up in mental constructions—numbers, charts, and development plans—that they treat those as reality and fail to spontaneously experience their true selves.

NAESS'S PLACE IN THE BUDDHIST TRADITIONS

The Zen Buddhist traditions are sometimes depicted as bizarre, even nonsensical. Some of its principal exponents in the West, such as D. T. Suzuki, characterize Zen as a form of anti-intellectualism totally grounded in Japanese culture. Suzuki neglected Soto Zen, however, Dogen's sect, and the principal influence on Naess's thinking. Dogen consciously looked back to Indian philosopher Nagarjuna for *arguments* against the ability of discursive reason to express the process of Self-realization. Naess's account of reason, going "back and forth, from precision to ambiguity," bears a strong resemblance to Nagarjuna's thought.

The fact that the Buddha espoused a rigorously practical and empirical account of experience did not prevent a variety of metaphysical schools from arising quickly after his death, schools that debated precisely the metaphysical questions the Buddha had refused to answer. Against these rival schools, Nagarjuna intervened to develop his Logic of the Middle based on the idea of emptiness, or thusness, to show that these metaphysical debates were vacuous since they distorted reason.

In the simplest terms, Nagarjuna found a way to dispense with competing metaphysical arguments by showing that both sides reduce to absurdity. Where the rival schools try to show that their conception of time or causality is absolute, for example, Nagarjuna shows that each school's terms presuppose the other. In the words of T. R. V. Murti, "Relation has to perform two mutually opposed functions: as *connecting* the two terms, in making them relevant to each other, it has to *identify* them: but as connecting the *two*, it has to *differentiate* them. Otherwise expressed, relation cannot obtain between entities that are identical with or different from each other" (Murti 1960: 13). So reason goes wrong, for example, in asserting either that the effect is contained in the cause, or that it is not contained in the cause. Put concretely, any distinction highlights only one aspect of a situation and shrouds the other, incompatible aspect. Nagarjuna's conclusion is that we may use reason, but we must suspect its ultimate efficacy.

The effect of Nagarjuna's arguments, as with the historical Buddha, is to drive us back to experience and away from the *entia rationis*. What we find here, again in Naess's terms, is the process of Self-realization among gestalts; in Buddhist terms we find "emptiness" or "thusness."

Naess has struggled to express the sense of self-in-relation that is both deeply connected to other beings and, yet, distinct. Time and again he rejects a substantial self in favor of the Buddhist no-self, but he then warns, "Such a formula must not be taken in the counter-intuitive sense that, for instance, I cannot be cold and hungry and somebody else warm and satisfied" (Naess Unpublished: 5). Neither the formula that there is self, nor the formula that there is no-self is precise. Like Nagarjuna, Naess proposes to find a path through this intellectual thicket not by further argument and clarification but by driving us back to immediate, spontaneous experience.

Following from Murti's characterization of Nagarjuna's position, we can see that the ambiguity we sometimes find in Naess's writings is not something that can be overcome with greater analytic precision. Whether we stress, in some contexts, the connectedness of beings, or, in other contexts, the distinctness of beings, we need to cultivate the suspicion of reason that reminds us that both depictions are merely tools to "facilitate [reason's] work."

Like the Buddhist tradition that runs from the earliest Buddhist writings, through Nagarjuna to Dogen, which drives us constantly back to immediate experience, I suggest that Naess's invitation to de-velop an ecosophy of our own can be seen as a recognition of the ulti-mate futility of stating any deep position in absolute terms. Some truths are only available through direct experience. The distinction Naess makes between his own version of deep ecological philosophy, Ecosophy T, and the other branches of deep ecology he invites others to develop is not simply an astute political move designed to make a political movement inclusive. We *must* all develop our own ecosophical visions because there is no choice. The suspicion of reason means we cannot do each other's work.

SELF-REALIZATION

Dogen was emphatic in his rejection of two faulty accounts of the self. The self is not an organic entity, like a seed, out of which other things grow. On this metaphor, Buddha-nature stands in a dualistic relation to its "fruit." Dogen therefore rejects a teleological explana-tion of self in the style of Aristotle. Self does not become real at the end of a long process. Rather, Buddha-nature is completely actual at each moment.

He also rejects an ancient view called the Senika heresy according to which there is a permanent self that is detached from change in the phenomenal world. Of those who espouse this view, he says, "they have not encountered their true self" (Waddell and Abe 1975: 100). Dogen's charge is phenomenological: such people have not yet had a certain experience; they have not "encountered" their true self as multiple, as interpenetrating other beings.

Dogen contends that the introspective search for an enduring, autonomous self is futile. To understand the self is to "forget" the Cartesian self. A famous passage from the *Genjokoan* of Dogen states this precisely:

> To study the Buddha way is to study the self. To study the self is to forget the self. To forget the self is to be actualized by myriad things. When actualized by myriad things, your body and mind as well as the bodies and minds of others drop away. No trace of realization remains, and this no-trace continues endlessly. (Dogen 1985a: 70)

To "forget" the self is to penetrate the delusion of the Cartesian self. It is to "Know that there are innumerable beings in yourself" (Dogen 1985d: 84) and thereby to realize one's true self in the cosmological dimension. Dogen makes a Humean point: careful phenomenological examination does not reveal a "singular" Cartesian self, but "innumerable beings" present to multiple spheres in which beings exist in relation to other beings.[2]

Dogen advises that to meet this true self, one must "just sit"; one must practice seated meditation (*zazen*). Zazen is a practice that reveals Buddha-nature through "undivided activity" (*zenki*), activity concentrated right here and right now. It brings one into the "presence of things as they are" (*genjokoan*). One of Dogen's most revealing descriptions of this state of direct presence reads:

> When you ride in a boat, your body and mind and the environs together are the undivided activity of the boat. The entire earth and the entire sky are both the undivided activity of the boat. (Dogen 1985d: 85)

What exists at that moment is the undivided activity of "the boat." Body, mind, boat, and environs are not separate. They are also not absolutely identical: "although not one, not different; although not different, not the same; although not the same, not many" (Dogen 1985d: 85–86).

This passage shows that there *is* a self for Dogen; the self does not disappear, or merge into the cosmos. He never denies that there are multiple, provisional, contextually defined borders that shape the sense of self. He maintains difference. Self is always experienced *in relation* to other beings, however, and those relations define what it means to be a self. Indeed, each person's set of defining relations at a given moment is unique.

The realized person, then, is neither a Cartesian unchanging self, nor an Aristotelian potentiality. A true self is one that practices undivided activity in the present moment, a practice that reveals the interpenetration (Buddha-nature) of all beings. In each moment there is full and complete realization, unlike the Aristotelian self; and, unlike the Cartesian self, there is direct experience of the non-substantiality of the self. Thomas P. Kasulis calls this "person as presence."[3]

DIRECTIONS FOR THE HEART OF THE FOREST

If Self-realization is a process that must be hinted at in various ways, this does not prevent some hints from being more revealing of experiential truths than others. In "Gestalt Thinking," Naess depends heavily upon Dogen's allusive writing to indicate what he means by "transcending the subject/object dualism" in the process of Self-realization. Naess's thought mostly coincides with Dogen's, but in one respect Dogen appears to go beyond Naess. Here I ask whether we should challenge Naess to take Dogen's "final" step.

Naess begins with a well-known Buddhist expression that is also quoted by Dogen: "Grass, tree, nations, and lands, all without exception attain Buddhahood" (Naess Unpublished: 3). In Buddhist terms, the idea is that Buddha-nature is all-pervading. All nature is concrete, relational processes.[4] In turn, the recognition of Buddha-nature in all beings allows us to experience compassion for and identify with these beings. In Naess's terms, only concrete relational processes (gestalts) may become Buddha, not the individual subjects of shallow, abstract thinking.

There is no question that Dogen and Naess are working in the same territory. However, Dogen's account of Buddha-nature is the most radical and characteristic facet of his work. It is therefore worthwhile to put his thought into slightly deeper context. Early in his masterpiece, the *Shobogenzo* (The Eye and Treasury of the True Law), Dogen takes up the question of Buddha-nature (*Bussho*) in a fascicle of the same name. Dogen's strategy was to begin with classical formulations of Buddha-nature that were well-known to his audience.[5] Then, while partially endorsing Buddhist tradition, he also transforms their meanings. As Norman Waddell and Abe Masao have noted, Dogen often sacrifices grammatical correctness in his translations from Chinese to Japanese for the illumination of an important and original philosophical point (Waddell and Abe 1975: 94).

Dogen begins by quoting from the *Nirvana Sutra*, the principal Mahayana sutra on Buddha-nature. The passage, in a traditional translation, reads, "All sentient beings without exception have the Buddha-nature." By referring to the *Sutra*, he acknowledges tradition. However, he also knew that this formulation is open to the charge of dualism. Saying that all sentient beings *have* Buddha-nature distinguishes Buddha-nature from the beings that have it, treating it as a potential quality of sentient beings.[6]

The traditional formulation also implies a distinction between daily practice and the actualization of enlightenment. Meditation and ordinary, daily practice would be maintained, accordingly, not as ends in themselves, but only for the sake of achieving a future end, an end that exists now only as a potentiality.

To remove these hints of dualism, Dogen twists the expression "All sentient beings without exception *have* the Buddha-nature," to read, "All sentient beings without exception *are* Buddha-nature" (Waddell and Abe 1975: 95, emphasis added).[7] Buddha-nature, for Dogen, is not a quality that sentient beings can *have* (or lack); rather, all sentient beings *are* Buddha-nature. Buddha-nature is fundamental reality.

A second feature of Dogen's nondualism is the scope of Buddha-nature. Buddhist tradition often restricted it to those beings that have the potential for enlightenment, either in this life (humans) or in a future life (other sentient beings that can be reborn as human beings). Nonsentient entities such as rivers and mountains are excluded. But Dogen refuses to accept the sentient/nonsentient distinction as fundamental. He says emphatically,

> Impermanence is in itself Buddha-nature. . . . Therefore, the very impermanency of grass and tree, thicket and forest, is the Buddha-nature. Nations and lands, mountains and rivers, are impermanent because they are Buddha-nature. Supreme and complete enlightenment, because it is the Buddha-nature, is impermanent. Great Nirvana, because it is impermanent, is the Buddha-nature. (Waddell and Abe 1975: 91, 93)

Dogen is both radical and traditional in his treatment of Buddha-nature. To be nondualist, he believes, Buddhist philosophy must commit to the fundamental reality of *all* beings as Buddha-nature, not just sentient beings. This is explained, however, by reference to the most traditional of Buddhist commitments: the impermanence of all being.

These ideas are expressed most strikingly and poetically in Dogen's great work, "Mountains and Waters Sutra" (*Sansui-kyo*). Here, Dogen challenges his audience to understand mountains and rivers themselves as sutras, as expressions of the Buddha. He quotes a Chinese source, "The green mountains are always walking; a stone woman gives birth to a child at night," and comments:

> Mountains do not lack the qualities of mountains. Therefore they always abide in ease and always walk. You should examine in detail this quality of the mountains' walking.
>
> Mountains' walking is just like human walking. Accordingly, do not doubt mountains' walking even though it does not look the same as human walking. The buddha ancestors' words point to walking. This is fundamental understanding. You should penetrate these words. (Dogen 1985c: 97–98)

Taken out of context, these lines might be read as an anthropomorphic projection: "Mountains' walking is *just like* human walking." But instead of implying that the mountains' being should be understood in terms of human being, the metaphor of walking points to a dehomocentric understanding of *all* being. Mountains and humans abide together in their impermanence.

Abe puts this dehomocentric reversal succinctly:

> When Dōgen emphasizes "all beings" in connection with the Buddha-nature, he definitely implies that man's samsāra, i.e., recurring cycle of birth and death, can be properly and completely emancipated not in the "living" dimension, but in the "being" dimension. In other words, it is not by overcoming generation-extinction common to all living beings, but only by doing away with appearance-disappearance, common to all things, that man's birth-death problem can be completely solved. Dōgen finds the basis for man's liberation in a thoroughly cosmological dimension. *Here Dōgen reveals a most radical Buddhist dehomocentrism.* (Abe 1971: 39, emphasis added)

We fail to understand life and death, the fundamental *human* problem, if we deal with it only in human terms. The life-and-death of human beings is subsumed by the generation-and-extinction (impermanence) of all sentient beings. We fail, as well, if we deal with it in terms of all sentient beings. In turn, the generation-and-extinction of all sentient beings is subsumed by what Abe calls the "appearance-and-disappearance" of *all* beings. There will be no release from human suffering, that is, until human beings experience themselves in the "cosmological dimension" of all beings, until they understand that "mountains' walking is just like human walking."

Through the level of "generation-extinction common to all living beings," Naess agrees with Dogen. But he then goes on to raise doubts about how far Buddha-nature can extend: "There is a question of how wide a range of beings may be said meaningfully to realize themselves. Animals: Yes. Plants: Yes. But a wider range dilutes further the very concept of realization and Self. There is a limit here" (Naess Unpublished: 3). Naess believes there is no problem in saying that Self-realization is a process of co-realization with all living beings. But he questions whether non-living beings co-realize. In Abe's terms, Naess questions whether the generation-extinction common to all *living* beings can be understood as a special case of the appearance-disappearance common to *all* things. The dilemma for Naess seems clear: to extend co-realization beyond living beings is to risk nonsense; not to do so introduces dualism, the distinction between beings we can identify with and have compassion for, and those that are beyond the "limit."

Dogen challenges us to take this most radical step. In this way he is exceptional, even within the Buddhist traditions. In traditional Buddhism, only human beings—sometimes only men—can "become Buddha" in this lifetime. Non-human sentient beings may be reborn as human beings, and become Buddha in a future lifetime. The traditional view distinguishes, however, between all sentient beings that can become Buddha, and non-sentient beings that cannot. A dog may become Buddha in a future life; a rock cannot.

Dogen saw this distinction as a crippling dualism that makes it impossible to say, as Naess does, that "*everything* may become Buddha." For Dogen, the self goes out to *co*-realize with what he calls "the myriad things." But the myriad things *also come forth to realize us.* This is what Abe calls Dogen's "dehomocentric reversal": we are realized by the mountains' "walking." The relations through which realization occurs move both ways, not only, as Naess often describes it, in circles of expanding identification starting with the self and moving out to other sentient beings.

Abe contends, and I agree, that to say "there is a limit here" beyond which co-realization cannot go is to stop at the level of the generation-extinction of all living beings.[8] In failing to push further to the "appearance-disappearance" of all things, Naess is committing to the kind of dualism that Dogen feared. It is to stay in the "living" dimension without hope of release from suffering, rather than pushing forth to the cosmological dimension.

Put in contemporary terms, Naess's position remains paradoxically close to the sphere of an animal rights position, such as Peter Singer's, according to which only sentient beings have moral standing. In refusing to push further toward a radical *environmental* ontology that goes all the way down to the ontological "roots" in the appearance and disappearance of all beings, Naess risks a crippling dualism.

If Naess did urge the concept of Self-realization to the deepest level, it would help him respond to several of the most important criticisms that have been lodged against him. Naess's hesitation, for example, is probably the source of the charge against him that his account of Self-realization remains anthropocentric (Plumwood 1991). Naess describes Self-realization as a process that pushes out from the human to embrace greater and greater realms of being, but has "limits" beyond the level of plants. Dogen provides an answer to this charge in a way that is consistent with deep ecological thinking.

Moreover, as Abe points out, the deepest level of co-realization is a "thoroughly cosmological dimension." This overcomes the charge that Self-realization is merely a psychological, anthropocentric projection. It accords perfectly with Naess's assertion that in speaking of gestalts as concrete, relational states, he is making an ontological, rather than psychological, point about Self-realization. It might help to use the term "co-realization" to mark this ontological dimension, in contrast to "Self-realization" which might be understood as a psychological process.

If Naess were willing to push his view further, he would coincide with another great "thinker to the roots," Gary Snyder, who elegantly expresses the truth of appearance-disappearance common to all things when he writes: "*All* beings are 'said' by the mountains and waters— even the clanking tread of a Caterpillar tractor, the gleam of the keys of a clarinet" (Snyder 1990: 115). There are no limits.

When Dogen deflates our anthropocentrism, saying, "If you doubt mountains walking you do not know your own walking," when we are enjoined to "think like a mountain," this is not mystical drivel. These expressions point toward a deep, coherent understanding of time, change, and causality. Yet, these truths appear spontaneously, in the moment before they are clouded by reason.

ETHICS WITHOUT GOOD AND EVIL

Naess has often characterized his writing as fundamentally ontological, making the surprising claim that he is not really interested in "ethics." Despite this, one of the basic commitments of deep ecology, after Self-realization, is to the intrinsic value of nature.[9] "Gestalt Thinking" gives insight not available in Naess's other writings into why he thinks of ethics as primarily an ontological enterprise. It helps to sort out the paradox of whether Naess's Ecosophy T is really an ethical position based on the intrinsic value of nature.

The final section of "Gestalt Thinking" connects the ontology of spontaneous experience with an ontology of value. Naess discusses an unpublished paper by Yasuaki Nara, "The Practical Value of Dogen's View of Nature" and Nara's use of two Japanese terms, *inochi* and *kuyo*. *Inochi* means, roughly, life, or the value of life. Nara notes that the Buddhist precept of nonharming is merged with Japanese culture through *inochi*. As Nara explains, however, this involves much more than a commitment to the nonharming of sentient beings. *Inochi* means the nonharming of "all beings."

We come to appreciate the scope of *inochi* when we understand how it functions within the Japanese custom of *kuyo,* memorial services to atone for harm done to all beings. Nara cites the example of the yearly service for eels, performed by restaurant owners and customers for taking the *inochi* of the eels. Notice, one does not swear off eating eels and become a vegetarian. The *kuyo* requires one to grant, however, that the eater exists in relation to the eel. To take the eel's *inochi* is an act of moral gravity.[10]

Nara goes on to point out that services for the taking of *inochi* are not limited to living things: "In the Edo period, the housewife and daughters of each home were supposed to do *kuyo* for the used or broken needles with a sense of regret for their lost *inochi,* thanks, and also with prayers for the enhancement of their sewing talents." *Kuyo* is also done for "old clocks, dolls, chopsticks, spectacles, tea-whisks, etc." Nara concludes, "To sum up the traditional view of nature in Japan, first of all do not make clear distinction between man, animals, and things. Though the individuality of each exists, all are felt to be part of the one world of the Buddha, each revealing its value" (Nara Unpublished: 8–9).

All beings have—better, *are*—their *inochi.* When one is spontaneously present to "concrete contents," as Naess calls them, in that moment before the clouding of reason, one cannot fail to be present to value(d)-being. Snyder, writing of the "Mountains and Waters Sutra," eloquently returns us to this original place:

> Dogen is not concerned with "sacred mountains"—or pilgrimages, or spirit allies, or wilderness as some special quality. His mountains and streams

are the processes of this earth, all of existence, process, essence, action, absence; they roll being and nonbeing together. They are what we are, we are what they are. For those who would see directly into essential nature, the idea of the sacred is a delusion and an obstruction; it diverts us from seeing what is before our eyes; plain thusness. Roots, stems, and branches are all equally scratchy. No hierarchy, no equality. . . . This, *thusness,* is the nature of the nature of nature. The wild in the wild. (Snyder 1990: 103)

For Snyder, we also see "directly into essential nature" when we are present to needles and dolls, chopsticks and tea-whisks, and Caterpillar tractors and clarinet keys. There is no hierarchy, no equality, at all.

Naess swallows hard and grants that "cruel parasites, inflicting slow painful death on their victims" are "'things' and therefore seem to be eligible for *kuyo.*" Significantly, he describes this "horizontality and anti-hierarchical way of feeling things" as "nearest to the truth and the [philosophy] which I feel at home with" (Naess Unpublished: 9).

I contend, however, that this way of feeling only makes sense if Naess agrees with the fundamental point of the previous section: there can be no limit to co-realization. To attain a truly horizontal feeling, we must affirm co-realization, not just Self-realization, and co-realization must occur among all beings, not just living beings. Naess's account of value is clearly within the ontological dimension, but his account of Self-realization remains psychological.

If Naess's account is ontological through and through, several important points become expressible. We must notice that *inochi* is a relational—although not relative—sense of value. We always stand in relation to the concrete contents of experience. When this becomes transparent to us, *kuyo* becomes necessary. One must atone for what one does because the context is relational: it includes the eel and the eater. But in becoming directly present to the eel, one does not create value, or "extend" moral standing from the human to the non-human. Rather, the choice is between recognizing and accounting for our responsibility—and eating gratefully—or failing to be directly present to the eel, and oneself—thereby eating with ingratitude. In Dogen's words, "If you doubt the mountains' walking, you do not know your own walking; it is not that you do not walk, but that you do not know or understand your own walking."

This co-relational account of value is not a form of relativism. The distinction between psychological Self-realization and ontological co-realization is critical here. If the Self simply extends itself to new realms of identification, values appear to be created relative to the state of the Self. But when we *and* the "myriad things" go forth to co-realize, this is a way of being in the world, not a mental construction.

We can now also see why Dogen would have rejected the distinction between (intrinsic) good and evil for reasons deriving from Nagarjuna: neither is absolute; to treat them as such is to invent an *entia rationis*. When we see directly into nature, we are *always* directly present to Buddha-nature, to value(d)-being. There is no distinction at this level between good and evil, between the good parasite and the bad parasite. Such distinctions come later. Intrinsic good and evil are, at most, "useful tools" required by reason to facilitate its work, and they are dangerous if we forget the suspicion of reason.

Instead of speaking of good and evil as intellectual categories, Dogen speaks of the practice in which we are directly present to things as they are (*genjokoan*), the dimension of "appearance and disappearance." Here "the resolve to do no evil continues as the act of not producing evil. When it comes to be that evils are no longer produced, the efficacy of one's cultivation is immediately presencing" (Kasulis 1981: 94–95). "Do no evil" becomes "The nonproduction of evil"; "Do good" becomes "The performance of good." Good and evil drop away. Practice remains in the presence of things as they are: pure thusness, without hierarchy.

There is an illuminating connection between Dogen's nondualistic practice and Naess's idea of beautiful actions. Naess has distinguished between what we conventionally mean by ethics—duty-bound actions that follow from moral laws—and beautiful actions which are done spontaneously and joyfully as an expression of Self. This reading of Naess's beautiful actions as joyful acts done in the presence of the *inochi* of *all* beings, not just motivated by the intrinsic value of *some* beings, appears sympathetic to his conclusion in "Gestalt Thinking." Naess considers that it is hard to know what to say about the "problem of evil," given the "conception of intrinsic value of all things." Surely, though, if we no longer know what to say of evil, we should also suspect its contrasting term: (intrinsic) good. Where Naess notes, "There is a need for clarification of the meaning of the intrinsic value conception, but I cannot go into the matter here" (Naess Unpublished: 9), I suggest that Naess give up the concept. It is merely an *entia rationis* which is sometimes useful for expressing the ontological point that humans do not create the value of nature. Morever, nature does not create the value of human beings.

I also see a strong connection among Dogen's nonproduction of evil, Naess's beautiful actions, and Spinoza's ethics. In the preface to the "Fourth Part of the Ethics: On Human Bondage, or the Powers of the Affects," Spinoza talks freely about the way the mind constructs concepts, concepts that may be useful but which also can be dangerous if we do not recall the specific way Spinoza uses them. He reminds us that, "Perfection and imperfection, therefore, are only modes of thinking, i.e., notions we are accustomed to feign because we compare individuals of the same species or genus to one another. This is why I said . . . that by reality and perfection I understand the same thing." There is here a nonhierarchical acceptance of the reality of all beings. Of good and evil, he says, "As far as good and evil are concerned, they also indicate nothing positive in things, considered in themselves, nor are they anything other than modes of thinking, *or* notions we form because we compare things to one another" (Spinoza 1985: 545). The great paradox of Spinoza's "Ethics" is that it is an ethic without good or evil.

If these suggestive readings make sense, it follows that it is a drastic misreading of Naess's work to depict him as an environmental philosopher whose moral obligations toward nature are derived from a basic commitment to intrinsic value. While he may *use* the language of intrinsic value as a helpful mental construction expressing his view that nature cannot be abused for shallow human purposes, his deeper view is that "*All* things have value" (Naess Unpublished: 7, emphasis added).

We may ask, then, in what way is Naess's "ethic" an *environmental* ethic? It does not privilege spotted owls over killer parasites, or wild rivers over Caterpillar tractors. My answer is that Naess is not an environmental ethicist. When he uses imprecise language like "*nature* has intrinsic value," he is open to the response "nature as opposed to what?" Naess is not saying anything that distinguishes "nature" from any other gestalt. But this is not a criticism. For Naess has said time and again that he is not interested in ethics; he is, rather, proposing a "new way of seeing the world." He is proposing a "pre-ethics" which springs spontaneously from the respect/compassion for the thusness of all beings.

Ecosophy T respects *all* beings. It just so happens that Naess lives at a time when human suffering is causing the eclipse of wild things. Unlike the environmental ethicist who intends to say something special about nature when using the phrase "*nature* has intrinsic value," Naess cannot be understood as saying something like "the value of nature trumps human concerns." This is where Naess's Buddhist compassion translates into a Gandhian nonviolent political agenda that includes both wild nature and human beings. It thus appears that Naess is not guilty of the charge that his use of the concept of intrinsic value pits humans against wild nature, although this is certainly true of the way other radical environmental philosophers have used the concept.[11]

Still, the charge might be made that direct presence to Buddha-nature makes for bad political movements. Deep ecology began out of the urgent need to stop environmental destruction. Yet, we all must do our own work at the roots of suffering, even if we can later reach consensus at a more abstract, imprecise, level. This does not make for quick political action.

Naess does not say that we must complete our own work before reaching consensus. He says that we must constantly work back and forth between "the heart of the forest" and the imprecise, but important, level of political consensus where we may use the language of intrinsic value to effect change. This is what a Buddhist calls "skillful means." The Buddhist realizes that we cannot say the truth to someone who has not yet had their experience in the heart of the forest. One can, however, use skillful means to direct someone to their own experience. While such means cannot be entirely "truthful"—they are not "precise"—they are motivated by compassion and the hope of relief from suffering. The environmental ethicist uses language to lay out clear and precise first ethical principles from which all duties follow. The environmental ontologist skillfully guides people toward the forest.

If Naess is not an ethicist, he is not really a holist either. "Nature is one" is not precise. "Nature is many" is not precise either. One finds both the single and the many in the heart of the forest.

I also think that, unlike the environmental ethicist, Naess is a pluralist. He is a cultural pluralist in the sense that he has warned against the attempt to subordinate the environmental beliefs of other cultures: "there is ample reason for supporters of the Deep Ecology movement to refrain from questioning each other's ultimate beliefs. Deep cultural differences are more or less cognitively unbridgeable and will remain so, I hope" (Naess 1995: 400). Naess is calling for a network of solidarity among plural cultures, not the reduction of all beliefs to a super-precise ethical formula.

Let me repeat: while a pluralist, Naess is *not* a relativist. That is, all human beings who are directly present to *any* being will work non-violently to relieve the suffering of that being. This is truth that cannot be doubted by those who dwell in the forest.

NAESS'S ATTITUDE TOWARD THE THIRD WORLD

This is, perhaps, one reading of Naess's Ecosophy T among many.[12] In developing Naess's relationship to Buddhist thought, however, it does help to illustrate Naess's response to the charges of Rama-chandra Guha against deep ecology, that it objectifies "The East" and advocates environmental justice over human justice.

It is surprising that Naess has become embroiled in this debate. Unlike Callicott, who began by staking out a "misanthropic" position that questioned the preciousness of human life, Naess has always shown keen regard for the third world. In one of his earliest essays on deep ecology, "The Shallow and the Deep, Long-Range Ecology Movements," Naess committed deep ecology to an anti-class posture (Naess 1973). The value of diversity includes the diversity of human communities. He constantly defends local autonomy and decentralization against the homogenizing tendencies of "developed" nations. On a personal level, Naess even reports that he so respected the wishes of Nepali villagers that foreign mountaineers not climb the sacred peak, Gauri Shankar, that he walked for a week with the chief of the community "to deliver a document addressed to the King of Nepal in Kathmandu, asking him to prohibit the climbing of Gauri Shankar. There was no reply. The rich Hindu government of Nepal is economically interested in big expeditions, and the opinion of the faraway Buddhist communities of poor people carry little weight" (Naess 1995: 405).

Naess's personal commitment to social justice has never been doubted. The question has always been whether his position on cultural diversity and autonomy actually follows logically from the commitments of deep ecology. Unlike various Green platforms, which explicitly feature social justice as an equal goal with environmental justice, deep ecology seemed to commit first to the intrinsic value of *nature*. Among the original set of eight basic principles is the call for "a substantial decrease of the human population" (Devall and Sessions 1985: 70).

Naess responded to the charges against him in "The Third World, Wilderness, and Deep Ecology." He followed Snyder in pointing out that "Throughout most of human history, all humans have lived in what we now call wilderness" (Naess 1995: 397). As Snyder reminds us, when European settlers arrived, "'North America was all *populated*. There were people everywhere'" (quoted in Naess 1995: 397). Since both human and natural diversity have "intrinsic value" "there is no inherent antagonism between human settlement and free nature, for all depends upon the *kind* of culture humans have" (Naess 1995: 399).

The problem is not that there is a contradiction in principle between human and ecological justice. Most human communities historically, and still most today, live lightly on the land. The problem is with consumerist cultures that trade material comfort for genuine quality of life: "What is considered a normal lifestyle in industrial countries is clearly incompatible with living in wilderness" (Naess 1995: 398).

If my previous reading of Naess is correct, everything has "intrinsic value." It would be incorrect to read his work, therefore, as espousing a misanthropic position. The problem is that if everything has intrinsic value this does not provide an ethical categorical imperative which can drive social policy. Unlike Callicott's early view, for example, in which nature—for better or worse—trumped human life, Naess has always argued for biocentric and human equality. Although there may be no inherent antagonism between human and environmental justice, the two are so out of balance in the late twentieth century that this observation offers no guidance in working out complex social policies that are often choices of the lesser evil.

Ramachandra Guha and others are correct in pointing out that deep ecology has an insufficient political analysis. The apparent metaphysical monism of deep ecology, based on the commitment to intrinsic value, stands in the way of granting the truth of pluralism, that social and ecological goods are inherently plural and require plural, although hopefully compatible, analyses. Put another way, deep ecology has not been sufficiently clear on whether it is proposing a monistic analysis (like Callicott has) that will be imposed on diverse communities, or whether its commitment to human diversity represents a genuine form of communitarianism in which ethics begins with the community, not abstract principles.

Again, Naess has said, "there is ample reason for supporters of the Deep Ecology movement to refrain from questioning each other's ultimate beliefs. Deep cultural differences are more or less cognitively unbridgeable and will remain so, I hope" (Naess 1995: 400). Perhaps it is an over-interpretation to suggest that Naess is here committing to a form of pluralism. However, I have argued in the previous sections that this would provide a consistent interpretation of Ecosophy T.

Beyond the confusion over monism versus pluralism, a second legitimate concern of Guha and others is the essentially *romantic* use of indigenous cultures one often finds in deep ecology. Unlike the stand Naess took with the Buddhist communities of Nepal, much deep ecological literature, in a way reminiscent of Callicott's *Earth's Insights,* simply uses purported environmental commitments of indigenous people to support a conception of first world environmental philosophy. Naess is not the only deep ecologist to show real concern for actual environmental conflicts that indigenous people have experienced. But it must be granted that in much of the deep ecological literature there is little evident concern for actual environmental problems. Guha is correct that when first world philosophers collect environmental wisdom for the purpose of providing philosophical demonstrations without engagement in real environmental issues, this is a form of intellectual colonialism.

Pluralism allows that communities within shouting distance of one another may possess very different kinds of environmental knowledge; they may engage the environment in profoundly diverse ways; and they may possess very disparate tools for addressing environmental conflict. Since pluralism is not offering a monist theory that describes what these various communities are "really thinking," it requires deep engagement in real situations.

If I am right in pushing a pluralist reading of Ecosophy T, however, this leads me to register a concern about the appearance that Naess's writing about non-Western cultures sometimes gives. In the end, while I am sympathetic to Naess's branch of deep ecology, I am uncomfortable that it may appear to readers as a universal account of "man's relationship to nature." From Nara we have some sense of what Self-realization might mean in Japanese culture. We even have a hint of what it would mean to a Nepali Buddhist to say that a mountain is sacred. What Naess does not give us is a vivid account of what Self-realization would mean for *us* in the West. Perhaps this is because he holds no hope for us. For us, the wild has become an abstraction, an *entia rationis*.

Unless we do the hard work of imagining a reconciliation of nature with *our* culture, however, the culture of political liberalism, we do risk a new kind of colonialism of the sort that worries Guha. It would be typical of cultural free-agents to imagine that we, alone, are uniquely untarnished by our culture's attitudes toward nature. But, far from escaping political liberalism, this view is a deeply unconscious and unreflective expression of the view it claims to reject. We must work through who we are *as a culture*. Failure to do so will mean that an environmental ethic will be marginal, the expression of a few disgruntled individuals.

8

Ecological Feminism and the Place of Caring

CRITICAL PLURALISM

Recall the image with which I began: as the sun sets across arid, marginal land, Nepali women are returning to a place that is not their home, having risked their lives to secure neat bundles of fire-wood taken from the forest which has been placed off limits to them. All this is in service to the demands of eco-tourism and a cash econ-omy. Women constantly find themselves caught in such borderlands, functioning between the demands of their traditional cultures and "progress," between the competing demands of men, between cash and barter economies, and between competing relationships of nature to culture. This matrix of competing demands is infinitely variable, as are the ways women choose to respond to such demands, sometimes working in consort with each other, sometimes divided by class or eth-nicity. There is no single "women's voice."

I have argued, paradoxically, that the greatest source of unity among women is found, not in a common culture, or in a single theory, but in their responses to the common demands of developmentalism as a global phenomenon. People in profoundly different cultural cir-cumstances are forced to respond to remarkably similar issues because of globalization. Plural voices can easily sound like a cacophony of noise, especially in comparison to the powerfully unified voice of a global neo-liberalism.

However, this is part of the paradox of ecofeminism. If it is true, as Bryan Norton points out, that "There are no important positive positions or tenets that unify pluralists" (Norton 1995: 345), then it is strange to identify any pluralist position as an "ism." Ecofeminism does not even attempt to provide necessary and sufficient conditions for an analysis of environmental or social goods. Perhaps because it does not attempt to satisfy the traditional philosophical requirements for theory-making, one of the most common criticisms of ecofeminism is that it "isn't anything." It does not come down to a single commitment to the intrinsic value of nature, or to the principle of biocentric egalitarianism. It appears, rather, to be nothing more than a collection of allied views.

According to one widely cited definition, "*eco-feminism* is a position based on the following claims: (i) there are important connections between the oppression of women and the oppression of nature; (ii) understanding the nature of these connections is necessary to any adequate understanding of the oppression of women and the oppression of nature; (iii) feminist theory and practice must include an ecological perspective; and (iv) solutions to ecological problems must include a feminist perspective" (Warren 1987: 4–5).

Perhaps the critical word here is "connections." Ecofeminism does not claim that there is a single Holy Grail of environmental ethics, a categorical imperative from which all our moral duties follow. Unlike the land ethic, whose goal is theoretical "closure," ecofeminism does not claim a single, reductive analysis of all environmental degradation. As a feminist position, it highlights a necessary, although not sufficient, element in the analysis of oppression. If race and gender are distinct categories, for example, and if even these categories are constructed differently in different times and places, ecofeminism claims only to reveal the variety of connections between the oppression of women and the oppression of nature. It does not claim that this ecofeminist analysis will replace an analysis of environmental racism. Ethics, as Karen J. Warren points out, is a quilt or collage of views that work in alliance with one another, not a single moral language. Ecofeminism "rejects the assumption that there is 'one voice' in terms of which ethical values, beliefs, attitudes, and conduct can be assessed" (Warren 1987: 139).

The danger of a pluralist position like this is that it will be misread as a kind of vacuous relativism. This is not only a theoretical danger, but a concern for practice since ecofeminism stands for the real interests of women and the ecocommunities in which they function. Despite it pluralism, it is committed to arguing *against* certain positions, and *for* others. Ecofeminism is not a form of relativism.

I believe ecofeminism is best viewed as a kind of *critical* pluralism. To draw out this critical dimension, first, I want to recall some of the threads of its critique of other views; second, I want to sketch at least one positive conception of an ecofeminist ethic.

Part of what some perceive to be ambiguity in ecofeminism is that ecofeminism may be approached in a variety of ways. It is even conceivable that ecofeminism could be thought of as a form of liberal feminism. However, many of the concerns I have expressed about political liberalism also apply to liberal ecofeminism. One concern about the compatibility of ecofeminism with a rights approach is that the rights approach is formalistic. It recommends a decision procedure by which those beings that have rights can be separated from those that do not. Its aspirations are universalistic. Feminist approaches to ethics, however, tend to be not only pluralistic, but contextual.[1] They tend to be based on actual interests in the narrative context of lived experiences.[2]

Second, the rights approach does not express feminist moral insights because it is inherently adversarial. As Joel Feinberg has said, "To have a right is to have a claim *to* something *against* someone" (Feinberg 1980: 139). Although conflict certainly may arise over a feminist understanding of morality, it does not begin from a theoretical assumption of conflict. Rather, a feminist understanding is more likely to be based in a pluralistic context that is dialogical and seeks mutual accommodation of interests (Benhabib 1987: section 4).

Third, connected to a dialogical understanding of ethics, feminist moral thought tends to reconceptualize personhood as relational rather than autonomous (Lugones 1987, and Curtin 1994). Whereas the rights approach requires a concept of personhood that is individualistic enough to defend the sphere in which the moral agent is autonomous, feminist approaches to ethics tend to see moral inquiry as an ongoing process through which persons are defined contextually and relationally.

In chapters 6 and 7, I encouraged skepticism about the Western assumption of a unified, autonomous (male) self. J. Baird Callicott's third position, in which he uses quantum theory to cast doubt on the Cartesian distinction between subject and object, and thus the central importance of the distinction between egoism and altruism, is an encouraging direction in his work. Similarly, at least on one reading of Arne Naess's Ecosophy T, we can understand Naess to be moving away from familiar liberal, masculine definitions of self.

While these directions represent important potentialities for these views, ecofeminism has taken a relational understanding of self as central to its project. Val Plumwood, for example, wrote in "Nature, Self, and Gender: Feminism, Environmental Philosophy, and the Critique of Rationalism":

> Thus it is unnecessary to adopt any of the stratagems of deep ecology—the indistinguishable self, the expanded self, or the transpersonal self—in order to provide an alternative to anthropocentrism or human self-interest. This can be better done through the relational account of the self, which clearly recognizes the distinctness of nature but also our relationship and continuity with it. On this relational account, respect for the other results neither from the containment of the self nor from a transcendence of self, but is an *expression* of self in relationship, not egoistic self as merged with the other but self as embedded in a network of essential relationships with distinct others. (Plumwood 1991: 20)

One of my concerns from the beginning has been to challenge the global applicability of the unified moral subject of political liberalism.

Fourth, whereas the rights approach has tended to argue that ethical judgments are objective and rational and do not depend upon affective aspects of experience, this has been questioned by feminist critics partly on the grounds that the conception of the purely rational is a myth, and partly on the grounds that this myth is inclined to marginalize the experiences of women by portraying them as personal rather than moral (Jaggar 1989: 139–43).

Finally, as a result of the emphasis on the rational in traditional moral theory, feminist insights concerning the body as moral agent have been missed. But as some feminist philosophers have argued (see Bordo 1989), the identification of woman with body has been one pretext on which women's lives have been marginalized.

Just as a rights approach is not a very promising route for expressing non-Western relationships to land, neither is it promising as a language that will allow women to articulate their local relationships to nature and culture. In a world where the language of rights is the common moral currency, there may be contexts in which it would be helpful for women (some of whom are feminists) to present their cases in the language of rights. However, this is akin to the requirement that we all speak English if we are going to communicate.

If one accepts that there is a deep connection between the oppression of nature and the oppression of women in Western culture, one must look to a distinctively feminist understanding of oppression. The analysis of much of the world's environmental destruction in terms of systemic and institutional violence is consistent with Warren's idea of an "oppressive conceptual framework" as "one that explains, justifies, and maintains relationships of domination and subordination" (Warren 1987: 127). Systemic and institutional violence can take many forms. Racism, sexism, naturism, and developmentalism are all forms of systemic violence that may necessitate the invention of social institutions. In the previous chapters I have drawn out the connections among these forms of exclusion.

Ecofeminism, or at least the form of ecofeminism I find most persuasive, is allied with the critique of globalization. From a feminist perspective it highlights the particular and unequal ways that the process of globalization affects women and their ecocommunities.

In chapter 5, I proposed a philosophy of material culture that emphasizes the roles that third world women actually are assigned by constructions of gender at the borders between nature and culture. If gender, unlike sex, is socially constructed, it follows that these roles will be highly various. As many ecofeminists have pointed out, being close to nature in a culture that exploits nature is dangerous business.

Some women, I believe, have privileged knowledge of the environment because their social roles necessitate such knowledge, often, as Vandana Shiva has written, for "staying alive." Where women are responsible for infant care, clean water is an important issue. Where women are farmers and medical practitioners, access to biodiversity is crucial. Where women's voices are excluded from decision-making, despite these critical responsibilities, it is impossible to develop informed public policies. "Expertise" is often, then, at odds with what women know about the local connections between culture and nature.

The positive form of ecofeminism that I find most persuasive might best be termed "transformative ecofeminism"[3] In first describing systemic and institutional violence, I characterized the transformative element in moral understanding. Since institutional violence is often advanced in the name of justice, and, yet, is experienced very differently by those outside the institutions, the movement from inside to outside requires an act of the moral imagination. Coming to experience the institutions from the outside demands a "phase shift" in moral understanding.

Since I think of transformative ecofeminism primarily in terms of a philosophy of material culture, I am not very sympathetic to certain (rare) forms of essentialist ecofeminism. Most women in the first world are no closer to nature, nor further removed from nature, than most first world men. Women are not closer to nature "by nature." Women sometimes oppress other women through identifying them with nature. In emphasizing the difficult material conditions under which women's environmental knowledge is produced, I hope to have arrived at a position that does not romanticize such knowledge. The last thing third world women need is to be colonized by first world intellectuals looking for ways to overcome their alienation from nature. I have also repeatedly questioned universalist claims for political liberalism, including the reduction of the moral domain to the sphere of rights. Caring for others, which often results from a transformative moral experience, is a more basic human capacity than rights since it is the "glue" that fosters and maintains community.

As I contend in the next chapter, abstract talk about rights becomes important when the normal bonds of community fail. So I am sympathetic to Jim Cheney, for example, when he writes of the differences between the ways self is defined in a gift economy and a market economy. "In a gift economy . . . selves tend to get defined in terms of what I call 'defining relationships'—where our relationships with others are central to our understanding of who we are" (Cheney 1987: 122).[4]

Having registered my fundamental sympathy for ecofeminist goals, I now focus on three concerns that still need to be addressed squarely if some form of ecofeminism is to play a role in helping women to articulate their concerns. The first is that, although my pluralism leads me to be sympathetic to a contextualized ethic of caring for the ecocommunity, unless we are quite clear about what this means, we are in danger of encouraging gender stereotypes: women's roles as caretakers free men to build "culture."

Second, to the extent that I am an ecocommunitarian (as defined more fully in the next chapter), I need to recognize that the internal standards of communities are often sexist. The traditions through which communities are constituted are frequently the very traditions that define repressive roles for women. But, as I assert in the next chapter, because a moral horizon begins in a community, we need not accept the moral boundaries of community. Communities change; sometimes they change through transformative shifts in our moral perspective.

Third, caring itself cannot capture the full range of human strengths required to resist "development" and build local communities. True caring, understood as human power to effect change and construct the bonds of community, can only function in combination with other powers. What we need, I argue, is a *critical ecocommunitarianism*, a pluralist ethic that begins with the authority of local communities to define their local values and participate in their transformation over time, but which also provides a critical function to values so we do not end up with a simple cultural relativism that is harmful to women and their communities.

A POLITICIZED ETHIC OF CARING FOR

A source for much of the Western feminist literature on women's psychological and moral development is Carol Gilligan's *In a Different Voice*.[5] Whereas the rights approach tends to emphasize identity of moral interests, formalistic decision procedures, an adversarial understanding of moral discourse, personhood as autonomous, and a valorization of the nonbodily aspects of personhood, Gilligan's research indicates that (at least some) women's moral experiences are better understood in terms of recognition of a plurality of moral interests, contextual decision-making, nonadversarial accommodation of diverse interests, personhood as relational, and the body as moral agent. Furthermore, for our purposes, an ethic of care has an intuitive appeal from the standpoint of ecological ethics. Whether or not nonhuman animals and ecosystems have rights, we certainly can and do care for them.

While an ethic of care does have an intuitive appeal, without further development into a political dimension, Gilligan's research may be turned against feminist and ecofeminist objectives. First, if not politicized, an ethic of care can be used to privatize the moral interests of women. In contrast to the rights model, which seeks to cordon off "my" territory over which I have control, the caring-for model may often suggest that the interests of others should, in certain contexts, come before one's own, and that knowing what to do in a particular situation requires empathetic projection into another's life. Putting the Other in front of oneself can easily be abused. The wife who selflessly cares for her husband, who cares only about himself, is only too well known.

In a society that oppresses women, it does no good to suggest that women should go on selflessly providing care if institutionally violent social structures make it all too easy to abuse that care. But consider, once again, the objections of Vandana Shiva and Mira Shiva to the International Conference on Population and Development in Cairo. They condemned first world liberals, including liberal feminists, whose concern for "individual sexual freedom" made it appear that "women's rights" are "antithetical to the rights of children and women's freedom as based on neglect of the family." "By ignoring the social, economic and family responsibilities that third world women carry, the exclusive focus on 'sexual and reproductive rights' is disempowering, not empowering, for third world women because it makes women appear socially irresponsible" (Shiva and Shiva 1994: 16). Notice, for the Shivas, a consistent ecofeminist position does not mean rejection of traditional roles of caring for children, community, and the environment. The Shivas are representative of every Indian feminist I have met in expressing their resentment of first world feminism to the extent that it seems to challenge Indian women to give up their traditional roles as caretakers. What these feminists want is not the rejection of responsibility for caring but a transformation in social conditions, both within India and from the outside, that make it dangerous to care.

The injunction to care must be understood as part of a radical political agenda that allows for development of contexts in which caring for can be nonabusive. It claims that the relational sense of self, the willingness to empathetically enter into the world of others and care for them, can be expanded and developed as part of a political agenda so that it may include those outside the already established circle of caring for. Its goal is not just to make a "private" ethic public but to help undercut the public/private distinction.

An ethic of care that is not politicized can be localized in scope, thereby blunting its political impact. Caring for resists the claim that morality depends upon a criterion of universalizability, and insists that it depends upon special, contextual relationships. This might be taken to mean that we should care for the homeless only if our daughter or son happens to be homeless. Or, it might mean that persons in dominant countries should feel no need to care for persons in dominated countries. Or, it might mean that we should care only for those of the same species. These were the problems we considered with Callicott's form of communitarianism according to which obligations decrease with distance.

Caring always operates on issues of scale. One can care about one's own children, the children of one's village, as well as children in general. There are also ecological issues of scale. One's primary locus of caring is within one's "home." This is where local expertise, understanding the internal values of a culture, is most effective. But issues of water purity, and access to safe water, cannot be simply local. This is particularly true in the context of developmentalism where there is a systemic bias toward large dams that centralize water collection and political power.

Of course, there can be deep conflicts over the scale of caring. This friction is especially pertinent where developmentalist policies have created what Hardin termed "the tragedy of the commons."[6] Caring becomes increasingly difficult in proportion to the privatization of the commons upon which traditional villages depend.

Is this a theoretical problem for an ethic of care? It is only if we have expectations for ethics such as Callicott's, that is, if we expect ethics to be equally communitarian and Kantian. We will then advance communitarian sentiments as long as they do not conflict with a universal algorithm from which all duties can be deduced. Ecological feminism, however, is making a point about ethics itself, an Aristotelian point: Ethics is not mathematics. Ethics is inherently messy. We should only expect the degree of clarity that critical examination of human affairs admits. If moral rationality is an element in social rationality, not the detached weigher of probabilities or rules of political liberalism, then we need to think of ethical reasoning contextually, in terms of the best position available from one's own position.

While contextual, caring itself is not altogether uncritical. A distinction can be drawn between caring *about* and caring *for* that helps clarify how caring can be expanded. Caring about is a generalized form of care that may have specifiable recipients, but it occurs in a context where direct relatedness to specific others is missing. For example, feminist perspectives may lead one to a sense of connection between oneself and the plight of women in distant locations. But if one has not experienced the condition of women in India, for example, and, more than that, if one has not experienced the particular conditions of women in a specific village in a specific region of India, caring remains a generalized caring about. As an element in a feminist political agenda, such caring about may lead to the kinds of actions that bring one into the sort of deep relatedness that can be described as caring for: caring for particular persons in the context of their histories.

Similar comments may be made about classic environmental issues. By reading about the controversy surrounding logging of old-growth forests, one might come to care about them. But caring for is marked by an understanding of and appreciation for a particular context in which one participates. One may, for example, come to understand the issue partly in terms of particular trees one has become accustomed to looking for on a favorite hike, trees that one would miss given changes in logging regulations. With these political and ecological considerations in mind, I conclude that an ethic of care can be expanded as part of a feminist political agenda without losing its distinctive contextual character. It can resist privatization and localization, retaining the contextualized character that is distinctive of caring for.

In summary, ecofeminist philosophy seeks not only to understand the condition of women but also to use that understanding to liberate women and nature from the structures of oppression. In achieving a new sense of relatedness of the sort that feminist and ecofeminist political philosophy can provide, one is enabled to enter into caring for relationships that were not available earlier. One may come to see, for example, that the white, middle-class American woman's typical situation is connected with—although not identical to—the condition of women in oppressed countries. Caring for can also be generated by coming to see that one's life (unknowingly) has been a cause of the oppression of others. The caring-for model does not require that those recipients of our care must be "equal" to us. It does also not assume they are unequal. It is built on developing the capacity to care, not the criterion of equality. The resultant caring for may lead to a new sense of empowerment based on cultivating the willingness to act to empower ourselves and others.

ECO-VIRTUES

True caring is best understood as one of a range of human virtues where virtues are understood as human powers that enable moral agents to achieve distinctively human goods. The definition of any virtue is always contextual; it depends upon whether the term names an actual human strength that can be exercised in a particular community. Part of the problem, then, is terminological: caring is not really caring in a specific context if it is not possible to care without being damaged, or subsumed by another's moral agency. Caring is only an actual virtue in communities where it is possible to care.

This does not mean that caring must be achieved without struggle. Perhaps what I admire most about village women in India is their struggle to care against great odds. It may even be these odds that turn such resistance into a strength. What is clear, however, is that effective caring must be allied with other virtues. Alone it is, at best, a partial description of what it means to function as a moral agent.

Consider humility. This is not a virtue often mentioned by feminists for the obvious reason that it is just as susceptible to abuse as caring. But this is only when we understand it as a weakness rather than a strength that has the subversive potential to deflate false ego and remind us of our citizenship in a larger community. If we are to achieve a relational sense of self, however, it cannot be without recognizing the strength of humble relationships to others who cannot be dominated. Part of my analysis of the effect of the green revolution is that it could only occur in a culture which lacks humility with respect to nature. The ways I characterized "women's agriculture" implied a sense of place, an attitude of respect, in relation to a larger community.

Practical wisdom is also a virtue that is typically overlooked by modern conceptions of what passes for expertise. This is the human strength of knowing what is appropriate given the options available in a particular context. It is not a matter of deducing obligations from universal rules. Rather, it involves concrete comparisons and weighing of options so that one's actions are better rather than worse. This is exactly the sort of reflection that operates in traditional agriculture, child rearing, and traditional medical care.

So, while the position I advocate here is resolutely ecofeminist, I am not *only* an ecofeminist. Women's roles as defined by definitions of culture and nature, their critical environmental expertise, are necessary for any adequate understanding of the dynamics of cultural and environmental change. Not every environmental issue is a feminist issue, however, just as not every form of oppression can be elucidated through the concept of race. A pluralist form of critical ecocommunitarianism seeks to discover and foster alliances among these positions.

A NOTE ON SOCIAL ECOLOGY

I want to close this review of three "radical," first world approaches to environmental ethics with a brief discussion of the fourth: social ecology. This approach, as originally articulated by Murray Bookchin, is consonant with many of the positions articulated here. However, it also appears to diverge at a critical point.

Social ecology, first, is a variety of naturalism. All beings are natural. Human life is seen as part of an evolutionary continuum. It thus rejects the untoward consequence of some versions of deep ecology which depict human beings as categorically distinct from nature, making all human intervention in nature "unnatural." One consequence of this view is that deep ecologists tend to regard *all* agriculture as anthropocentric ecological violence. This leaves no room for a distinction between *kinds* of agriculture. One of the contradictions of deep ecology is that it repeatedly claims traditional cultures as conceptual ancestors, but only selectively, when they do not engage in agriculture.

Social ecology sees environmental violence largely in terms of what I call institutional and systemic violence. Environmental violence is, thus, connected to other forms of violence: racism, sexism, and colonialism. Social ecology resists the invitation of deep ecology to reduce all environmental violence to one cause: anthropocentrism.

It also resists deep ecology's solution to the ecological crisis: the need to move to a biocentric egalitarianism. This complete leveling of the evolutionary process prevents any account of the uniqueness of human culture.

Social ecology locates a powerful source of systemic violence in the tendency of capitalism to "commodify" reality, to produce a homogeneous world culture. It contests globalization and offers a solution very similar to the vision suggested in chapter 7, the need to move toward a critical ecocommunitarianism.

Finally, social ecology criticizes the liberal conception of freedom as simply "being left alone" to advance one's subjective preferences. Instead it attempts to offer a positive conception of freedom which connects freedom with the ability to achieve valuable ends.

I am profoundly in agreement with all these positions social ecology espouses. They all function, however, within a world-historical narrative that is disturbing in the way it reproduces a dialectic of center and margin between "advanced" and traditional cultures. One finds this especially in the Hegelian and Marxist influence on Bookchin's writing.

Bookchin describes his view as rejecting the "linear thinking" of much Western thought. He advocates a "form of 'nonlinear' or organic thinking [that] is developmental rather than analytical, or, in more technical terms, dialectical rather than instrumental" (Bookchin 1993: 356). Non-human nature is defined as "an evolving process, as the *totality,* in fact of its evolution." Human beings are an extension of this natural continuum.

Humans are always rooted in what Bookchin calls "first nature," our biological, evolutionary heritage. But human beings also produce a unique social nature of their own, which Bookchin calls "second nature." This evolutionary continuum accounts for both our continuity with all of nature, but also our uniqueness as creators of culture.

This "developmental" view is Hegelian, and Marxist, in the sense that it lays out a single historical path through which humans can achieve their full potential as humans. We began in simple, tribal cultures that enjoyed a kind of naive unity with nature. As "second nature" developed it became riddled with the contradictions of modern human consciousness. When these contradictions are overcome, we will emerge into a new form of human life where human potentialities are fulfilled and we are able to live together in a new "ecological society" which celebrates both our continuity with nature and the uniqueness of human ecological consciousness.

Bookchin's account of the transformation from nature to culture, from first nature to second nature, is embedded in a deeply prejudicial account of traditional cultures that is a familiar feature of European philosophy. At the transition between nature and culture there were tribes whose "mores . . . were based on an unreflected body of *customs* that seemed to have been inherited from time immemorial." "Only later," Bookchin tells us, "beginning with the ancient Greeks, did *ethical* behavior emerge, based on rational discourse and reflection" (Bookchin 1993: 361).

The rational reconciliation of nature with human culture occurs only through the gateway of contradictions that are characteristic of the modern, Western consciousness. In the ecocommunities to come, we will have "a shared community of human beings rather than ethnic folk—a community of citizens rather than of kinsmen" (Bookchin 1993: 361).

We recognize here an old ploy of colonialism which underpins the thinking of philosophers such as the Mills on one end of the spectrum of Western philosophy and Georg Wilhelm Hegel and Karl Marx on the other end. Whether a "linear" thinker such as Mill or a "dialectical" thinker such as Hegel, Marx, and Bookchin, traditional people are first identified with nature and then patronized for their pre-rational, folkish identification with nature. Despite their many differences, Bookchin and Callicott both pretend to critique the relations of nature and culture from a hegemonic position of rationality at the end of time.

In the last three chapters I have considered a range of proposals for an environmental ethic with several questions in mind: Do they simply assume familiar Western approaches to ethics which are then represented as universal, or do they engage the concrete realities of diverse cultures as they mediate the borders between culture(s) and local conceptions of nature? Are they content with abstract theorizing about nature, or do they account for our immediate, plural connections to place? Do they so emphasize environmental justice that they become prejudicial in their treatment of issues of human justice: population, access to biodiversity, and gender, race, and class?

I am deeply sympathetic to pluralist versions of ecofeminism and social ecology, although I think ecofeminism needs to be expanded, and social ecology goes wrong when it surrenders to the call for a grand evolutionary narrative of human progress. The land ethic is seriously paradoxical since it is defined as a radical alternative to utilitarian resource management, but in most of its versions it simply assumes familiar Western conceptions of moral agency and the purpose of ethics, assumptions it shares with the utilitarian view it claims to reject. How the land ethic reads the relationships of nature and culture in the third world is as clear a case as one could ask for of contemporary Western environmental neocolonialism. Finally, I have attempted to understand Arne Naess's version of deep ecology as escaping the charge that he simply projects first world views of ethics onto the third world, although even here he may object to the ways I push him toward a still more radical view.

Out of these readings of the state of Western environmental philosophy emerges the broad outlines of an answer to the basic questions of this book. In the two concluding chapters, I work out an approach to the reconciliation of nature and culture that is both deeply pluralistic and critical. It begins with the central authority of local cultures to express, defend, and participate in the transformation of their mediations of culture with nature. As with the distinction between caring *for* and caring *about*, this approach sees issues of nature and culture as inherently issues of scale. A way of life that mediates between culture and nature begins in its local dimension. However, it must also be critical, since life, even at the local level, is burdened by conflicts, and conflicts only tend to increase at larger scales.

At last we can approach the most difficult question: If an environmental ethic must not simply colonize other ways of mediating culture and nature, if it must be "home-grown," what would an environmental ethic look like for us, the heirs of the Enlightenment? Where is our place?

Part 3
Democratic Pluralism

9

Democratic Discourse in a Morally Pluralistic World

THE LANGUAGES OF CONFLICT

A recent newspaper headline read:

Human Rights Divide U.S., Third World:
Christopher says cultural traditions shouldn't be refuge for repression.
(*Minneapolis Tribune*, June 15, 1993)

At the World Conference on Human Rights in June 1993, former secretary of state Warren Christopher defended human rights as the universal moral language, charging that "cultural relativism [has] become the last refuge of repression." When some third world countries protested that the language of individual human rights is inappropriate to communalistic cultures, Secretary Christopher replied that such "cultural traditions" are not ethical systems.

We can imagine how third world countries reacted to the news that there is one true moral language which emanates from the first world, all else being "cultural traditions." The language of individual rights, like the language of calculable utilities, is undeniably the invention of the industrialized West.[1] While it has found its way into the founding documents of many third world countries, and has sometimes played a constructive role there,[2] it often connects uneasily with indigenous ethical traditions. Although Secretary Christopher undoubtedly saw himself as defending human dignity, we should now be able to sympathize with those who received his words as all too familiar examples of systemic violence. The Kantian distinction between cultures that have ethics and those that merely have "traditions" has been a basic ploy in the colonial agenda for centuries.

Incidents such as these may lead us to question whether democratic discourse is possible where colonialism has caused legacies of dialogical inequality and distrust. Perhaps the very desire for cross-cultural ethical discourse is a colonizing demand. Why, after all, *should* the colonized speak with those who have colonized them? Furthermore, when deep cultural differences mean there is no common moral language, what cross-cultural criteria can we appeal to for mediation of moral disputes? Under such conditions, what would count as agreement?

Without the possibility of cross-cultural ethical discourse, however, we are left with two alternatives, both unacceptable. Failure of such discourse sometimes produces outright physical violence, as in Chiapas and Bangalore. More often, institutionalized violence results when we accede to the view that cross-cultural relations are mediated either by the ethically neutral language of utilities, or the universal language of rights. Such relations are then mediated either by the supposed ethically neutral scientific or economic expert, or they are reduced to a language so abstract that it is incapable of expressing unique relationships of culture and place. People and their environments then become commodities.

When this happens, the best arguments we are left with are not very good. We may argue, for example, that the fate of Kayapo Indians of Brazil should be left largely to themselves, not because of the integrity of diverse cultures and their environments, but because the rainforest, and the ecological knowledge of its inhabitants, are economically valuable. (The "Ben and Jerry's" argument.)

I cannot accept either Christopher's liberal imperialism, nor the relativist response to Christopher that defends third (and fourth) world autonomy by denying that ethical discourse is possible across cultures. Unlike the relativist, I believe genuine cross-cultural ethical discourse is possible. Yet I believe the moral spheres of life are far more diverse and pluralistic than Christopher's reductionist argument allows. While I grant there are secondary roles for the language of rights and utilities in cross-cultural discourse, neither is helpful at the primary level in fostering cross-cultural moral understanding, or in mediating out-of-context ethical disputes. In fact, as we have seen, expectations about the very nature of moral reasoning set up by deontological and utilitarian theories sometimes *cause* failure in moral communication.

The question that confronts democracy is: "In a world of ethical pluralism, how can we foster democratic discourse worldwide when there is no common moral language?" By "democratic" I obviously do not mean the culturally specific institutions created by Western political liberalism. I refer, simply, to the normative dialogical space that opens up through transformative moral experiences in which grievances can be mediated nonviolently.

My project in this chapter is to lay out a non-relativist alternative to both versions of political liberalism. First, I ask why cross-cultural ethical discourse is problematic, finding reasons within the structure of ethical practices themselves. Next, I provide reasons for thinking ethical pluralism is a genuine and irreducible feature of the moral domain. In the final section I argue that ethical discourse is possible even when common criteria are lacking.

THE OPACITY OF MORAL REASONS

Setting aside often-cited political and economic reasons for subverting democratic ethical discourse, I believe there are deeper, less understood systemic and institutional reasons within the domain of ethics that make cross-cultural ethical discourse difficult to achieve. These reasons concern the ways practices internal to a local form of moral life shape what counts as a compelling ethical reason.[3]

Let me begin with an abridged version of Alasdair MacIntyre's definition of a practice: "By a 'practice' I am going to mean any coherent and complex form of socially established cooperative human activity through which goods internal to that form of activity are realized" (MacIntyre 1981: 187). There are two things I particularly want to notice about this passage. First, practices are cooperative forms of human activity having an internal structure and logic that places demands on any individual participant in the practice. "To enter into a practice," MacIntyre says, "is to accept the authority of those standards and the inadequacy of my own performance as judged by them. It is to subject my own attitudes, choices, preferences, and tastes to the standards which currently and partially define the practice" (MacIntyre 1981: 190).

For MacIntyre, farming and baseball are practices, but growing vegetables and throwing a baseball, to the extent that they are individual and not social activities, are not. Architecture is a practice; bricklaying is not. The patterns of scientific inquiry that are characteristic of physics, chemistry, and biology, as well as the work of the historian, philosopher, painter, or musician, are practices. Cooking and mothering are also practices (Curtin and Powers 1994; Curtin and Heldke 1992; Ruddick 1989).

Second, MacIntyre distinguishes between internal and external goods. External goods—MacIntyre mentions prestige, status, and money—can be achieved in alternate ways, not necessarily through the practice. One might achieve these three external goods, for example, by cheating to win the World Series. By cheating, however, one does not engage in the practice for its own sake. One does not, therefore, achieve the characteristic goods of the practice. Since external goods can be achieved outside the practice—even at the expense of the practice and those who engage in it—they are individual goods. There is only a limited amount of prestige, status, and money to go around. When "rights" to these individual goods are violated, we have no difficulty recognizing individual violence.

Not so with internal goods: "Internal goods are indeed the outcome of competition to excel, but it is characteristic of them that their achievement is good for the whole community who participates in the practice" (MacIntyre 1981: 190). Such goods can only be achieved through developing and exercising the characteristic excellences of the practice itself. So, in a given year only one team can win the World Series, but the excellence represented by the Series (won honestly) is valuable for the practice of baseball. It sets the standard by which the practice is measured.

It follows from this distinction between internal and external goods that there is a critical difference between insiders and outsiders to a practice in the ways that moral reasons are understood. One understands the internal goods to the extent one functions as an insider. To the extent one is an outsider, these reasons for internal goods will be opaque. The instructions a master violinist gives to her advanced pupil, for example, tend to be short and cryptic. The pupil may ask how to achieve a particular intonation, and the master may simply move slightly her student's hand position on the bow. The change may be both momentous in terms of achieving goods within the practice and imperceptible to the outsider.

On a more popular level, consider how little accomplished athletes often have to say about their practices to outsiders. A batter on a hitting streak may appear stone-like when the sports reporter asks for an explanation. There is just not much that *can* be said to the outsider. We are often told that the batter is "seeing the ball," as if new contact lenses were the answer. In contrast to the opacity of these reasons to the outsider, insiders to the practice probably would not have asked the question in the first place. If one has to ask, one probably will not understand.

Drawing on the familiar distinction between knowing-that and knowing-how, we see that what is easily communicable to outsiders is bits of knowledge which can be separated from the practice without much loss in cognitive content: knowledge-that.[4] Significantly, this includes knowledge that is amenable to quantification, whether scientific or economic. It also includes knowledge of individual goods that are achievable without social cooperation.

What really needs to be communicated, however, if the ethical density of the situation is to be conveyed, is process knowledge. Knowing-how is hands-on knowledge. It is local knowledge that involves the development of skills within a tradition which provides criteria for those skills. It is precisely these deep, messy, difficult-to-explain reasons constituting a practice that cannot be taken out of context without great loss of meaning. Yet, it is precisely these reasons that are neglected in much ethical discourse between "worlds." Such discourse usually concentrates on external goods.

We thus have a deeper way of solving one of the basic puzzles of this book: how social and environmental justice in one context can become unjust in another context. How can a social system appear—perhaps *be*—nonviolent from within, yet violent when transported elsewhere? How can the green revolution earnestly be advocated as the agent of progress in one context, and simultaneously be the agent of destruction of an ecological community in another context? The danger of economic liberalism is not that it has entirely misidentified human goods. There *are* external goods, and these are sometimes important to all people. What liberalism misses—or refuses to grant in its reductionist zeal—is that there are other goods, the internal goods which constitute ecological communities.

THE IRREDUCIBILITY OF ETHICAL PRACTICES

If MacIntyre is right, we must all be pluralists about human goods. The moral sphere is simply messier than reductionists would like. We must always balance individual goods against social goods. So, in this section I want to get at the sense in which various practices are not only different, when they have different internal goods and different epistemic grounds, but irreducible. We cannot assume, as does Secretary Christopher, that diverse practices must be reducible to a single, abstract norm, and that all other practices are nothing more than confused versions of the one norm. Ethical pluralism is a genuine, irreducible feature of the moral sphere(s) of life.

There are three reasons for thinking that practices have what I will call "objective positional integrity." The first is epistemological: objectivity can be understood as the best account of internal goods from within a practice. The second is ethical: functioning as a moral self *is* functioning from within the horizon of reasons and capabilities available through a set of goods. Third, following from these epistemological and ethical considerations, I conclude that cross-cultural ethical discourse seeks to apprehend the narrative of the concrete Other; it is not about the application of abstract or quantifiable rules.

Objective Positional Integrity

I have emphasized that each practice includes an internal fabric of reasons and explanations that is available to insiders. I now want to draw out the sense in which these reasons are objective. Amartya Sen has argued that objectivity is positional. He begins with the elementary observation that from a position on earth, the belief that the moon and sun are the same size is objective. If one lacked any information available from other positions, if one judged solely on the basis of that single position, it would be *irrational* to believe the sun and moon are different sizes. From a particular position on earth during a solar eclipse, for example, the moon covers the sun almost entirely.

To say that a belief is positionally objective, however, is not to say that it is true. There is the need for "'trans-positional' assessment—drawing on but going beyond different positional observations" (Sen 1993: 130). In contrast to the well-known view of Thomas Nagel according to which objectivity is a "view from nowhere" (Nagel 1986), Sen reconstructs objectivity as the best account from a position. There are, in Sen's terms, "objective illusions": "The notion of 'objective illusion' invokes both (1) the idea of positionally objective belief, and (2) the diagnosis that this belief is, in fact, mistaken" (Sen 1993: 132).

Sen intends this analysis to apply not only to observational beliefs, but, in a very powerful way, to social and ethical beliefs. He contrasts the Indian state of Kerala, where longevity is high (67.5 years for men, 73 years for women), with states like Bihar and Uttar Pradesh, where longevity is very low. Despite these differences, residents of Bihar and Uttar Pradesh do not think of themselves as dying prematurely. Keralans, on the other hand, are much more aware of their own morbidity because of higher literacy and more awareness of health care in

Kerala. Residents of Bihar and Uttar Pradesh, then, because of lower literacy rates, are both positionally objective about their longevity compared to others in their position, given what they know about longevity, and mistaken in their belief that they live long, at least when compared to others (Sen 1993: 134–35).

I want to extend Sen's idea by connecting it with my earlier remarks on the difference between insiders and outsiders to a practice. Where Secretary Christopher regards difference as a mark of relativity (except for his own position, which is objective), I find positional objectivity within *all* practices. A practice includes, by definition, a coherent system of reasons in the minimal sense that it must capture the attention and imagination of its insiders if it is to thrive and gain adherents. The set of internal goods must be sufficiently compelling—for at least some insiders—that it can order a pattern of life.

It does not follow from this that every cultural self-explanation is correct. Sen is correct that we can be positionally objective, and our account can be the best available from a position—and, yet, we can be mistaken. Put more broadly, cultural relativism does not follow from the fact that all self-interpretation is place based.

Moral Horizons and Human Functioning

The nonreductivist approach to epistemic and cultural diversity can be advanced further, I believe, by showing that the objective position from which one operates is not optional. While horizons may evolve, functioning within *some* ethical horizon is constitutive of what it means to function as a human being. If this is correct, it highlights the mistake in Christopher's reductivist argument according to which some deep human functionings are ethical, while others are merely "traditions." In a certain sense, if we are human we cannot fail to function ethically.

I find Charles Taylor's *Sources of the Self* extraordinarily insightful on this point. Taylor summarizes:

> I want to defend the strong thesis that doing without frameworks is utterly impossible for us; otherwise put, that the horizons within which we live our lives and which make sense of them have to include these strong qualitative discriminations. Moreover, this is not meant just as a contingently true psychological fact about human beings, which could perhaps turn out one day not to hold for some exceptional individual or new type, some superhuman of disengaged objectification. Rather the claim is that living within such strongly qualified horizons is constitutive of human agency,

that stepping outside these limits would be tantamount to stepping outside what we would recognize as integral, that is undamaged human personhood. (Taylor 1989: 26–27)

A moral horizon, or framework, for Taylor is nothing less than the context in which we have an identity, a sense of self. "To know who you are," Taylor says, "is to be oriented in moral space, a space in which questions arise about what is good or bad, what is worth doing and what is not, what has meaning and importance for you and what is trivial and secondary" (Taylor 1989: 28). Without such an orientation, we would not know how to discriminate better and worse; we would not know what questions to ask of ourselves and others; we would be, quite literally, without an identity.

Taylor believes that our identity is not the invention of a solitary individual, but a function of our relationships to our surroundings. He says emphatically, "One is a self only among other selves. A self can never be described without reference to those who surround it" (Taylor 1989: 35).[5] For Taylor, frameworks "inescapably pre-exist for us"; they pose questions independently of our ability to answer.

To function within a horizon is to allow discriminations, not just of good or bad, but of better or worse. It is to allow that one can be closer to or farther away from the ideal of personhood as expressed within the framework. Moral reasoning of this sort is substantive, not merely formal or procedural. It deals with the content of a good human life judged by the goods of the practice. Aristotle's phronesis, practical wisdom, is an example of substantive moral reasoning. Like Aristotle, Taylor is concerned not so much with what we do, but with who we are, or strive to become, within a moral horizon.

Perhaps it helps to see what Taylor rejects here. He contrasts his view with ethical naturalism, according to which functioning within a moral horizon is optional. We, at most, invent a horizon; and if we invent one, we can just as well operate without one. We see this in classical utilitarianism which denies all qualitative distinctions, gradations of better and worse, that are available within a moral horizon. As Taylor says, "The aim of this philosophy was precisely to reject all qualitative distinctions and to construe all human goals as on the same footing, susceptible therefore of common quantification and calculation according to some common 'currency'" (Taylor 1989: 22–23). When all human goals are on the same footing, judged according to a single quantifier, discriminations of better and worse are impossible. The will triumphs over ever-deepening self-understanding.

One of Taylor's criticisms of a hedonistic calculus is that it cannot adequately account for the utilitarian's actual practice of moral agency. The "utilitarian ideologue," as Taylor says, unconsciously operates from a framework that includes ideals of rationality and benevolence. The utilitarian admires those who live up to this ideal and condemns those who do not (Taylor 1989: 31–32). Yet, the utilitarian calculus itself is set up to exclude such considerations.

RATIONAL TRANSPARENCY
AND THE CONCRETE "OTHER"

If these conclusions about the inevitability of functioning within a horizon can be accepted, we are in a position to address a further tenet of naturalist reductionism. Secretary Christopher appeared to argue that insiders to third world cultures are radically mistaken about the enterprise in which they are engaged. That is, they are not just mistaken about this or that moral conclusion, but, at a very deep level, they are misguided about what they are up to in life: they thought all along that they were functioning as moral beings, but it turns out they only have "cultural traditions." According to this view, experience as it is actually lived "from the inside" can be explained through reduction to the "objective" view of the outsider.

Both utilitarian and deontological approaches encourage us to understand moral reasons apodictically. Apodictic reasoning refers a particular to the universal. To view the situation objectively, we need to set aside everything particular and individual, and refer to a transcultural universal. The mark of objective understanding is that one always remains an outsider. Participation compromises objectivity.[6] We have seen that when moral reasoning is decontextualized in this fashion, only the external goods get communicated.

Returning to a question raised at the beginning of the chapter, I believe ethical discourse is not *itself* culturally imperialistic, but certain expectations about it are, namely that all moral reasons are apodictic, and that they appeal exclusively to quantities or to abstract rules. These expectations about moral rationality, which are certainly embedded in aspects of Western moral culture, make the outside expert possible: the expert, such as James Mill in India, is one who does not need to be a partial insider, one who does not need to understand a culture's narrative. Ethics is a matter of decontextualization.

Rather than a decision procedure that has recourse to some abstract criterion, I suggest cross-cultural ethical discourse is the dimension of moral life in which the Rawlsian veil of ignorance fails most dramatically (chapter 1; Rawls 1971). Instead of suspending reference to the full-blooded story of the concrete Other, as embodied in the ways one functions according to the internal goods of a practice, this is the point at which the full concreteness of a practice must be addressed (Benhabib 1987). We need to reserve judgments about what will count as moral reasons from the other side. We must suspend judgments about what is within the moral domain of the concrete Other. We simply do not know what will count as part of the practice.

Often it is the well-meaning assumption that "we're all the same," that we *must* share some common culture, or the same basic human nature, if we are to communicate at all which corrupts the possibility of genuine communication. The very expectation that we will find deep reservoirs of commonality may cause us to invent what we want to find, and thereby ignore serious points of divergence. It is only when we begin from the possibility that others are unimaginably different, that we are open to the surprise of genuine understanding.[7]

As Martha Nussbaum has remarked, at this point we need to ask "some of our most basic and ordinary questions, such as 'Who *are* these people? What are they trying to do? What general abilities and circumstances do they have?'" This approach, she says, "urges the parties involved in the argument to ask themselves what aspects of living they consider so fundamental that they could not regard a life as a fully human one without them. Put this way, it is not a request for a matter of metaphysical or biological fact, but a request for a particularly deep and searching kind of evaluative inquiry" (Nussbaum 1993: 327).

The argument that self-explanation may be eliminated through appeal to objectivity and universality is an example of what Donald Davidson calls "changing the subject" (Davidson 1980). We cannot explain the complex network of people's goals and aspirations within a practice by saying they are deluding themselves. Self-interpretation is irreducible because all interpretation must begin with the best account from the position of the insider. As Taylor puts it:

> What we need to *explain* is people living their lives; the terms in which they cannot avoid living them cannot be removed from the explanandum, unless we can propose other terms in which they could live them more clairvoyantly. We cannot just leap outside of these terms altogether, on the grounds that their logic doesn't fit some model of "science" and that we know a priori that human beings must be explicable in the "science." This begs the question. (Taylor 1989: 58)

Pluralism cannot be ruled out a priori by changing the subject. Modification of a best account is itself positional. This process begins with reasons that could be accepted from within the positionally objective account of the practice. In such "ad hominem" moral reasoning, the concrete Other is not set aside; we do not win an argument by referring to abstract moral criteria. Rather, moral discourse focuses on providing reasons the concrete Other can accept within the narrative of his or her practice. To reason effectively, one must understand well enough the goods internal to a practice to provide reasons that will "take" within the matrix of those goods. Moral reasoning is transitional in the sense that it provides a *better* account of life, not the incomparably best account. To function as a human being is to compare one's own moral horizon with met horizons. Moral reasoning involves "comparative propositions" (Taylor 1989: 72; Taylor 1993).

Recalling Sen, good reasons need not endorse the set of internal goods from which moral reasoning begins. Indeed, reasons may provide evidence of shortcomings that cannot be appreciated from within the objective position the practice occupies. Reasons may expose objective illusions. Despite the positional objectivity of practices, the strong sense that one is either inside or outside, there are also internal critics. The position of the internal critic is often seen by attending to differences of gender, class, caste, or race. In patriarchal practices, women are typically both insiders and outsiders. They are insiders in the sense that they were born and raised within a practice, but outsiders in the sense that they are systematically excluded from its full benefits. It is arguable that this trans-positional status can give women's knowledge privileged status. They know the practice from the inside, but function from multiple positions.[8] Marginalized knowledge often plays a transformative role in providing criticism from within.

ETHICAL REASONS AS CULTURAL NARRATIVES

Now the critical issue: "How should we understand democratic discourse in contexts of deep ethical pluralism, contexts having different centers of discourse, each with its own objective positional integrity, its own best account of the practice from within, but where there are no universal, trans-cultural criteria to which appeal can be made?"

It follows from my earlier account of the difficulty of understanding reasons for the goods internal to a practice that one must become at least a partial insider to a practice to claim authority. One must cultivate at least some of the knowing-how through which the network of reasons becomes available. The partial insider is often the one who can provide the best ad hominem arguments through which a practice evolves.

The work of the partial insider is the work of translation. Just as there are translators of literary texts who are sensitive and understand the limitations of what they do, so there is the accomplished translator between moral worlds.[9] Given that what we are trying to communicate about is process knowledge of the concrete Other, knowledge that is available first and primarily to insiders, the best way to represent such knowledge without distortion is through a temporal unfolding, a narrative. I suggest we think of ad hominem reasoning as the unfolding to a partial outsider of a cultural narrative. The process of understanding for the outsider is progressive, marked by the increasing sense that the unfolding narrative is becoming "my" story.

I argue both that such cross-cultural ethical discourse is very difficult and that it happens all the time. Were it impossible, we would never be able to learn to play the violin, for instance. We can and do enter into new practices, slowly developing the ability to judge better and worse. Yet, while it happens all the time, it is also exceedingly difficult, as we see in the number of failed interventions in third world and tribal cultures. The massive destruction of biological diversity and indigenous people when the rainforests are destroyed for short-term economic gain is the most notable example of this failure.

I want it to be clear that I do not suggest there is no role for reference to utilities, moral laws, or the language of rights in these situations. There are cases in which third world and indigenous people might gain by learning to speak the language of rights. In response to GATT initiatives concerning intellectual property rights, for example, Indian indigenous activists are trying to implement a system of communal intellectual property rights to protect indigenous knowledge against the intervention of first world pharmaceutical companies (Khanna 1993; Shiva 1993). They are encouraging the extension of the idea of rights from individuals to groups.

However, I must point out that these activists are not defending indigenous interests through moral resources available within their own cultural narrative. There is a certain loss when communalistic cultures are forced to defend themselves in a foreign language. In cases like this, there is no mutual moral understanding of the kind that comes after the cultural narrative unfolds and we begin to understand the dimensions of the moral from within a culture. It is simply a matter of learning to speak a foreign language in the interest of self-defense.

While rights and utilities may have roles to play, they are conceptually secondary. They are useful, but they have no transcendental standing.

As a pluralist I do not deny the relevance of utilitarian and deontological thinking. I am not committing the sins of liberal imperialism in reverse by saying that only the perspectives of traditional communities count, never the individualism of Western liberalism. The difficulty rests with specifying the variety of important roles that forms of moral discourse play. One approach that attempts to do this has been advanced by Michael Walzer, originally in *Spheres of Justice: A Defense of Pluralism and Equity* and more recently in *Thick and Thin: Moral Argument at Home and Abroad* (Walzer 1983; Walzer 1994). Walzer's goal is to defend both equality and cultural pluralism. Unlike the liberal, who wishes to begin with what Walzer terms a "thin" account of ethics, Walzer believes morality begins thick, deeply culturally imbedded. That is, where Rawls conceives the original position in minimalist terms that disallow any knowledge of one's culture, for Walzer, "Morality is thick from the beginning, culturally integrated, fully resonant, and it reveals itself thinly only on special occasions, when moral language is turned to specific purposes" (Walzer 1994: 4). Only in special cases where our normal, culturally resonant moral intuitions fail us, does morality "thin out" its cultural basis.

Instead of viewing the 1948 Universal Declaration of Human Rights[10] and similar international ethical conventions as stating metaphysical truths, then, we might view them as instructive social criticism. While originally hegemonic, in Ranajit Guha's sense, since no third world countries were even consulted, the declaration has been followed by gradually increasing levels of participation by third world and indigenous men and women. Subsequent international charters have covered biodiversity and cultural diversity, the rights of indigenous people, the rights of women, and food security. The arrogance of liberal imperialism could conceivably be replaced by constructive social criticism in which all sides transparently see themselves as engaged in the process of "thinning out" their thickly imbedded sets of culturally specific goods. But this is an exercise in social ethics; it cannot be legislated in the "idiom of Improvement."

It might even be that there is a place for the language of rights in a postcolonial world. Shorn of its universalism and individualism, it may be possible to argue that there is a right to culturally specific development which indigenous cultures exercise within a particular ecological niche. Sen, for example, argues that authentic human development should be understood in terms of a person's "capability to function" within a particular context.[11] "Capability rights," as he terms them, are defined in relation to basic functionings and capabilities within a cultural context. Whereas the language of inalienable human rights does not guarantee a person's actual capability to function, the notion of capability rights requires that guarantees coincide with actual capabilities.

A pluralist approach to social justice might grant that the caste system is a system of social and ecological "justice" in the sense that it provides a coherent set of social meanings for the distribution of social and ecological goods (Walzer 1983). While this consequence seems paradoxical to the liberal mind, the pluralist can emphasize that, being plural, all systems of distribution are subject to change. They are also subject to criticism from within and from the outside. Unlike political liberalism, however, the pluralist approach understands all good criticism to be immanent rather than transcendental. The goal is a "fusion of horizons" (Taylor 1989) rather than reduction to a single language of evaluation. It may be that both "rights protest," now understood as representing the thick moral aspirations of a particular culture, and Dharmic Protest can play roles in challenging local patterns of distribution.

On this view, for example, there is no universal right to an abortion imbedded in human nature. In some contexts, abortion may increase a woman's ability to function within her community. In other contexts, as the Shivas point out, the claim to such a right may actually undercut a woman's social position, lessening her capability to function. The pluralist approach also allows us to mention that in most third world contexts, a woman's ability to function effectively within her community has much more to do with maintaining access to the biological commons than with a right to an abortion. Perhaps this is another way of expressing the Shivas' protest that when population issues are dislodged from their broader context of authentic human development, women's capabilities are usually thwarted.

Still, the political liberal will ask, "Are there not times when we want to say, in the most powerful terms, that a foreign social practice is morally abominable?" Since the Mills, the Indian caste system has served as an example. More recently, the example of female genital mutilation in certain African communities has become popular. As a critical ecocommunitarian, I reject the analysis of these situations in terms of a violation of transcendental rights. However, I reserve the possibility that one may achieve the understanding of a partial insider to such cultures, to understand something of the internal goods and practices of profoundly different cultures, and still come to the conclusion that such practices are abhorrent. The important point, so that we do not, once again, sneak in the all-knowing Western observer, is that there are also internal critics of such practices. One does not need to be a modern Western liberal to come to the conclusion that there is something wrong with mutilating women's bodies, dousing them with kerosene and burning them alive in their kitchens . . . or in the sexist subculture in the United States that condones date rape.

The same considerations hold for the exportation of American attitudes toward wilderness of the sort that Ramachandra Guha has identified. The idea that American national parks are "our greatest export" that should be implemented globally is a plain example of cultural imperialism. One can easily imagine, however, having taken time to understand the internal goods that define a culture's relationship to nature, that something like wilderness could, and does, function as an internal good. The virtue of ecological humility might imply that all of nature should not be remade in the image of one's culture. A relational sense of self-functioning within a healthy environment can value beings and processes that are different from oneself. In fact, coming to be partial insiders to these communities, we might come to a vivid recognition of the cultural limitations of the American legal definition of wilderness as places "untrammeled by man, where man himself is a visitor who does not remain" (Wilderness Act 1964: section 2c). We might learn from traditional Indian communities that have witnessed what were their original biological commons fenced off in a system of "reserve forests," first for the purposes of British colonialism and then for the new Indian nationalists, that there are dangers inherent in thinking of wilderness areas as a sort of prison (Birch 1990).

Finally, the pluralist perspective I have arrived at strongly encourages the recent attempt of American philosophers to accommodate political liberalism to the demands of pluralism. Such debates about renewing the bonds of community after a period of exclusive focus on external goods mark the healthy evolution of an open and democratic culture. Just as tribal cultures must have the authority to see themselves reflected in the alteration of their internal goods, so, we must use our own traditions as a source of renewal. In a postcolonial world, however, these internal debates cannot be isolated from cross-cultural issues of moral and cultural identity. Such identities exist only in relation to one another.

REITERATIVE AND TRANSFORMATIVE VALUE

If an ethical viewpoint issues from a coherent social identity,[12] and the assumptions we are entitled to make "thin out" as discourse expands from this center, then perhaps the very functions of ethical discourse are plural. We can distinguish two such functions: the *reiterative* and *transformative*.

To function within an ecological community is to function within a thick moral context that translates to the outside only with difficulty. The borders of the moral domain are matters of local knowledge. To function on the inside is to be partially constituted by the way the borders of the moral domain are drawn locally. The values of any community—whether or not the inhabitants define themselves in relationship to place—are largely *reiterative.* When a newly married couple has to apply to the village for permission to cut branches for a new home, and they are taken to the forest, told they can cut only certain branches, and that they must plant and care for two trees in return, this is a matter of cultural reiteration. These values are constitutive of what it means to function as a member of the community. To be partially constituted by the narrative of one's community constitutes, in large part, what it means to function as a moral being. Without such a pre-existing constitution we would have no intuitions about how to begin a moral life.

Unlike the reiterative function of value, *transformative* value can never be anticipated. Such values strike at the heart of the individual. Unlike the reiterative values that bind a culture together, transformative values threaten to become anti-social, especially when cultural narratives have become routine. Transformative values challenge the comfortable assumptions of reiterative value that have become "second nature," and in doing so drive us back to original questions. Reiterative values constitute us as social beings. Transformative values are revolutionary; they disrupt comfortable lives from the edges.

The transformative moral imagination is subversive in its openness to new ways of knowing. It becomes critical to culture when cultural reiteration has become stagnant, when it functions to hide rather than to reveal the character of its citizens. This might be called the discourse of liberation, reserving this term for deep ethical reflection on the concrete Other (Taylor 1982: 133). Since traveling to the world of the concrete Other is an act of the moral imagination, this discourse is liberating.

Transformative values require an act of the moral imagination. The outsider must engage in an act of imagination that alters the moral self. This happens when another's story becomes partially one's own. Deep reflection on the concrete Other requires partial loss of self; it requires existential risk. Moral communication is not simply "ethical," in the narrow sense of the term, but aesthetic. Real moral communication is not just objective interpretation, but participation in which selves are transformed. A mark of a truly democratic society is its openness to transformative challenges, while, at the same time, being loyal to the reiterative values that constitute one's local moral identity.

Mahatma Gandhi, for example, understood that moral claims can be compelling precisely in cases of great dialogical inequality. But what made his appeal so powerful, I believe, was that he spoke the language of liberation, not a discourse of rules.[13] Gandhi was successful because he used the language of liberation to force recognition of the concrete Other.

Arthur Danto, in his book *The Transfiguration of the Commonplace*, helps us capture this opening to transformative experience. Drawing on Aristotle, Danto points out that metaphors, whether verbal or visual, depend upon a suppressed middle term which the speaker or viewer must actively supply. To "get" the visual metaphor "Napoleon-as-Roman emperor," we must "know how in general Napoleon would have dressed, know that it was historically wrong for Napoleon to have dressed that way, know that Roman emperors were supposed to have dressed that way, and so on." The visual metaphor "Napoleon-as-Roman emperor" is, as Danto describes it, a "provocation to participation" at the "*living edge* of language" (Danto 1981: 171). Metaphors are windows that require an act of the synthetic imagination.

One way of articulating what has gone wrong with Western moral discourse is that it radically diminishes the moral domain by blurring the distinction between these two kinds of discourse. That is, it takes legitimate, often admirable, local values—the values of political liberalism—and treats them as if they were universal, transformative values. In refusing to speak transparently *from a place,* we make our values look hypocritical, unexamined, and neocolonial.

We do participate in a thick moral culture. We are at least partial[14] insiders to thick moral culture, the culture of bourgeois political liberalism, whose ancestors are the figures of the Enlightenment. However, it is characteristic of our culture that we do not allow ourselves the pleasure of our own narratives. They are regarded not simply as the narratives that constitute who we are, the "way we do things," but as the logic of a universal culture. What might have revealed who we are acts to conceal. When such narratives become hardened into mere routine, when actions are divorced from their original reasons, a culture loses its self-transparency. A key to regaining this self-transparency about our life projects is to reinvigorate our narratives, connecting them to future meanings in a crowded world. We need a transformative sense of value. (Perhaps we also need to take ourselves less seriously.)

Because we in the West are "homeless," internal critics of this culture often tend to appropriate those aspects of indigenous cultures that are useful to us, those aspects which "travel well" because they inspire our liberal imaginations. My extensive reference to the caste system as a complex, indigenous arrangement of ecological preservation is intended to be a reminder of the crucial need for a sober, balanced account of indigenousness. As with the utilitarians, the caste system does not fire our Western moral imaginations. The uncritical use of other cultures to address our own lack of cultural meaning is dangerous if it encourages a kind of New Age colonialism.

As I turn to the task in the final chapter of imagining the outlines of an *American* ethic of environmental communities, it is helpful to remember the critical position that guides this task. I have proposed a *critical* ecocommunitarianism. This means that all values begin in local moral identities. When internal critics or issues of scale cause these values to intersect with others, we face two creative tasks. Looking outward, we face the task of integrating these deeply held values at larger scales of reference. Looking backward, toward our core values, we must accept the possibility of transformation of our own values. We may find that, although objective, we are mistaken. Freedom in a crowded world means reflection on, and participation in, transformation of local moral identity at a spatial scale in which one can make a difference, where one's choices can be reflected in what that world becomes. Freedom also presupposes a *rate* of change that allows for transformation, not dislocation.

10

Putting Down Roots
Ecocommunities and the Practice of Freedom

CHINNAGOUNDER'S CHALLENGE

Let me conclude as I began, with a story.

Forty years ago, an Indian friend of mine came to know a group of tribal (Adivasi) people in Southeast India. The Malaiali villages were inaccessible by road, and the trail up through the hills where they lived was slippery with leaves and mud from the monsoon rains. As he negotiated his way up the steep switchbacks, he and an acquaintance from the tribe encountered a boulder that blocked the trail. Progress required that they slide from root to branch along the slippery slope, in danger at every moment of losing control. Finally, when they regained the trail on the far side of the boulder, my friend turned to his acquaintance and asked why they did not just shove the boulder down into the valley. Clearly taken aback by this question, the man responded, "Just as all people have their proper place in the world, so the boulder has its proper place, and it would not be right to move it because it is unsafe for human beings."[1]

Now, I will not pretend to know what this ethic of "respect for boulders" meant to these people. I do know that my friend quickly learned to set aside certain familiar, utilitarian values when he passed to the far side of the boulder, values such as "the best route is always the shortest distance between two points." He came to believe that the respect for boulders was indicative of deep cultural commitments (as well as a very pragmatic desire to make travel difficult for outsiders). Later, he was anguished when the boulder was moved; he took this to be a mark of the destruction of an ecological community.

I came to know the Malaialis many years later when I visited their villages with a group of American students. These villages are famous in India for an indigenous form of medicine called siddha. Unlike the far more famous ayurveda, which arrived in India with the Aryan invasions, siddha is truly indigenous. It exists only within a small group of villages in Southeast India.

With expectations high, the students set out the first day to visit Muluvie, a village of about eighty families. We eagerly asked to hear about siddha medicine, and were told that they had never heard of it. We retreated to consider a new strategy. Over the next few days we visited several other villages, some of whose residents admitted that they did have siddha medicine. We often found ourselves standing in the middle of what appeared to be patches of weeds along a road where women would casually point out several plants that had medicinal uses.

With such experiences in tow, the students returned to Muluvie and asked not whether they had siddha but whether they had *any* form of medicine that depended upon plants. Of course, they granted, but we had not asked *that.* Siddha is "foreign" medicine. It is practiced "over there," they said, pointing a few yards away to the village on the next ridge. Muluvie's medicine was secret; if the next village heard about it, they told us, it would lose its power.

A final vignette: In the village of Nagalur, we spoke to a man named Chinnagounder. He did not know his age, but recollected events placed him at more than one hundred years. He lived at the back of a stable on sheets of cardboard. He was deeply bent, his hair bright yellow and stiff like straw. His skin was deeply rutted, like a field wracked by drought. To communicate, we placed an ear horn directly into his ear and shouted.

Chinnagounder told us that his family had once been prominent in the village. His father had twenty-three hectares of land. Strangers had gotten his father to place his thumbprint on a sheet of paper he could not read. He realized later that he had sold his land to a coffee plantation for 70 rupees, still today worth only about $2. During his lifetime he had seen the coffee plantations "buy" literally all the land, so that the small villages at the tops of ridges were touching the last row of coffee plants. Forests had been replaced by neat rows of silver oaks that provided shade for the coffee plants below. Adults now worked on the plantations for 50 cents a day; children over age ten worked for 30 cents.

As we were about to leave, Chinnagounder said he had one question for us. He had met "chemical prospectors" sent by drug companies to find out what the Malaialis know about siddha. The case of the neem tree, whose chemical properties had been patented by an American scientist based on indigenous knowledge of the tree, was known by every indigenous person I met, no matter how remote (Shiva and Holla-Bhar 1996). Chinnagounder wanted to know what drug company we worked for, since that was the only reason he could imagine for wanting to know about siddha.

Well, we were not in Nagalur representing the East India Company or its contemporary incarnations, but his question was discomforting nevertheless. Why were we there? Why did we want to know about siddha? What uses did we have for this knowledge? Particularly since their ecological knowledge is local, even to the point of differing from one hilltop to the next, how could it be applicable to vastly different lives in the United States? While we were all genuinely concerned for the welfare of the people we met, we were also conscious of the fact—since they reminded us of it almost daily—that we would get on an airplane and leave, carrying our knowledge with us.

I recall these stories not to produce paroxysms of liberal guilt as we drink our morning cups of coffee, but to indicate that the position of the Westerner who attempts to put the category of "indigenousness" to use in Western environmental ethics is in a complicated position. It would be a mistake to conclude from these stories that all Western philosophical interest in indigenous cultures is colonizing. Since most of the world's cultural and biological diversity intersects in a narrow band around the earth's equator, and because most of the cross-cultural environmental conflicts of the next century will grow out of this intersection, Western environmental philosophers urgently need a sober, yet sympathetic, account of indigenousness. Yet, the history of Western philosophical interest in indigenousness, from James Mill and John Stuart Mill to J. Baird Callicott and Murray Bookchin, is hardly unblemished. Little wonder philosophers occupy a social standing in India reminiscent of our standing in the United States.

Alfred W. Crosby put the problem succinctly when he began his book *Ecological Imperialism* with the words, "European emigrants and their descendants are all over the place, which requires explanation" (Crosby 1986: 2). We are, perhaps, the lone people that has never succeeded in becoming native to any place. Five hundred years after the European settlement of North America, Wes Jackson can still write, "It has never been our national goal to become native to this place. It has never seemed necessary even to begin such a journey. And now, almost too late, we perceive its necessity" (Jackson 1994: 2).

In *The Rediscovery of North America*, Barry Lopez laments the opportunity lost when Columbus and his men violently pursued gold to the exclusion of true wealth: "The true wealth that America offered, wealth that could turn exploitation into residency, greed into harmony, was to come from one thing—the cultivation and achievement of local knowledge. It was in the pursuit of local knowledge alone that one could comprehend the notion of a home and its attendant responsibilities" (Lopez 1992: 23).

As an academic, I have always tried to take seriously the obligation to "profess." My travels, however, have made me see the rootlessness of what we often profess. An education these days is usually a passport to placelessness. Given my own travels, it should be no surprise that many of my students want an undergraduate degree for the freedom it grants them to *move,* and move again. Something is wrong if that is what it means to be educated.

Our culture is probably unique in the singularity of its focus on external goods. If all goods are reduced to external goods, then the entire world must be remade as a resource. It may seem to contradict our very nature to ask, "Can we become native to place?" One is tempted to say, in the fashion of Parmenides: "One either is, or is not." We happen to be the people who have "leapfrogged around the globe." Our place is no place—and every place.

When we pursue Jackson's "becoming native" question more deeply, however, quick dismissal may turn out to be shortsighted. Although the question raises thorny issues that are easily subject to misinterpretation, it is not contradictory—or a matter of false consciousness or historical amnesia—to ask whether the cultures of the Enlightenment can find a home. Consider, before the first trickle of human beings passed over the Bering land bridge sometime between twelve and twenty thousand years ago, *no* ecological communities in the Western Hemisphere included humans. Prior to three million years ago, no beings of the genus *Homo* were indigenous to this earth. One can *become* native.

The real question is not whether becoming native is possible, but whether we see it as valuable, as an expression of an ideal to which we aspire. The true value of putting down roots is two-fold: it defines who we are, where we belong; it also defines who we are not, places where we are strangers. Perhaps what we find difficult as a culture is the humility that commitment to a place requires. To inhabit a place is implicitly to reject the idea of "the universal man," the single evolutionary outcome of "progress" whose place is every place. To admit that there are other viable narratives is to define oneself honestly and transparently in relation to other viable beings. It is to admit that one's culture has made choices that were contingent, and that these were choices among actual alternatives about valuable ways of organizing a life, not simply reflections of the one universal constitution.

American writer, director, and actor Woody Allen is, among other things, a tribal thinker. Recall his character, Zelig, who thinks people will accept him if he becomes a human chameleon. The completely "acceptable" person is the one who is a perfect reflection of those around him, Zelig thinks. So, sitting next to an Orthodox Jew, his beard flourishes. Hospitalized, he becomes a doctor. Put under analysis, he analyzes the analyst. Far from becoming "everyman," he becomes the misfit who is lost no matter where he goes. Paraded around fascist Germany by his sister, he escapes, only to be recognized at a political rally standing next to Hitler.

Who is Zelig: Nazi or Jew? We cannot answer. To belong everywhere is to belong nowhere. Tellingly, Zelig begins to recover when his analyst, played by American actor Mia Farrow, firmly insists that *she* is the analyst, not Zelig. Deprived of those qualities, at least, coming to recognize who he is *not*, Zelig is left to confront the question of who he *is*.

We are like Zelig. The dream of a universal culture waiting at the end of progress has severed us from the contingency of our human identities. Like Zelig, we can begin to recover who we are by asking who we are not, and where we do not belong. Recovering who we are and where we belong are two ways to look at the same problem.

I inquire about the meaning of indigenousness without the slightest longing for a utopian future. Living "in-place" does not put an end to imperialism. As Crosby recalls, "All these peoples have expanded geographically—have committed acts of imperialism, if you will—but they have expanded into lands adjacent to or at least near to those in which they had already been living" (Crosby 1986: 2). Given population pressures, it is unlikely that such expansion will end soon.

The reference to fascist Germany causes us to recall the frightening connections between romanticized longings for place and extreme politics. More recently, in Eastern Europe after the fall of the Soviet Union, we witnessed the resurgence of seemingly irreconcilable claims to place and the violence that sometimes results from such claims.

One need only stand in the Jewish Quarter of Jerusalem, first glancing down at the Western Wall where Jews go to pray at the remains of the Second Temple and then letting one's gaze shift up to the golden dome of the mosque built on the remains of the temple where Mohammed is said to have ascended to heaven, to visualize the problems of conflicting claims to place.

In India itself, the fifty-year experiment with democracy is often contested by claims to ethnic identity. Kashmiris resent that they were not given the right to determine their own future after independence. Tribal groups in the northeastern state of Assam have been engaged in a violent movement for independence. Even some conservative Hindus (most notably those associated with the Bharatiya Janata Party [BJP]) complain that too much has been done for minority populations. Despite its overlay of democracy, India has different legal codes for different ethnic groups. We will probably never understand such conflicts until we grant that these are new (and very old) kinds of disputes that can no longer be contained by the universalist politics of either the former Soviet Union or the United States.

If a place-based ethic does not offer a utopia, it also does not redeem past misdeeds and purify our spirits. Probably the last thing Native North Americans need is the New Age appropriation of indigenous traditions (Smith 1997: 31ff). In pointing out that the Malaialis' narratives are *theirs,* in claiming the irrelevance of Malaiali narrative to those who are not interested in new colonies, Chinnagounder is throwing us back on our own resources. He is forcing us to ask the most difficult question: "What are the resources for a place-based ethic within the culture of Western political liberalism?" The legacy of colonialism, whether in the United States or India, makes Chinnagounder's challenge to us urgent: "How do we intend to use the category of indigenousness for the task of constructing a Western environmental ethic?"

Chinnagounder's challenge regards moral knowledge. He is forcing us to ask not just which moral rules we are willing to be bound by, but who we are, what we believe to be constitutively important. To claim a transformative place-based ethic we need to be open to the conception of moral reflection as self-understanding. Genuine self-understanding of the sort that true freedom requires is open to the challenge of knowledge from the margins.

So, what would it mean to imagine a new *ecological* community? Whatever it means, it will be something fresh. Our task, for the first time, is to effect a shift in the moral imagination that expands the borders of *our* thickly constituted moral domain. Our issues derive from John Muir and Gifford Pinchot. Our task, however, is new.

Thinking back to the beginning of the book, we can now see that the question Jackson is asking—what it would mean to "become native" to North America—has animated two distinct, often antagonistic, responses. Each is distinctively American. The alternatives represented by Muir and Pinchot still function as our basic options.

Muir's heirs continue to regard the defense of wild nature against the incursions of a (capitalist) human culture as the litmus test of an authentic environmental ethic. Since nature and human culture are opposed, an environmental ethic must defend wilderness against the human plague of agriculture. Max Oelschlaeger, author of *The Idea of Wilderness*, writes of the transition from the "Paleolithic mind" to the "Neolithic mind," the transition from hunter/gatherer societies to agricultural societies, ten thousand years ago: "Rather than attempting to live in harmony with wild nature, as hunter-gatherers had done since time immemorial, farmers literally rose up and attempted to dominate the wilderness" (Oelschlaeger 1991: 28). Although Oelschlaeger's account registers powerfully with many who are alienated from contemporary industrial culture, the "dominating farmer" motif of American environmental philosophy is too simplistic. It erases the differences among kinds of farming: *all* farming intends to dominate "the wilderness." This perspective also lumps together all relationships between nature and culture evolved over the last ten millennia. Traditional and indigenous farmers might as well be the multinational corporation Cargill.

While well-intended, the "ten-thousand-year thesis" has viciously anti-environmental consequences. It obscures the fact that *our* problems really only arose in the last two hundred to five hundred years with the Industrial Revolution and the subsequent invention of industrialized farming. Its positive recommendation for the future amounts to neo-primitivism, the need to go back ten thousand years to recover an environmentally responsible lifestyle. Like Callicott, who has no interest in Native American cultures after the arrival of European cultures, Oelschlaeger diverts our attention from a practical analysis of where we must go given our present character. This thesis also neutralizes gender as a category of analysis.

Finally, this approach is based on an oppositional understanding of environmental ethics. We have already noted Callicott's early position: "The extent of misanthropy in modern environmentalism thus may be taken as a measure of the degree to which it is biocentric" (Callicott 1989: 27). Callicott hence became entwined in one of the major issues of chapter 6: how to reconcile human and environmental justice. Because his early land ethic is resolutely ecocentric in recognizing the moral standing of whole ecosystems, this response claims to be an authentic environmental ethic; yet it threatens to become undemocratic in its resistance to human culture. An *authentic* environmental ethic, according to this approach, must risk being undemocratic in its defense of nature against culture.

The second response to Jackson's question has the opposite intuition. Pinchot's original formulation of the problem for an American environmental ethic was democratic in its concern to foster the public good in contrast to the European model which reserved environmental access to the rich. However, critics question its authenticity as an *environmental* ethic since it is anthropocentric in viewing nature as nothing more than a resource for human progress. Furthermore, in an age of trans-national corporations whose intellectual property rights are protected by the GATT, even when they conflict with the democratic interests of nations, Pinchot now seems hopelessly naive.

Like contentious claimants to the same place, the two sides seem irreconcilable. From a logical point of view, nature either has, or does not have, intrinsic value. If it has intrinsic value, then environmental justice trumps human justice. If it does not, human justice trumps environmental justice. Similarly, either our attitude toward nature is ecocentric or it is anthropocentric. It often appears that there is no middle ground, either in philosophy or in politics. Let us hope that these positions are not just irreconcilable, but outdated. If our alternatives require a ten-thousand-year regression to pre-agricultural times to regain an authentic relationship to place, or a capitulation to the language of capitalism without borders, then we really are lost. Are we at such an impasse?

Stated in such polarized terms, it is easy to miss how much Pinchot and Muir had in common. Both were top-down thinkers, at least when it came to public policy. Despite their important differences, both Pinchot and Muir were convinced that a *national* response was required to the challenge of unrestrained capitalism. As valuable as the national parks and national forests have been in preserving something of North America's original natural legacy, both Pinchot and Muir began from the assumption that an American environmental ethic will not be local. This must be a large part of what seems strange to other cultures when the national park model is exported on the assumption that no localized environmental ethic exists. Yet, we have seen in the remarkable consistency of resistance movements to "development" that there often are local communities with strong place-based conceptions of the moral standing of the ecocommunity. What we attempt to export is frequently not needed locally.

It should come as no surprise, then, that in the United States we now have movements on opposite ends of the political spectrum defending local values against (national) environmental policy. Greens defend bioregionalism as a new idea, and it is probably new in a Euro-American context. Communities in Utah and Idaho, as well as those surrounding the Boundary Waters Canoe Area Wilderness in Minnesota, resent politicians in Washington, D.C., who assume the right to decide what they can do "in their own backyards." Both movements are responding to the American tradition of top-down environmental policy that negates the possibility of a bottom-up ethic of ecocommunities expressing their internal goods at larger and larger scales of interaction.

In retrospect, neither Pinchot nor Muir offered a fully developed environmental ethic. Both substituted valuable, short-term, defensive measures in response to an immigrant culture educated in the American ideal of ethnic neutrality. To be an American, in short, was to forget one's connection to place. An environmental ethic in America meant defense against the excesses of a culture with vast resources and no traditions regulating wise access to the biological commons. Admirable as both these defensive measures were, we are still a culture in need. We need an environmental ethic.

AMERICAN ENVIRONMENTAL ETHICS

It is time to move past the friction of the Muir/Pinchot debate to a new American vision of ecological community. This vision must be both democratic *and* authentic in its commitment to reconciling culture with nature. It must be democratic, I suggest, in the sense that an American environmental ethic is an ethic appropriate to what it means to be a citizen. Care for and understanding of nature must come to function as an internal good, constitutive of what it means to function as a citizen. Just as there are issues of scale inherent in any environmental issue, so citizenship is an issue of scale. Each begins, although neither ends, at a local level, with local knowledge.

An American environmental ethic must be *authentic*, furthermore, in that it must capture what ethical inherentists are getting at with the idea of intrinsic value. Citizenship in an *ecological* community must mean the recognition of pre-existing commitments to *both* human and ecological justice.

An American environmental ethic must grow consciously and deliberately out of reflection on its own context, taking its place alongside plural conceptions of ecocommunity that emerge from the world's diverse cultures. This distinctively American form of ecocommunitarianism must begin from a reawakening of traditional, coherent conceptions of internal goods that define freedom in connection to place. However, it must also wisely anticipate a future with at least twice the number of human beings now alive, a future where eco-humility will be ever more difficult to practice.

It must strive not to be marginal, or to reflect simply the solitary alienation of those who have entirely rejected American culture. It must, therefore, be a public ethic in the sense that it represents the aspirations of an American democratic community. It must respond to the longing for meaning that is characteristic of the life of a citizen, but which is often shunted aside in modern life.

In observance of the ideas of positional objectivity and local expertise, it must seek out expertise in all sectors of the population, in farming communities as well as among wilderness advocates, in cities as well as in towns. If it is to be distinctively American, it must think through the category of meaningful *work* as an expression of culture's mediation with nature.

One of the greatest historical sources for such an American tradition is in Jeffersonian agrarian republicanism. Thomas Jefferson's reputation has been subject to reinterpretation in recent years. Certainly, as a critic of historical amnesia, I do not suggest that we forget the aspect of his agrarian ideal which was based on a slave economy. In retrospect, his attitude toward Native Americans seems a hopeless artifact of the Enlightenment. Jefferson advocated "civilizing" Indians by encouraging them to take up agriculture, a typical Enlightenment example of the identification of hunting and gathering with nature, and agriculture with culture.

The question, nevertheless, is whether Jefferson's legacy can still provide a glimpse of a distinctively American conception of internal goods that is source material for a coherent narrative with contemporary relevance. The Jeffersonian heritage requires us to take the ideal of an *ecological* community to heart. For Jefferson, intimacy with place is the foundation of civic virtue. In his *Notes on Virginia*, Jefferson wrote, "Those who labor in the earth are the chosen people of God, if ever He had a chosen people, whose breasts He has made His peculiar deposit for substantial and genuine virtue" (Jefferson 1993: 259).

Jefferson opposed the industrialists of his day because he thought that certain kinds of work are alienating in that they bolster economies of scale which rob workers of their sense of investment in their own work. Unlike the "ten-thousand-year thesis," that is, which appears to depict *all* human labor as anthropocentric environmental destruction, Jefferson maintained a distinction among kinds of labor. Some labor is alienating because it forces a separation between worker and place. It disables achievement of a responsible human identity as a citizen in an ecological community. Other labor can be seen as an internal good of the ecological community. True democracy is essentially a matter of scale, beginning with commitment to place in the fullest sense of that term.[2] Citizenship has both natural and cultural dimensions.

A Jeffersonian ideal contends, also, that liberty depends upon sharing in self-government. In Michael Sandel's words, "It requires a knowledge of public affairs and also a sense of belonging, a concern for the whole, a moral bond with the community whose fate is at stake. To share in self-rule therefore requires that citizens possess, or come to acquire, certain qualities of character, or civic virtues. But this means that republican politics cannot be neutral toward the values and ends its citizens espouse" (Sandel 1996: 5–6). The citizen is previously "encumbered" by the obligations of community membership. Civic virtues are powers required by a citizen to act on such obligations.

Much would need to be said to fully draw out what remains relevant in Jefferson's vision for the United States. In addition to rethinking work as a category of authentic engagement with culture and nature, one would also need to rethink spirituality, as I have begun to do in my discussion of Arne Naess. The Western visual arts since the Renaissance also often mark an attempt to control nature, and have recently come to function as a commodity in American culture. However, some art, including certain aspects of Japanese and Chinese art, are arguably motivated by a sense of ecological community. The sciences, too, which have been influenced by the Baconian attempt to control nature, are undergoing a transformative process, as seen in many conceptions of conservation biology. I hope to be able to thoroughly address these ideas in the future.

Perhaps it is optimal at this point, however, to anticipate three contemporary challenges to a new Jeffersonian ideal. According to the first, the ideal is not authentic in its commitment to the environment. The second holds that it is no longer relevant. The third challenge grants the contemporary relevance of a Jeffersonian ideal, but denies that it is the best option for a future conception of ecological citizenship. Let me consider each of these challenges briefly in reverse order.

It is really this broadly Jeffersonian model that in recent years has been challenged by the two versions of contemporary political liberalism, Rawlsian liberalism and utilitarianism, as the best option for a public philosophy. We have seen that, despite their profound philosophical differences, the effect of both approaches is to displace community from the framework of moral deliberation. Community is either fictitious, nothing more than the sum of individual preferences, or it becomes important only as a matter of pre-cultural choice of principles. The life of the citizen is admirable only if the solitary will chooses it. Choosing it makes it valuable.

Since the only model of moral deliberation that political liberalism offers is the psychological inventory of one's pre-existing needs and wants, community cannot stand as an independent standard. Internal goods are not counted as shaping one's moral identity. Whether one accepts community becomes a matter of whether it already exists in one's psychic inventory.

Yet, we must ask, can either a preferential or a procedural individualism capture the sense of connectedness to place that an ecological community requires? This is highly doubtful. For the liberal, Self is not defined in relationship to place as an issue of citizenship. Liberalism leaves us only the option that individuals can freely choose to define themselves in relation to place as a personal expression of who they are. This encourages a kind of solitary, almost mystical, understanding of what some deep ecologists call Self-realization. It makes such a choice "subjective," just one more preference we might choose to optimize in a consumer society. Disputes with those who choose to optimize other preferences become intractable.

Critics of political liberalism, such as Charles Taylor, Michael Walzer, and Michael Sandel, have joined with Cornel West and Martha Nussbaum in calling for a public philosophy that re-engages questions of civic virtue. While they have been concerned to reinvigorate the meaning of *human* community, this debate opens the possibility of re-covering an original Jeffersonian meaning of community that extends beyond the boundaries of the human community.[3]

Michael Sandel's recent book *Democracy's Discontent: America in Search of a Public Philosophy* is perhaps the most explicit in connecting the new public philosophy with a Jeffersonian ideal. Speaking of political liberalism, Sandel says, "The public philosophy by which we live cannot secure the liberty it promises, because it cannot inspire the sense of community and civic engagement that liberty requires" (Sandel 1996: 6). Both strands of contemporary liberalism defend an ideal of freedom in terms of the "unencumbered self," the self defined prior to its engagement in culture. Sandel is correct if he is suggesting that the fundamental malaise we feel rests with the vague feeling that the meaning of freedom has been lost. We have never been more "free." We have never been less clear about what kind of life is worth living.

Although Americans tend not to fully understand what is happening to them under the GATT and the global economic court of the WTO, they have no doubt that they are losing control over their lives. When environmental policy intervenes in local communities—whether the policy of greater resource exploitation or greater protections for "wilderness" against capitalist exploitation—these policies are experienced as interventions from above that do not represent the interests of communities to participate in decisions over their future.

Perhaps because American environmental policy has always been national in scope, there is little confidence that local communities, given the chance, would make wise local decisions. Certainly the attitude "we will do what we want to do in our own backyards" reflects the exclusivity of the private property model rather than environmental wisdom. We lack confidence in an alternative tradition of the shared commons, what Wendell Berry calls the sacred grove, which makes environmental decisions elsewhere a matter of public policy rather than personal preference.

Mark Sagoff, however, argues that the American public is still capable of distinguishing between the environmental policies appropriate to a *consumer* and to a *citizen* (Sagoff 1988: 50–57). We are, in effect, still capable of shifting paradigms in response to the kind of question we are asked. It may well be that the consumer framework seems "natural"—even inevitable—to most citizens only because of the power of *Homo economicus.* We are rarely *encouraged* to respond as citizens.

Sagoff's insight is a breakthrough in American environmental ethics understood as an ethic of citizenship. However, he sees himself as advancing a Kantian theory of environmental values that is not broad enough to deal with out-of-context environmental conflicts. Bryan G. Norton and Bruce Hannon have taken Sagoff's insights further by offering a place-based environmental ethic founded on the idea that an orientation toward place is a feature of *all* human experience of the environment. Environmental ethics, then, requires a "tri-scalar" system through which environmental values can be analyzed (Norton and Hannon 1997). Much of what I have said here is consistent with Norton's democratic, pragmatic approach to environmental ethics. However, rather than arguing for a kind of "weak anthropocentrism,"

I am suggesting that the anthropocentrism/non-anthropocentrism debate is ultimately misguided. A citizen's moral identity may be previously encumbered by both nature and culture.

Despite these differences among like-minded options, the core of my response to the third challenge is that a contemporary Jeffersonian ideal remains the best option since it urges us to address our deepest concerns "for the loss of self-government and the erosion of community" (Sandel 1996: 3). A contemporary Jeffersonian ideal speaks to the search for meaning. Jeffersonian republicanism is a public ethic that engages questions of substantive goods of the ecological community.

To the second challenge, that the Jeffersonian ideal is no longer relevant, I respond that we do, indeed, need to rethink what it means to be a Jeffersonian in contemporary America. Jefferson's fears concerning the urbanization of American culture have largely come true. The family farm is becoming rare, and it will only become rarer still under the provisions of the Freedom to Farm Act. This act, which continues the dissembling tradition of the Peacekeeper Missile, brings third world development strategies to the American farm. Farm towns that once depended upon a rural economy are suffering from the invasion of a Wal-Mart retail culture whose headquarters are elsewhere. The migration to cities raises critical questions about the scale of democracy and self-government.

Jefferson could not have imagined our issues. However, his deepest concerns for the *scale* of democratic practice are relevant in ways that continue to surprise. Recently, for example, New York City residents defended their neighborhood gardens for the sense of community and a commitment to place that they foster. Whatever a contemporary Jeffersonian ideal comes to mean, it will no longer represent only the ideals of Virginia's gentlemen farmers. A contemporary Jeffersonian ideal cannot simply be a nostalgic longing for old relationships to land. It must be practical in the ways it addresses citizens' needs for place. A critical reexamination of the relationship of nature and culture would include the ways urban residents relate to place—their own and the commons that make democratic practice possible.

Finally, ecocentric ethicists will likely continue to challenge the authenticity of the Jeffersonian ideal since it may still appear anthropocentric in its focus on democracy, its concern for the centrality of *human* relatedness to place. In recasting the nature/culture issue, contemporary Jeffersonianism does refuse to take the ecocentric/anthropocentric split as basic. It is, in fact, motivated by what it perceives to be the failure of traditional Western categories of moral philosophy to provide a workable environmental ethic that integrates theory with practice. It refuses to reiterate the notion that culture and nature are inherently opposed.

But radical democratic environmental philosophy is not entirely unsympathetic to radical environmentalism either. To be encumbered by residency in an *ecological* community means that one has pre-existing relations that are *both* cultural and ecological. If genuine democratic practice assumes issues of scale, if true freedom can only occur at the level at which one can function as a human and natural being, then democracy can only flourish from a place. A democratic ethic *is* an environmental ethic. A critical problem with what passes for democracy is that it occurs at such a large scale that character formation is impossible. We engage in the work of building character, but we do not see ourselves reflected in the commons. In the words of Barry Lopez, "To be intimate with the land . . . is to enclose it in the same moral universe we occupy, to include it in the meaning of the word 'community'" (Lopez 1992: 34).

Furthermore, a radical democratic environmental ethic is just as resolute as non-anthropocentric inherentism in demanding recognition that all goods are not reducible to external goods. Economic reductionism is wrong. The view that nature is simply a resource for human exploitation is wrong. However, these views are wrong not because they violate a moral rule, but because they corrupt the meaning of freedom without which we cannot even begin to articulate what it means to engage in a democratic practice. They defend an impoverished account of the moral imagination.

WENDELL BERRY AND THE CRISIS OF CHARACTER

Philosophers are beginning to imagine a new, distinctively American, environmental ethic.[4] But it is possible that such a new Jeffersonianism has already been articulated. It is worth asking, for example, where a writer such as Wendell Berry fits into the Muir/Pinchot debate. Berry does not share Pinchot's utilitarianism, yet his primary orientation is toward agriculture, not wilderness. Like Muir, Berry condemns the view that nature is simply a resource for human exploitation. Unlike Muir, Berry does not think of nature and culture as inherently opposed, even within the last ten thousand years.

It is striking, furthermore, how different their conceptions are of an authentic engagement with nature. We think of Muir wandering alone through the Sierras, worshipping in "temple wilderness," furious at the intrusion of domesticated sheep which he depicts as "hoofed locusts" (Muir [1911] 1987: 56). For Berry, in contrast, agricultural *work* bridges the nature/culture divide: "People are joined to the land by work. Land, work, people, and the community are all comprehended in the idea of culture." (Berry 1983: 73). With Berry a certain kind of work, work that is not alienating, transforms nature in an authentic way. Through work one comes to see oneself in a broader horizon. Authentic work reflects the natural order.

Berry is a nonconformist. He does not fit neatly into either of the received categories for an American environmental ethic. We might understand his nonconformity as hinting that he offers passage beyond the false dilemma of the American nature versus culture debate. At the least, as we search for distinctively American concepts of place, it is worth rereading him in this light.

Wendell Berry often has written that the ecological crisis is a crisis of character. This focus on character provides the third ethical alternative that is neither deontological nor teleological. Berry follows neither Immanuel Kant nor the Mills. An environmental ethic must be an ethic of character, according to Berry, not an abstract ethic of rules, or a calculus of quantities.

For Berry, character and culture are inward and outward aspects of connected organizing principles:

> [O]ur decisions can also be informed—our loves both limited and strengthened—by those patterns of value and restraint, principle and expectation, memory, familiarity, and understanding that, inwardly, add up to *character* and, outwardly, to *culture*. Because of these patterns, and only because of them, we are not alone in the bewilderments of the human condition and human love, but have the company and comfort of the best of our kind, living and dead. (Berry 1983: 67)

Character is principled engagement in community. The knowledge that issues from character is not just correct information, although it does include that, but *familiarity* gained through long experience: "the sort of knowledge that might properly be called familiarity, and the affections, habits, values, and virtues (conscious and unconscious) that would preserve good care and good work through hard times" (Berry 1983: 72).

A place-based ethic of character operates out of familiarity with a particular place. Its care and good work radiate from this place in dimensional scales of time and space. Berry's relationship to his newly bought farm began "in love that [was] more or less ignorant" (Berry 1983: 69). Over years of proper cultivation, the land shapes character, growing familiarity is reflected outwardly in greater acceptance by the land. In Berry's words,

> [O]ne's first vision of one's place was to some extent an imposition on it. But if one's sight is clear and if one stays on and works well, one's love gradually responds to the place as it really is. . . . Vision, possibility, work, and life—*all* have changed by mutual correction. Correct discipline, given enough time, gradually removes one's self from one's line of sight. One works to better purpose then and makes fewer mistakes, because at last one sees where one is. (Berry 1983: 70)

Seeing where one *is* implies that one's character is formed *here*, not somewhere else. In a beautiful image, Berry recalls that the A string of a violin vibrates at 440 vibrations per second. If an A is played near the violin, the violin's A string may "hum in sympathy." Berry concludes, "For as common wisdom holds, like *speaks* to like" (Berry 1983: 76). We can only truly speak *with* what we care *for*. One can care *about* distant places only because one cares *for* one's own place.

The "practical harmony" that results from familiarity with place results in *health,* an important and recurring category for Berry. In a poem titled "Healing," Berry writes:

> The grace that is the health of creatures can only be held in common.
> In healing the scattered members come together.
> In health the flesh is graced, the holy enters the world.

He goes on to criticize mere "originality," where the "would-be creator works alone." "Novelty," Berry says, "is a new kind of loneliness." In contrast, "To be creative is only to have health; to keep oneself fully alive in the Creation, to keep the Creation fully alive in oneself" (Berry 1990c: 9).

Health is an achievement that requires the strength of virtues. Berry speaks of many virtues in his writing, but the two most commonly cited are humility and fidelity. Without proper humility one suffers from an arrogant mind: "There are some things the arrogant mind does not see: it is blinded by the vision of what it desires" (Berry 1983: 71). Fidelity is a kind of constancy of commitment to a place one speaks with and cares for.

Although Berry is known primarily for his reflections on agriculture, an account of the importance of wilderness follows equally from his thoughts on humility:

If we are to be properly humble in our use of the world, we need places that we do not use at all. We need the experience of leaving something alone. We need places that we forbear to change, or influence by our presence, or impose on even by our understanding. . . . We need what other ages would have called sacred groves. (Berry 1977: 30)

Responsible agriculture itself needs wilderness. Berry reminds us of Albert Howard's thought in *An Agricultural Testament,* drawn from his observations of Indian cultivators, that farmers ought to "pattern the maintenance of their fields after the forest floor" (Berry 1977: 30).

Nevertheless, while "wilderness must stand at the apex of the conservation effort," "most of [nature] we will have to use" (Berry 1977: 29, 30). The question, then, is not *whether* we use nature, but *how* we use it. Berry's answer, once again, is character, properly humble, and committed to place through long familiarity.

Although Berry considers himself a wilderness advocate, he is quick to criticize the American wilderness movement, or at least one of its major expressions in the 1980s and 1990s. This movement, he believes, divides nature from culture and defines conservation in terms of nature preservation only. The "environment" thus becomes something separate from human culture, and the conservation movement is "variously either vacation-oriented or crisis-oriented" (Berry 1977: 27).

Perhaps this challenge to "the environmental movement" also motivates Wendell Berry's spirited, and, to those who read his work superficially, unexpected, defense of Edward Abbey against his environmentalist acolytes. "Mr. Abbey," Berry announces, "is not an environmentalist." Why not? Well,

He is, certainly, a defender of some things that environmentalists defend, but he does not write merely in defense of what we call "the environment." Our environmental problems, moreover, are not, at root, political; they are cultural. As Mr. Abbey knows and has been telling us, our country is not being destroyed by bad politics; it is being destroyed by a bad way of life. (Berry 1990b: 37)

People want Abbey to be "an environmentalist," and then "who shows up but this *character.*" Berry decides that what Abbey really is is an autobiographer: "he remains Edward Abbey, speaking as and for himself, fighting, literally, for dear life" (Berry 1990b: 39).

Then let Berry *and* Abbey show us the way: what we face is a crisis of character. We are being destroyed by a bad way of life. The environmental movement, when it separates nature from culture, is (almost) as much an obstruction to right living as those who advocate "wise use."

Berry's warning about politics might also serve as a warning about philosophy: we should not think that there is some single, missing categorical imperative that will solve the environmental crisis. What we need is the fine modulation of character to place. Here, it is worth recalling a story from Plato's *Republic*. Socrates is conversing with an old acquaintance named Cephalus, who has defined justice as speaking the truth and repaying one's debts. Socrates quickly produces a story that puts this definition into question: suppose a friend has deposited a weapon with you when he was sane, but returns when he is "out of his mind," demanding return of the weapon. "Should you return the weapon?" Socrates asks. "No," he responds, in this case justice requires that you lie and break your promise (Plato 1974: 327c).

Unlike Kant, who tells us one must never break a promise, Socrates tells us that we must cultivate the right sort of character to know what is appropriate in a given situation. The moral person is the one who knows when to follow the rules, but also when to break them. For Socrates, moral rules are, at best, rules of thumb, helpful generalizations based on the past experience of morally developed human beings.

Questions of the relative weight of human and environmental justice will always be judgment calls. There is no formula from which a universally applicable set of duties can be deduced. Given the growth rate of human populations and the massive extinction of biodiversity, many choices will necessarily be tragic. We have gotten ourselves into a situation in which the best choices are only "less bad" than other choices. But ethics is not, as moral monists would have us believe, an exact science that neatly spins out a complete, consistent set of moral injunctions. Ethics, as Aristotle knew, is far messier than that. Especially in these times, we should hope for wise, humane, and scientifically informed counsel that simply represents the best our judgment has to offer.

In light of this reading of Berry, let us now think back to the monumental debate over the intrinsic/extrinsic issue. Exactly what is the issue here? Even the most ardent deep ecologists admit that nature sometimes functions as a resource. If we are to use these terms at all—as mental constructions—we must admit that nature, like a good education, has both intrinsic and extrinsic value. The view that nature has *only* intrinsic value is strangely anti-ecocentric since it implies that humans are not part of nature.

Furthermore, if I am right that Naess's more basic commitment is to Self-realization, his continuing reminder that *everyone* must engage in their own process of realizing Self, Naess comes close to Berry's commitment to character. Through character, we can "hum in sympathy" with a place. In challenging the explanatory power of a theory of intrinsic value, and in pushing Naess toward a more radical account of Self-realization in chapter 7, we can see Naess also as moving beyond the Pinchot/Muir impasse.

Berry's term "character" sounds dusty and confining to the imagination in contrast to Naess's "Self-realization." However, Berry uses it to draw out something important that is sometimes missing in Naess's work: the proper response to the ecological crisis operates in a polarity between *community* and place. Not just any place, but *this* place that has shaped one's character. Naess's sometimes indiscriminate references to *atman* and a variety of other ideas foster his attempt to think globally, but they sometimes obscure the fact that we must all do our own work, and we must do it beginning with the horizon of our community. We cannot just "go native" and co-opt another culture. We have the harder task of imagining a place-based ethic, given the historical and cultural density of our own place.

Non-anthropocentric inherentists may still not be satisfied with assurances that a radical democratic environmental ethic is up to the job of defending nature. What, for the inherentist, was a distinction of *kind* between intrinsic and extrinsic value becomes an issue of the wise balance between competing demands consistent with what it means to function as a citizen in an ecological community. The non-anthropocentrist will worry that, without a distinction in kind, the balance between encumbrances to nature and culture will shift in favor of human culture. Here, it may be that we still have different views about the function of ethics. My view is that the best guarantee we have of preserving the wildness of nature is through cultivating an informed and humble citizenry that is genuinely committed to preservation. Then, theory and practice coincide. What the inherentist holds out for, an imperative that will command individuals to do the right thing, simply does not exist. And if it did, there would be no guarantee that individual moral commitment would translate into effective public policy. There really is no alternative to the dirty work of attempting to provide the most convincing arguments in a democratic forum.

Another legitimate concern is that communities are sometimes oppressive. Perhaps for feminist reasons, some will find the reference to character and community as the basis for an environmental ethic too confining politically. I have already drawn extensive reference to the ways institutional and systemic forms of violence in a community shape one's identity against one's will. Most actual communities are not healthy places for the moral identities of at least some of their members. But we should notice that, in Berry's hands, character is the principal instrument of *resistance* to misappropriations of one's identity. Much of his work is about the question of living a meaningful life when identity is defined by global capitalism:

> People whose governing habit is the relinquishment of power, competence, and responsibility, and whose characteristic suffering is the anxiety of futility, make excellent spenders. They are the ideal consumers. By inducing in them little panics of boredom, powerlessness, sexual failure, mortality, paranoia, they can be made to buy (or vote for) virtually anything that is "attractively packaged." (Berry 1977: 24)

Berry has long distinguished, for example, between the responsible consumer and "consumers who are merely organized." Consumers' rights organizations can defend one's rights, but they cannot serve one's responsibilities. "[R]esponsiblity," Berry rightly says, "is intransigently a personal matter" (Berry 1977: 24). Being a responsible consumer puts one's character into play. The responsible consumer is critical, moderate, and distinguishes needs from wants. This is the same point that Berry makes about Abbey: Abbey frustrated environmentalists because he refused to allow his identity to be defined by environmental rights organizations. "A responsible consumer," Berry says, "*is*, of course, a responsible conservationist" (Berry 1977: 25).

Although Berry has been criticized by feminists—certainly his discussion of fidelity will seem unnecessarily heterosexual—his account of caring, and surprisingly, to some, his account of the body, may resonate with some ecofeminist orientations (Berry 1990a; Berry 1990d). Berry, as much as Michel Foucault, resists the industrial appropriation of the body. In his own way, Berry talks about the re-enchantment of sexuality as a meaningful expression of what it means to be human.

A place-based environmental ethic also gives us a way of stating what is *right* about both Muir and Pinchot. Just as international agreements can be seen as representing a forged consensus as substantive conceptions of goods "thin out" at higher scales of organization, so the national model of environmental preservation can be read as the thinning out of a place-based ethic as it functions at a larger scale. Since scalar issues of time and place radiate out from an ecological community, it follows that not all environmental issues can be addressed strictly at a local level. Global warming, at least in one of its dimensions, is inherently a global issue.

What is unique about the American situation is that its ethic for the environment has been truncated. Whereas elsewhere the internal goods of ecological communities shape the issues at stake, here national policy is the defense against the lack of such local goods.

If Sagoff is right, it may not be too late for an American environmental ethic. What we have lost temporarily is the ability to make deeply considered decisions that are reflective of the internal goods characteristic of what it means to function as a citizen in an ecological community. A truly American environmental ethic offers what we must hope and believe is our deepest aspiration: a conception of our own freedom that is consistent with the freedom of others, both human and more-than-human.

NOTES

1. TURNING SOUTH

1. Of course, it "makes sense" only if we forget that much of what Europeans regarded as wilderness was not unsettled. See the discussion later in this chapter concerning the terms "first world" and "third world."

2. For a retrospective look at the national park system, see the special issue of *Orion* 1997.

3. One of the oddities of utilitarianism is that while it supported a colonial agenda in India, it also anticipated the animal liberation movement. If the ability to experience pain and pleasure is the criterion for moral standing, then it is hard to exclude non-human animals. See Singer 1990 for a sophisticated position of this kind.

4. Here I mean "wilderness" as defined legally. The question of how to reconcile real ecosystems protection with human justice is perhaps the most profound issue of our time. Much of my evaluation of American environmental philosophy in part 2 is in terms of a position's ability to foster this reconciliation.

5. I am not suggesting that there is no concept of wild nature in Asia. In India, for example, there is an ancient tradition which links wisdom with wilderness. It is also not true that all Western conceptions of wilderness exclude the presence of human beings. Gary Snyder has written eloquently about the place of people in wilderness. Native Americans often have no sense of the wild as categorically separate from the human. These are clearly minority traditions, however, within the paradigm that regards nature as separate and therefore available for exploitation. Also, as I will use the term "third world," it is not a geographical term but a conceptual construction marking distance from a "center." In this sense there is a third world in the first world, and this includes native peoples of the Americas.

6. This earlier debate was an attempt to save utilitarianism from unsavory consequences. It appeared, for example, that utilitarianism may be committed to endorsing slavery (despite the utilitarian's reformist commitments) when slavery is seen to produce the greatest good for the greatest number of people. An important distinction was introduced between rule and act utilitarianism. Rule utilitarianism attempted to block the apparent endorsement of slavery by showing that courses of action should be chosen because they support the general rule that would produce, if adopted as a matter of public policy, the greatest good for the greatest number. Slavery adopted as a public policy has little utility value since, for example, all citizens may wonder when they will be enslaved. The basic motivation of rule utilitarianism is to establish a consequentialist theory which has the advantages of a deontological theory's insistence that some actions or policies are wrong in principal. On the distinction between two forms of utilitarianism, see Rawls 1955. For an important

collection of essays published at the time that both versions of utilitarianism were coming under doubt, see Sen and Williams 1982.

7. For liberals' view of Rawls's work, see Kymlicka 1989; Kymlicka 1995b; Kymlicka 1995c; Mouffe 1992b; Mouffe 1993. For critics who reject liberalism, see Sandel 1996; Taylor 1992; Walzer 1983; Walzer 1994.

8. Some aspects of the liberalism/communitarianism debates could qualify as out-of-context. Will Kymlicka and Charles Taylor, as Canadians, have been concerned to address the Quebec separatist movement, and demands for the cultural integrity of indigenous groups, such as the Cree and Inuit. While sometimes relevant, however, these are debates under the umbrella of a common set of laws deriving from the liberal tradition, and a history of treaties (not always rigorously enforced).

9. Iris Marion Young proposes a conception of otherness based on the idea of "political togetherness in difference" that avoids regarding another culture as either utterly different or as identical to one's own. Her view is relational: "a social group exists and is defined as a specific group only in social and interactive relation to others" (Young 1995: 161).

10. I extend my appreciation to Alan Nash, who brought this problem to my attention.

11. I discuss traditional methods of environmental protection later. See chapters 3 and 5.

12. When an apparently disgruntled member of the World Bank staff leaked Summers's internal memorandum to the press, Summers defended himself by claiming that he was only writing to stimulate thought. Whatever we make of this response (why would someone even find it valuable to *think* about this), the problem is that such thoughts are not confined to the rarified atmosphere of the World Bank. Such ideas often concretely define what happens to poor people in the third world. One certain consequence of the GATT and NAFTA agreements, for example, is increased dumping of first world pollutants in the third world. No side agreements on the environment can alter the result that the third world will be treated as a garbage dump.

13. Niccolò Machiavelli and Henry Kissinger are familiar representatives of this position. For a careful exposition of this position in comparison to just warism (the position that war must be morally justified) and pacifism, see Cady 1989.

14. This taxonomy was worked out in collaboration with Bob Litke for a co-edited volume, *Institutional Violence* (forthcoming).

15. Such holes in the standard measures of development have been widely noted by economists. Remarkable among these is Amartya Sen who has proposed the Human Development Index (HDI) as a more accurate measure of development.

16. "Dalit" means "the oppressed." It is often preferred as a more descriptive term than either "Untouchable" or "Harajin" (Mahatma Gandhi's term meaning "children of God").

2. THE BRITISH UTILITARIANS AND THE INVENTION OF THE "THIRD WORLD"

1. This is doubly significant, as we shall see, because agricultural labor in the third world has traditionally been women's labor.

2. C. A. Bayly argues that the Permanent Settlement grew out of the influence of "agrarian patriotism" in Britain, which tried to forge a conservative consensus among large landowners, small farmers, and the professional

classes around the idea of agrarian improvement (Bayly 1989: 80–81). We should not lose sight of the fact that the classes on which such a British policy depended at home did not exist in India.

3. These policies were most notably carried out by Thomas Munro who became governor of the Madras presidency in 1820, two years after the publication of Mill's *History.* On the "Munro System," see Beaglehole 1966.

4. Because of their conviction that the land rent system is the natural inheritance of the state that—so it is claimed—does not impede economic progress, the Mills and Jeremy Bentham were able to convince themselves that India was not a colony. In such essays as "Emancipate Your Colonies!" Bentham considered whether emigration and colonization were effective means for dealing with problems of overpopulation. He decided that colonies were not effective and should be emancipated. But what he meant by a colony was the Greek model involving the actual emigration of populations in over-crowded states to colonial outposts. Since this was not British policy in India, and theoretically the land rent was claimed not to impede progress, India was not considered a colony.

In practice, land rent levied such a heavy burden on good and bad soils that its effect was to further dispossess subsistence farmers, arguably creating unstable social conditions in Bengal and the Madras presidency which led to dramatic population increases. This is far from the only case of "the fallacy of misplaced concreteness," as economist Herman E. Daly calls the tendency to think that the world must be the way our theories say it is (Daly and Cobb, Jr. 1989: 35–43).

5. Here we also see the influence of Herbert Spencer's view that the laws of evolution require "an adjustment of political and moral principles to the level of any given civilization" (Guha 1989: 280, 243).

6. Perhaps we can also detect here an anticipation of John Stuart Mill's famous test for "higher" qualities of pleasures that satisfy his version of the hedonic calculus. One of the criticisms of utilitarianism which he was most concerned to address was that hedonic theories reduce human beings to the level of pigs. As he said, "better to be Socrates dissatisfied than a pig satisfied" (Mill [1861] 1957: 14). Mill's attitude was that when there are disputes over higher and lower pleasures, we need to defer to the competent judge who has experienced both kinds of pleasures, namely such "civilized" judges as Mill himself. The hedonic calculus is decidable only by the intuitions of the "civilized."

7. Bentham's intimations that moral standing may even be extended to animals on the basis of their sentience has been picked up by contemporary utilitarians, such as Peter Singer, as the foundation for the animal welfare movement (Singer 1990).

8. This explains, perhaps, why Gandhi never repudiated the caste system, but tried to appeal to a revived sense of responsibility of the upper castes to the lower castes as a source of resistance to colonialism. See Nandy 1987a for an important account of Gandhi's critique of the West, including his use of the caste system as a source of revolutionary change.

3. WAR AND PEACE

1. See the distinction between individual and institutional violence in chapter 1.

2. I do not intend these remarks to romanticize indigenous women's agriculture. Violence does exist within indigenous communities. This violence,

however, is immeasurably worsened by the effects of the green revolution. "Women's agriculture," is not the name of an essential category. My approach is nonessentialist, as will become clear in this chapter. Women are not inherently closer to nature than men. Men are not the sole perpetrators of environmental violence. Nevertheless, I do not want to overgeneralize in presenting a broad overview. Any generalization, however nuanced, risks losing sight of the diversity of women's lives. Yet this concern generates a dilemma: women's practices are often invisible to development experts. Without some degree of generalization, they will remain invisible.

3. One reason the Punjab was chosen as the site for transfer of green revolution technology is that it already had a system of irrigation based on partial diversion of rivers (Shiva 1991: 122).

4. See Kenney 1986 and Kloppenburg 1988. The impact of these technologies is suggested by the juxtaposition of two facts: in five years during the latter half of the 1960s, consumption of inorganic nitrogen fertilizer in India increased from 58,000 metric tons to 1.2 million metric tons. During that decade, India's currency was devalued by 37.5 percent as a result of its rising foreign debt (Borlaug 1971: 233; Shiva 1991: 30).

5. For a collection of essays on the history and legacy of the World Bank after fifty years, see Danaher and Yunus 1994.

6. For the history of the issue in Mexico, see Lappé and Collins 1978: 112–16; Pearse 1980: 33–37.

7. The fragility of such genetic information cannot be overstated. As one observer commented, "The genetic heritage of a millennium in a particular valley can disappear in a single bowl of porridge." Once lost, it is lost forever. This has, in fact, happened. A cache of wheat-germ plasm stored at the International Maize and Wheat Improvement Center in Mexico was destroyed when an Institute refrigerator shut down during a power outage (Lappé and Collins 1978: 174).

8. At a political level, green revolution techniques marginalize third world countries in other ways. Products such as DDT that have long been banned in the first world because of their known damage to human health and the environment are still widely sold in the third world. Pesticide accidents among people who are illiterate and cannot read directions for recommended use are responsible for 40,000 deaths each year, primarily in the third world.

4. GANDHIAN LEGACIES

1. In 1998 Cargill sold its seed genetics business to Monsanto.

2. Precedent already exists in a ruling of the GATT Commission which Mexico filed against the United States. The U.S. Congress had passed a ban on Mexican tuna because of the use of purse seine nets, which catch dolphins and other marine life. Mexico filed a grievance claiming this was a barrier to free trade, and the GATT Commission sided with Mexico. Environmental legislation which Congress passed was overruled by the commission. The difference between this case and cases of indigenous autonomy is that indigenous people are not parties to the GATT.

5. RECOGNIZING WOMEN'S ENVIRONMENTAL EXPERTISE

1. I owe this example to Kristin Cashman, Center for Indigenous Knowledge for Agriculture and Rural Development, Iowa State University.

2. This chapter takes its inspiration from feminist standpoint theory,

which argues that there are typically women's ways of categorizing, experiencing, and valuing the world (Hartsock 1983). Hilary Rose observes that "feminist epistemology derives from women's lived experience, centred on the domains of inter-connectedness and affectual rationality. It emphasizes holism and harmonious relationships with nature, which is why feminism has links with that other major social movement of our time, ecology" (Rose 1986: 162–63). A feminist standpoint organizes the world precisely through a revaluation of those practices that sexist categories marginalize, practices that are pushed to the periphery of what has counted as important. Thus, like the meal that miraculously appears on the table every night and only becomes important when it is *not* there, these practices are often invisible to those who benefit from them.

3. The program was offered by WIDA (Integrated Rural Development of Weaker-Sections in India). I extend my appreciation to Dr. K. Rajaratnam, director of the program, and to Sasi Prabha, director of women's programs, for assistance in helping me to understand WIDA's programs.

6. CALLICOTT'S LAND ETHIC

1. For example, consider the recurring dispute over access to the Boundary Waters Canoe Area Wilderness in northern Minnesota.

2. Granting that J. Baird Callicott is logically correct, I would only point out that the "problem" of altruism becomes a problem only given certain assumptions common to Western moral discourse according to which the autonomous moral agent is categorically distinct from nature. The problem of altruism then becomes the issue of whether we can "cross over" this posited divide and value something that is categorically distinct from us. Callicott himself, as we shall see in examining his "third position," begins to explore this supposition by showing that the fundamental questions of environmental philosophy are based on Cartesian/Newtonian assumptions that are investigated in quantum mechanics. In short, the third position deconstructs the first and second positions by exhibiting that the fundamental questions in the origination story of environmental ethics are inquiries only given certain questionable assumptions.

3. I agree with much of what Jim Cheney has written, but I do not agree with him that environmental ethics must be postmodern. There is a distinction between the postmodern and the postcolonial.

4. Callicott has recently begun defending "sustainable development" as an alternative to "the wilderness idea," partly as a response to Ramachandra Guha's essay. I will consider this in the next section, only noting here that Callicott is still supporting a linear idea of "development."

5. Under pressure from communitarians, Rawls has lately altered his view as expressed originally in Rawls 1971. See Rawls 1993b. I consider these issues in chapters 9 and 10, where I develop a communitarian alternative to intrinsic value theories inspired by the work of Michael Walzer and Charles Taylor.

6. It is strange that Callicott never draws on the potential of David Hume to question the autonomy of self as it has been assumed in Western moral philosophy. In *A Treatise of Human Nature*, Hume challenged the Cartesian idea of a self that remains identical through time, saying, "For my part, when I enter most intimately into what I call *myself*, I always stumble on some particular perception or other, of heat or cold, light or shade, love or hatred, pain or pleasure. I never can catch *myself* at any time without a perception, and never can

observe any thing but the perception" (Hume 1888: 252). Introspection simply did not reveal to Hume the substantial self that remains identical through time.

Of course, Callicott is well aware of Hume's position, but he fails to make use of the insight Hume opened in his characterization of the moral self. If there is no substantial moral self that remains self-identical through time, can the problem of egoism and altruism arise? This problem seems to presuppose a clear division between Self and Other.

7. Although I am sympathetic to Norton's pragmatic characterization of practical ethics, I also deepen my account of such ethical deliberation in chapter 9. There I depict such deliberation as reflective of a cultural practice.

7. A STATE OF MIND LIKE WATER

1. I thank Arne Naess for providing me with this paper in response to my article "Dogen, Deep Ecology, and the Ecological Self" (Curtin 1994). For the sake of simplicity, I have removed diacritical marks except when they occur in direct quotations.

2. See Dogen 1985b for the two methods of studying the Buddha way. Dogen accepts the traditional Buddhist understanding of body as "the four great elements" (earth, water, fire, and air) and the five skandhas (form, feeling, perception, impulses, and consciousness). The five skandhas are the mental and physical aggregates from which the phenomenal world is analyzed. The point of the analysis is to show that there is no substantial self.

3. There is no better philosophical introduction to Dogen's thought than Kasulis's book (Kasulis 1981: 87–103).

4. Given the previous section, perhaps one reminder is in order: apparently such categorical statements should be read as clues toward direct experience.

5. Readers interested in the ways Dogen connects with and departs from Buddhist tradition should consult Heinrich Dumoulin's two volume *Zen Buddhism: A History.*

6. This idea, however, was not original with Dogen. See LaFleur 1978 for some fascinating background on this issue.

7. Norman Waddell and Abe Masao's translation of the second sentence is "All sentient beings-whole being is the Buddha-nature." I have kept the translations parallel here. On the radicalization of Buddha-nature, see Dumoulin 1990: 79ff.

8. Naess does say, "There is a limit here. Not a definite [limit], and the options where to trace it are many" (Naess Unpublished: 3). He does not explicitly address these options, but it does seem clear that he questions whether we can go beyond plants.

9. This has led David Rothenberg, for example, to question whether Ecosophy T includes an ethical position (Rothenberg 1993: 153–59).

10. I develop a co-relational account of eating along these lines in Curtin 1991 and Curtin and Heldke 1992.

11. See Guha 1989 for this charge, and Naess 1995 for Naess's response. I take Callicott's early work to be a classic case of the objectionable use of intrinsic value when he says, "The extent of misanthropy in modern environmentalism thus may be taken as a measure of the degree to which it is biocentric" (Callicott 1989: 27). His more recent attempt to provide an evolutionary account of ethics in which human and environmental concerns coincide does

nothing to provide a decision procedure for such cases. Where Naess is an environmental ontologist, Callicott is an environmental ethicist.

12. For other readings, see the special issue of *Inquiry: An Interdisciplinary Journal of Philosophy* (39, no. 2 [1996], Andrew Light and David Rothenberg, eds.) dedicated to Arne Naess's environmental thought.

8. ECOLOGICAL FEMINISM AND THE PLACE OF CARING

1. See Iris Marion Young, "Impartiality and the Civic Public: Some Implications of Feminist Critiques of Moral and Political Theory," where she connects deontological theories with what Theodor Adorno called the logic of identity which "eliminate[s] otherness" by denying "the irreducible specificity of situations and the difference among moral subjects" (Young 1987: 61).

2. Not all feminists would agree that a feminist ethics should be inherently contextual. Susan Moller Okin has recently argued that the rights perspective can include both the requirement of universalizability and empathetic concern for others. She proposes that the rights approach may be contextualized; thus she doubts whether there is a "different voice" in morality. I question whether she has succeeded in showing this, however, since her suggestion that the rights perspective requires us "to think from the point of view of everybody, of every 'concrete other' whom one might turn out to be" still entails "*equal* concern for others" (Okin 1990: 32, 34, emphasis added). This is still not fully compatible with the care perspective, which allows that a particular context of caring may include caring that is *un*equal. Even if contextualized, a rule-based ethic still proceeds by finding cross-situational identity. There is a difference between contextualizing a rule-governed theory, and a "theory" that is inherently contextualized. I therefore tend to side with those who argue that there is a distinctively feminist ethic of care that cannot be reduced to the justice perspective.

In fact, I would be sympathetic to a position that is even more pluralistic than the alternatives of rights or care. Charles Taylor argues that there are moral perspectives based on personal integrity, perfection, and liberation (Taylor 1982: 133). These may not be reducible either to rights or care. I would suggest that an ecofeminist ethics of care is most appropriately developed in dialogue with what Taylor calls the liberation orientation rather than the rights orientation. I intend to do this by arguing in the next section that the care perspective needs to be politicized.

3. Karen J. Warren uses this term in Warren 1987: 17–20, and Lisa Heldke and I use the term in Curtin and Heldke 1992.

4. In Curtin and Heldke 1992, I argued for just such a feminist sense of self as might arise from mindfulness about our defining relationships to food.

5. See Kittay and Meyers 1987 as well as Sunstein 1990 for useful collections of essays illustrating the influence of Carol Gilligan's research. Owen Flanagan and Kathryn Jackson give a helpful overview of the large body of literature on this subject (Flanagan and Jackson 1990). They point out several changes that might be helpful to Gilligan's theory. For example, whereas Gilligan depicts the alternative between a rights perspective and a care perspective in terms of a gestalt shift, Flanagan and Jackson argue that this does not accurately represent the shift which occurs between the two perspectives. A gestalt shift, such as the duck-rabbit, only allows the image to be seen as either a duck or a rabbit. But research suggests that most people can see a particular moral situation from the perspective of either rights or care but that

one of these perspectives is regarded as more important, and the distinction in importance tends to be gender based—women emphasizing care, men emphasizing rights (Flanagan and Jackson 1990: 38–40). This suggests the two perspectives are psychologically, not inherently, mutually exclusive, although one may find contexts in which the perspectives do conflict.

6. Of course, for Garrett Hardin it was greedy villagers over-grazing their cattle that causes the tragedy, not the centralizing powers of developmentalism.

9. DEMOCRATIC DISCOURSE IN A MORALLY PLURALISTIC WORLD

1. Significantly, Secretary Christopher made this extraordinary claim during the period when third world countries were being pressured into signing the GATT and NAFTA agreements, agreements designed to force third world communities to accept the language of individual property rights.

2. In South Africa and Tibet, for example, oppressed populations have gained by learning how to speak the language of individual rights as a way of protesting torture and unjust detention.

3. In beginning with consideration of ethical practices, I am not committing to a full-blooded communitarianism. If we mean by communitarianism the view that ethics resides solely within cultural practices, I clearly disagree. This chapter is raising the question of moral discourse across practices. I refer to the structure of practices assuming that practices are important features of ethical life, and that part of the reason for the failure of first world/third world ethical discourse is the inability of utilitarian and deontological theories of ethical reasoning to capture the richness of cross-cultural ethical discourse.

4. Stephen A. Marglin makes a similar point in terms of the distinction between techne and episteme (Marglin 1990).

5. I explore this sense of self-in-relation in Curtin 1994 as well as in Curtin and Heldke 1992.

6. Onora O'Neill argues powerfully that a Kantian conception of justice can be sufficiently contextual to deal with issues of difference. The problem lies with the misapplication of Kantian moral laws through "idealization." The problem is not one of abstraction. I cannot deal with her argument here, but see the response by Martha Nussbaum (Nussbaum 1993; O'Neill 1993).

7. Iris Marion Young made something like this point during a session at the 1994 Central Division Meeting of the American Philosophical Association on Seyla Benhabib's *Situating the Self.* Also see Lingis 1994, where he argues that "the intruder" is one who concerns us precisely because of his or her otherness.

8. Nancy Hartsock argues for feminist standpoint theory in a way that is similar to my argument in this chapter concerning the special position of gender in practices. María Lugones argues that "world-travelling" is distinctive of feminist consciousness (Hartsock 1983; Lugones 1987). Nussbaum and Sen emphasize that such criticism comes from the inside (Nussbaum and Sen 1989).

9. On the roles of insiders and outsiders in international development, see Crocker 1991.

10. For a fine summary of this process, see Kelsay and Twiss 1994, especially chapter 3, "Universality vs. Relativism in Human Rights."

11. See Crocker 1991 for an overview of Sen's development ethic.

12. By "social" I do not necessarily mean "exclusively human." If the dis-

cussion of Naess and Buddhist philosophy suggests anything, it is that the notion of an exclusively human social identity is a prejudice of the Enlightenment.

13. It may seem odd that, until the last section, I have confined my references (with the exception of Sen) to first world moral theorists. This was deliberate. I want to show there are resources within Western traditions for dealing with cross-cultural ethical discourse.

14. The word "partial" becomes critical later. Of course, not all insiders to the culture of bourgeois political liberalism were full insiders. Not all were included in the Enlightenment vision of moral progress. Nevertheless, even slaves and women were partial insiders—even if this happened against their will. Their position "on the border" makes their ability to shift between the reiterative and transformative powerful.

10. PUTTING DOWN ROOTS

1. I offer my thanks to Bennet Benjamin for this story.

2. Thomas Jefferson's contradictions have been widely noted, especially his unwillingness, as a Virginia farmer, to free his slaves. Jefferson also set off the greatest land rush ever with the Louisiana Purchase and the Louis and Clark Expedition, the latter to map the new territory and discover a trade route to the Pacific. Although he respected Native Americans more than his African slaves, no one would claim that he really understood indigenousness.

3. Chantal Mouffe is one of the rare critics of traditional liberalism who connects citizenship with the environment. Speaking of radical democracy, she says, "In short, it has to meet the challenge of the 'new movements' and acknowledge concerns relating to ecology, gay issues, ethnicity and others, as well as the struggles around class, race and gender" (Mouffe 1992a: 4). Although she recognizes the connection, the reconciliation of American culture with nature is not her major concern.

4. Paul B. Thompson is one of the rare environmental philosophers who takes agricultural practice seriously. Thompson's critical discussion of Wendell Berry awakened me to the possible relevance of his work to the question of a distinctively American environmental ethic that reconciles agriculture with wilderness (Thompson 1999: chap. 4).

REFERENCES

Abe, Masao. 1971. Dogen on Buddha Nature. *Eastern Buddhist* 4:1.

Bayly, C. A. 1989. *Imperial Meridian: The British Empire and the World, 1780–1830.* London: Longman.

Beaglehole, T. H. 1966. *Thomas Munro and the Development of Administrative Policy in Madras, 1792–1818.* Cambridge: Cambridge University Press.

Benhabib, Seyla. 1987. The Generalized and the Concrete Other: The Kohlberg-Gilligan Controversy and Feminist Theory. In *Feminism as Critique: On the Politics of Gender,* edited by S. Benhabib and D. Cornell. Minneapolis: University of Minnesota Press.

Bentham, Jeremy. [1789] 1970. *An Introduction to the Principles of Morals and Legislation.* Edited by J. H. Burns and H. L. A. Hart. *The Collected Works of Jeremy Bentham.* Reprint, London: The Athlone Press.

Berry, Wendell. 1977. *The Unsettling of America: Culture and Agriculture.* San Francisco: Sierra Club Books.

———. 1983. People, Land, and Community. In *Standing by Words.* Berkeley: North Point Press.

———. 1990a. Feminism, the Body, and the Machine. In *What Are People For?* San Francisco: North Point Press.

———. 1990b. A Few Words in Favor of Edward Abbey. In *What Are People For?* San Francisco: North Point Press.

———. 1990c. Healing. In *What Are People For?* San Francisco: North Point Press.

———. 1990d. Why I Am Not Going to Buy a Computer. In *What Are People For?* San Francisco: North Point Press.

Birch, Thomas H. 1990. The Incarceration of Wildness: Wilderness Areas as Prisons. *Environmental Ethics* 12 (1): 3–26.

Bookchin, Murray. 1993. What Is Social Ecology? In *Environmental Philosophy: From Animal Rights to Radical Ecology,* edited by Michael Zimmerman et al. Englewood Cliffs: Prentice Hall.

Borlaug, Norman. 1971. The Green Revolution, Peace, and Humanity. In *Les Prix Nobel en 1970.* Stockholm: Imprimerieal Royal P. A Norstedt & Söner.

Boserup, Ester. 1970. *Woman's Role in Economic Development.* London: Allen and Unwin.

Botkin, Daniel. 1990. *Discordant Harmonies: A New Ecology for the Twenty-first Century.* New York: Oxford University Press.

Brennan, Andrew. 1992. Moral Pluralism and the Environment. *Environmental Values* 1: 15–33.

Brower, David, ed. 1965. *Not Man Apart.* New York: Ballantine Books.

Brown, Lester R., ed. 1993. *State of the World.* New York: W. W. Norton.

Butalia, Urvashi. 1985. Indian Women and the New Movement. *Women's Studies International Forum* 8.2: 131–33.

Cady, Duane. 1989. *From Warism to Pacifism: A Moral Continuum.* Philadelphia: Temple University Press.

———. 1991. War, Gender, Race, and Class. *Concerned Philosophers for Peace Newsletter* 11 (2): 4–10.

Callicott, J. Baird. 1989a. American Indian Land Wisdom? Sorting Out the Issues. In *In Defense of the Land Ethic: Essays in Environmental Ethics,* edited by J. B. Callicott. Albany: State University of New York Press.

———. 1989b. Animal Liberation: A Triangular Affair. In *In Defense of the Land Ethic: Essays in Environmental Philosophy,* edited by J. B. Callicott. Albany: State University of New York Press.

———. 1989c. Intrinsic Value, Quantum Theory, and Environmental Ethics. In *In Defense of the Land Ethic: Essays in Environmental Ethics,* edited by J. B. Callicott. Albany: State University of New York Press.

———. 1989d. On the Intrinsic Value of Nonhuman Species. In *In Defense of the Land Ethic: Essays in Environmental Philosophy,* edited by J. B. Callicott. Albany: State University of New York Press.

———. 1989e. Traditional American Indian and Western European Attitudes toward Nature: An Overview. In *In Defense of the Land Ethic: Essays in Environmental Ethics,* edited by J. B. Callicott. Albany: State University of New York Press.

———. 1990. The Case against Moral Pluralism. *Environmental Ethics* 12 (2): 99–124.

———. 1994a. *Earth's Insights: A Multicultural Survey of Ecological Ethics from the Mediterranean Basin to the Australian Outback.* Berkeley: University of California Press.

———. 1994b. The Wilderness Idea Revisited: The Sustainable Development Alternative. In *Reflecting on Nature: Readings in Environmental Philosophy,* edited by L. Gruen and D. Jamieson. New York: Oxford University Press.

———. 1995. Environmental Philosophy *Is* Environmental Activism. In *Environmental Philosophy and Environmental Activism,* edited by D. Marietta and L. Embree. Lanham, Md.: Rowman and Littlefield.

Chabousson, F. 1986. How Pesticides Increase Pests. *Ecologist* 16 (1): 29–36.

Cheney, Jim. 1987. Eco-Feminism and Deep Ecology. *Environmental Ethics* 9: 145–55.

———. 1989a. The Neo-Stoicism of Radical Environmentalism. *Environmental Ethics* 11: 293–325.

———. 1989b. Postmodern Environmental Ethics: Ethics as Bioregional Narrative. *Environmental Ethics* 11: 117–34.

Crocker, David. 1991. Functioning and Capability: The Foundation of Sen's Development Ethic. In *Ethical Principles for Development: Needs, Capacities, or Rights,* edited by K. Aman. Upper Montclair, N.J.: Institute for Critical Thinking.

Cronon, William. 1995. The Trouble with Wilderness; or, Getting Back to the Wrong Nature. In *Uncommon Ground: Toward Reinventing Nature,* edited by W. Cronon. New York: W. W. Norton.

Crosby, Alfred W. 1986. *Ecological Imperialism: The Biological Expansion of Europe, 900–1900.* Cambridge: Cambridge University Press.

Crump, Andy. 1991. *Dictionary of Environment and Development.* London: Earthscan Publications.

Curtin, Deane. 1991. Toward an Ecological Ethic of Care. *Hypatia* 6.1: 60–74.

———. 1994. Dogen, Deep Ecology, and the Ecological Self. *Environmental Ethics* 16 (2): 195–213.

———. 1995. Making Peace with the Earth: Indigenous Agriculture and the Green Revolution. *Environmental Ethics* 17 (Spring): 59–73.

Curtin, Deane, and John Powers. 1994. Mothering: Moral Cultivation in Buddhist and Feminist Ethics. *Philosophy East and West* 44 (1): 1–18.

Curtin, Deane W., and Lisa Heldke, eds. 1992. *Cooking, Eating, Thinking: Transformative Philosophies of Food.* Bloomington: Indiana University Press.

Daly, Herman E., and John B. Cobb, Jr. 1989. *For the Common Good: Redirecting the Economy toward Community, the Environment, and a Sustainable Future.* Boston: Beacon Press.

Danaher, Kevin, and Muhammad Yunus, eds. 1994. *50 Years Is Enough: The Case against the World Bank and the International Monetary Fund.* Boston: South End Press.

Dankelman, Irene, and Joan Davidson, eds. 1988. *Women and Environment in the Third World.* London: Earthscan.

Danto, Arthur. 1981. *The Transfiguration of the Commonplace: A Philosophy of Art.* Cambridge: Harvard University Press.

Davidson, Donald. 1980. Mental Events. In *Essays on Action and Events,* edited by D. Davidson. Oxford: Oxford University Press.

De Bary, Wm. Theodore, ed. 1972. *The Buddhist Tradition in India, China, and Japan.* New York: Vintage Books.

Devall, Bill, and George Sessions. 1985. *Deep Ecology: Living As If Nature Mattered.* Salt Lake City: Peregrine Smith Books.

Dogen. 1985a. Actualizing the Fundamental Point (Genjokoan). Translated by Robert Aitken and Kazuaki Tanahashi. In *Moon in a Dewdrop,* edited by K. Tanahashi. Berkeley: North Point Press.

———. 1985b. Body-and-Mind Study of the Way (Shinjin Gakudo). Translated by Dan Welch and Kazuaki Tanahashi. In *Moon in a Dewdrop,* edited by K. Tanahashi. Berkeley: North Point Press.

———. 1985c. Mountains and Waters Sutra. Translated by Arnold Kotler and Kazuaki Tanahashi. In *Moon in a Dewdrop,* edited by K. Tanahashi. Berkeley: North Point Press.

———. 1985d. Undivided Activity (Zenki). Translated by Ed Brown and Kazuaki Tanahashi. In *Moon in a Dewdrop,* edited by K. Tanahashi. Berkeley: North Point Press.

Dogen, Zenji. 1975. *Shobogenzo* (The Eye and Treasury of the True Law). Translated and edited by Kosen Nishiyama. Tokyo: Nakayama Shobo.

Dumoulin, Heinrich. 1990. *Zen Buddhism: A History.* 2 vols. Translated by James W. Heisig and Paul Knitter. Vol. 2. New York: Macmillan Publishing Company.

Durning, Alan Thein. 1992. Guardians of the Land: Indigenous Peoples and the Health of the Earth—An Abstract. *International Journal of Sustainable Development* 1 (3): 61–68.

Dussel, Enrique. [1980] 1985. *Philosophy of Liberation.* Translated by Aquilina Martinez Christine Morkovsky. Maryknoll, N.Y.: Orbis Books.

Feinberg, Joel. 1980. The Rights of Animals and Unborn Generations. In *Responsibilities to Other Generations,* edited by E. Partridge. Buffalo: Prometheus Books.

Flanagan, Owen, and Kathryn Jackson. 1990. Justice, Care, and Gender: The Kohlberg-Gilligan Debate Revisited. In *Feminism and Political Theory,* edited by C. R. Sunstein. Chicago: The University of Chicago Press.

Frye, Marilyn. 1983. *The Politics of Reality: Essays in Feminist Theory.* Trumansburg, N.Y.: Crossings Press.

Gadgil, Madhav, and Ramachandra Guha. 1992. *This Fissured Land: An Ecological History of India.* Delhi: Oxford University Press.

Garver, Newton. 1968. What Violence Is. *The Nation* 209 (24 June): 819–22.

Guha, Ramachandra. 1989. Radical American Environmentalism and Wilderness Preservation: A Third World Critique. *Environmental Ethics* 11 (1): 71–83.

———. 1990. *The Unquiet Woods: Ecological Change and Peasant Resistance in the Himalaya.* Berkeley: University of California Press.

Guha, Ranajit. 1989. Dominance without Hegemony and Its Historiography. In *Subaltern Studies VI: Writings on South Asian History and Society,* edited by R. Guha. Delhi: Oxford University Press.

Hardin, Garrett. 1968. The Tragedy of the Commons. *Science* 162: 1243–48.

———. [1974] 1994. Lifeboat Ethics. In *Environmental Ethics: Readings in Theory and Application,* edited by L. P. Pojman. Reprint, Boston: Jones and Bartlett Publishers.

Hartsock, Nancy. 1983. The Feminist Standpoint: Developing the Ground for a Specifically Feminist Historical Materialism. In *Discovering Reality,* edited by S. Harding and M. Hintikka. London: D. Reidel.

Howard, Sir Albert. [1943] 1972. *An Agricultural Testament.* Rodale Press Edition. London: Oxford University Press.

Human Rights Divide U.S., Third World. *Minneapolis Tribune,* June 15, 1993.

Hume, David. 1888. *A Treatise of Human Nature.* Edited by L. A. Selby-Bigge. Oxford: Clarendon Press.

India, Government of. 1993. *India 1992: A Reference Annual.* New Delhi: Publications Division, Ministry of Information and Broadcasting.

Jackson, Wes. 1987. Meeting the Expectations of the Land. In *Altars of Unhewn Stone: Science and the Earth.* San Francisco: North Point Press.

———. *Becoming Native to This Place.* Washington, D.C.: Counterpoint, 1994.

Jacobson, Jodi. September 1992. *Gender Bias: Roadblock to Sustainable Development.* Paper 110. Washington, D.C.: Worldwatch Institute.

Jaggar, Alison M. 1989. Love and Knowledge: Emotion in Feminist Epistemology. In *Gender/Body/Knowledge: Feminist Reconstructions of Being and Knowing,* edited by Alison M. Jaggar and Susan R. Bordo. New Brunswick, N.J.: Rutgers University Press.

Jefferson, Thomas. 1993. Notes on Virginia. In *The Life and Selected Writings of Thomas Jefferson,* edited by A. Koch and W. Peden. New York: The Modern Library.

Kasulis, Thomas P. 1981. *Zen Action, Zen Person.* Honolulu: University of Hawaii Press.

Kelsay, John, and Sumner B. Twiss, eds. 1994. *Religion and Human Rights.* New York: The Project on Religion and Human Rights.

Kenney, Martin. 1986. *Biotechnology: The University-Industrial Complex.* New Haven: Yale University Press.

Khanna, Anjani. 1993. India's Miracle Tree Ready to Storm Markets. *Down to Earth,* April 15, 1993, 37–39.

Kheel, Marti. 1989. From Healing Herbs to Deadly Drugs: Western Medicine's War against the Natural World. In *Healing the Wounds: The Promise of Ecofeminism,* edited by J. Plant. Philadelphia: New Society Publishers.

Kittay, Eva Feder, and Diana T. Meyers, eds. 1987. *Women and Moral Theory.* Lanham, Md.: Rowman and Littlefield.

Kloppenburg, Jack Ralph. 1988. *First the Seed: The Political Economy of Plant Biotechnology, 1492–2000.* Cambridge: Cambridge University Press.

Kymlicka, Will. 1989. *Liberalism, Community and Culture.* Oxford: Clarendon Press.

——. 1995a. Introduction. In *The Rights of Minority Cultures,* edited by W. Kymlicka. Oxford: Oxford University Press.

——. 1995b. *Multicultural Citizenship: A Liberal Theory of Minority Rights.* Oxford: Oxford University Press.

——, ed. 1995c. *The Rights of Minority Cultures.* Oxford: Oxford University Press.

LaFleur, William. 1978. Sattva: Enlightenment for Plants and Trees in Buddhism. *CoEvolution Quarterly* 19: 47–52.

Lappé, Frances Moore, and Joseph Collins. 1978. *Food First: Beyond the Myth of Scarcity.* New York: Ballantine Books.

Leopold, Aldo. [1949] 1977. *A Sand County Almanac: And Sketches Here and There.* Oxford: Oxford University Press.

Levins, Richard. 1986. Science and Progress: Seven Developmentalist Myths in Agriculture. *Monthly Review* 38 (3): 13–20.

Lewontin, Richard. 1982. Agricultural Research and the Penetration of Capital. *Science for the People* 14 (1): 12–17.

Lingis, Alphonso. 1994. *The Community of Those Who Have Nothing in Common.* Bloomington: Indiana University Press.

Lopez, Barry. 1992. *The Rediscovery of North America.* New York: Vintage Books.

Lugones, María. 1987. Playfulness, "World-Travelling," and Loving Perception. *Hypatia* 2 (2): 3–18.

Luttwack, Edward. 1993. *The Endangered American Dream.* New York: Simon and Schuster.

MacIntyre, Alasdair. 1981. *After Virtue: A Study in Moral Theory.* 2d ed. Notre Dame: University of Notre Dame Press.

Majeed, Javed. 1992. *Uncovered Imaginings: James Mill's The History of British India and Orientalism.* Oxford: Clarendon Press.

Malthus, T. R. [1815] 1969. *An Inquiry into the Nature and Progress of Rent and the Principles by Which It Is Regulated.* Reprint, New York: Greenwood Press.

Malthus, Thomas Robert. [1798] 1965. *First Essay on Population.* Reprint, New York: Augustus M. Kelley.

——. [1872] 1971. *An Essay on the Principle of Population or a View of Its Past and Present Effects on Human Happiness.* 7th ed. New York: Augustus M. Kelley.

Marglin, Stephen A. 1990. Losing Touch: The Cultural Conditions of Worker Accommodation and Resistance. In *Dominating Knowledge: Development, Culture and Resistance,* edited by F. A. Marglin and S. A. Marglin. Oxford: Clarendon Press.

Mies, Maria. 1986. *Patriarchy and Accumulation on a World Scale.* London: Zed Books.

——. 1988. Class Struggles and Women's Struggles in Rural India. In *Women: The Last Colony,* edited by Maria Mies, Veronika Bennholdt-Thomsen, and Claudia von Werlhof. London: Zed Books.

Mies, Maria; Veronika Bennholdt-Thomsen; and Claudia von Werlhof, eds. 1988. *Women: The Last Colony.* London: Zed Books.

Mill, James. [1817] 1858. *The History of British India.* Edited by H. H. Wilson. 5th ed. 10 vols. London: James Madden, Piper, Stephenson and Spence.

Mill, John Stuart. [1861] 1957. *Utilitarianism.* Edited by O. Piest. Reprint, Indianapolis: The Bobbs-Merrill Company.

——. 1965. *Principles of Political Economy.* Edited by J. M. Robinson. 3 vols. Vol. 3. Toronto: University of Toronto Press.

——. 1990. *Writings on India.* In *Collected Works of John Stuart Mill,* edited by John M. Robson, Martin Moir, and Zawahir Moir, vol. 30. Toronto: University of Toronto Press.

Mouffe, Chantal. 1992a. Democratic Politics Today. In *Dimensions of Radical Democracy: Pluralism, Citizenship, Community,* edited by C. Mouffe. London: Verso.

——, ed. 1992b. *Dimensions of Radical Democracy: Pluralism, Citizenship, Community.* London: Verso.

——. 1993. *The Return of the Political.* London: Verso.

Muir, John. [1911] 1987. *My First Summer in the Sierra.* Edited by E. Hoagland. Reprint, New York: Penguin Books.

Murphy, Patrick D. 1988. Sex-Typing the Planet: Gaia Imagery and the Problem of Subverting Patriarchy. *Environmental Ethics* 10 (2): 155–68.

Murti, T. R. V. 1960. *The Central Philosophy of Buddhism: A Study of the Madhyamika System.* London: Allan and Unwin.

Naess, Arne. 1973. The Shallow and the Deep, Long-Range Ecology Movement: A Summary. *Inquiry* 16: 95–100.

——. 1995. The Third World, Wilderness, and Deep Ecology. In *Deep Ecology for the Twenty-first Century,* edited by G. Sessions. Boston: Shambhala Publications.

——. Unpublished. Gestalt Thinking and Buddhism.

Nagel, Thomas. 1986. *The View from Nowhere.* New York: Oxford University Press.

Nandy, Ashis. 1987a. From Outside the Imperium: Gandhi's Cultural Critique of the West. In *Traditions, Tyranny and Utopias: Essays in the Politics of Awareness.* Delhi: Oxford University Press.

——. 1987b. *Traditions, Tyranny and Utopias: Essays in the Politics of Awareness.* Delhi: Oxford University Press.

Nanjudaswamy, M. D. 1993a. Our Goal is Self-Reliance in Seeds. *Third World Resurgence* 39: 23.

——. 1993b. Farmers and the Dunkel Draft. *Economic and Political Weekly* June 26: 1334.

Nara, Yasuaki. Unpublished. The Practical Value of Dogen's View of Nature.

Nelson, Joyce. 1993. The Great Global Greenwash. *Third World Resurgence* 37: 5–10.

Norton, Bryan. 1987. *Why Preserve Natural Variety?* Princeton: Princeton University Press.

——. 1991. *Toward Unity among Environmentalists.* New York: Oxford University Press.

——. 1995. Why I Am Not a Nonanthropocentrist: Callicott and the Failure of Monistic Inherentism. *Environmental Ethics* 17 (4): 341–58.

Norton, Bryan G., and Bruce Hannon. 1997. Environmental Values: A Place-Based Theory. *Environmental Ethics* 19 (3): 227–45.

Nussbaum, Martha. 1993. Onora O'Neill: Justice, Gender, and International Boundaries. In *The Quality of Life,* edited by M. Nussbaum and A. Sen. Oxford: Clarendon Press.

Nussbaum, Martha, and Amartya Sen. 1989. Internal Criticism and Indian Rationalist Traditions. In *Relativism: Interpretation and Confrontation,* edited by M. Krausz. Notre Dame: University of Notre Dame Press.

Oelschlaeger, Max. 1991. *The Idea of Wilderness.* New Haven: Yale University Press.

Okin, Susan Moller. 1990. Reason and Feeling in Thinking about Justice. In *Feminism and Political Theory*, edited by C. Sunstein. Chicago: University of Chicago Press.

Omo-Fadaka, Jimoh. 1990. Communalism: The Moral Factor in African Development. In *Ethics of Environment and Development: Global Challenge, International Response*, edited by J. R. Engel and J. G. Engel. Tucson: University of Arizona Press.

O'Neill, Onora. 1993. Justice, Gender, and International Boundaries. In *The Quality of Life*, edited by Martha C. Nussbaum and Amartra Sen. Oxford: Clarendon Press.

Orion: People and Nature. 1997. 16 (2). Special issue of "Parks Americana."

Pearse, Andrew. 1980. *Seeds of Plenty, Seeds of Want: Social and Economic Implications of the Green Revolution*. Oxford: Oxford University Press.

Philips, C. H., ed. 1977. *The Correspondence of Lord William Cavendish Bentinck*. Vol. 1. Delhi: Oxford University Press.

Pinchot, Gifford. 1947. *Breaking New Ground*. New York: Harcourt, Brace.

Plato. 1974. *Plato's Republic*. Translated by G. M. A. Grube. Indianapolis: Hackett Publishing Company.

Plumwood, Val. 1991. Nature, Self, and Gender: Feminism, Environmental Philosophy, and the Critique of Rationalism. *Hypatia* 6 (1): 3–27.

Porter, Eliot, ed. 1967. *In Wildness Is the Preservation of the Earth*. New York: Ballantine Books.

Public Interest Research Group. 1993. Cargill's Bitter Salt. Delhi: Public Interest Research Group.

Quarrie, Joyce, ed. 1992. *Earth Summit '92: The United Nations Conference on Environment and Development, Rio de Janeiro 1992*. London: The Regency Press.

Raghavan, Chakravarthi. 1990. *Recolonization: GATT, the Uruguay Round and the Third World*. Penang, Malaysia: Third World Network.

Rawls, John. 1955. Two Concepts of Rules. *The Philosophical Review* 64: 3–32.

———. 1971. *A Theory of Justice*. Cambridge, Mass.: Harvard University Press.

———. 1985. Justice as Fairness: Political not Metaphysical. *Philosophy and Public Affairs* 14: 223–51.

———. 1987. The Idea of an Overlapping Consensus. *Oxford Journal of Legal Studies* 7: 1–25.

———. 1988. The Priority of Right and the Ideas of the Good. *Philosophy and Public Affairs* 17: 251–76.

———. 1993a. The Law of Peoples. In *On Human Rights: The Oxford Amnesty Lectures, 1993*, edited by S. Shute and S. Hurley. New York: Basic Books.

———. 1993b. *Political Liberalism*. New York: Columbia University Press.

Regan, Tom. 1982. Environmental Ethics and the Ambiguity of the Native American Relationship to Nature. In *All That Dwells Therein: Animal Rights and Environmental Ethics*, ed. Tom Regan. Berkeley: University of California Press.

———. 1983. *The Case for Animal Rights*. Berkeley: University of California Press.

Rose, Hilary. 1986. Women's Work, Women's Knowledge. In *What is Feminism?* edited by J. Mitchell and A. Oakley. New York: Pantheon.

Rosset, Peter, with Shea Cunningham. April 7, 1994. Understanding Chiapas. From Zapatista National Liberation Army (EZLN), Declaration of the Lacandon Jungle, 1993. Internet: native-l@gnosys.svle.ma.us

Rothenberg, David. 1993. *Is It Painful to Think? Conversations with Arne Naess*. Minneapolis: University of Minnesota Press.

Rowe, Robert D.; R. C. D'Arge; and D. Brookshire. 1980. An Experiment on the Economic Value of Visibility. *Journal of Environmental Economics and Management* 7: 1–19.

Ruddick, Sara. 1989. *Maternal Thinking: Toward a Politics of Peace.* New York: Ballantine Books.

Sagoff, Mark. 1988. *The Economy of the Earth.* Cambridge: Cambridge University Press.

———. 1993. Doing the Numbers: Demographic Trends and Global Population. *Report for the Institute for Philosophy and Public Policy* 13 (4): 7–11.

Sandel, Michael. 1982. *Liberalism and the Limits of Justice.* Cambridge: Cambridge University Press.

———. 1996. *Democracy's Discontent: America in Search of a Public Policy.* Cambridge, Mass.: Harvard University Press.

Sen, Amartya. 1981. *Poverty and Famines: An Essay on Entitlement and Deprivation.* Oxford: Oxford University Press.

———. 1990. More Than 100 Million Women Are Missing. *New York Review of Books* 37 (20): 61–66.

———. 1993. Positional Objectivity. *Philosophy and Public Affairs* 22 (2): 126–45.

Sen, Amartya, and Bernard Williams, eds. 1982. *Utilitarianism and Beyond.* Cambridge: Cambridge University Press.

Shiva, Vandana. 1988. *Staying Alive: Women, Ecology and Development.* London: Zed Books.

———. 1991. *The Violence of the Green Revolution: Third World Agriculture, Ecology and Politics.* London and Penang, Malaysia: Zed Books and Third World Network.

———. 1993. Farmers' Rights, Biodiversity and International Treaties. *Economic and Political Weekly* 28 (14): 555–60.

Shiva, Vandana, and Radha Holla-Bhar. 1993. The Rise of the Farmers' Seed Movement. *Third World Resurgence* (39): 24–27.

———. 1996. Piracy by Patent: The Case of the Neem Tree. In *The Case against the Global Economy: And for a Turn toward the Local,* edited by J. Mander and E. Goldsmith. San Francisco: Sierra Club Books.

Shiva, Vandana, and Mira Shiva. 1994. Was Cairo a Step Forward for Third World Women? *Third World Resurgence* (50): 13–16.

Simon, Julian. 1981. *The Ultimate Resource.* Princeton: Princeton University Press.

Singer, Peter. 1990. *Animal Liberation.* 2d ed. New York: New York Review of Books.

Smith, Andy. 1997. Ecofeminism through an Anti-Colonial Framework. In *Ecofeminism: Women, Culture, Nature,* edited by K. J. Warren. Bloomington: Indiana University Press.

Snyder, Gary. 1990. *The Practice of the Wild.* San Francisco: North Point Press.

Spinoza, Benedict de. 1985. Ethics. In *The Collected Works of Spinoza,* edited by E. Curley. Princeton: Princeton University Press.

Stanley, Autumn. 1982. Daughters of Isis, Daughters of Demeter: When Women Sowed and Reaped. In *Women, Technology, and Innovation,* edited by J. Rothschild. New York: Pergamon.

Stokes, Eric. 1989. *The English Utilitarians and India.* Delhi: Oxford University Press.

Stone, Christopher D. 1988. Moral Pluralism and the Course of Environmental Ethics. *Environmental Ethics* 10 (2): 139–54.

Summers, Lawrence. Let Them Eat Pollution. *The Economist* 322.7745: 66 (1).

Sunstein, Cass R., ed. 1990. *Feminism and Political Theory.* Chicago: University of Chicago Press.

Taylor, Charles. 1982. The Diversity of Goods. In *Utilitarianism and Beyond,* edited by A. Sen and B. Williams. Cambridge, Mass.: Harvard University Press.

———. 1989. *Sources of the Self.* Cambridge, Mass.: Harvard University Press.

———. 1992. The Politics of Recognition. In *Multiculturalism and the "Politics of Recognition,"* edited by A. Gutmann. Princeton: Princeton University Press.

———. 1993. Explanation and Practical Reason. In *The Quality of Life,* edited by M. C. Nussbaum and A. Sen. Oxford: Clarendon Press.

Taylor, Paul W. 1986. *Respect for Nature: A Theory of Environmental Ethics.* Princeton: Princeton University Press.

Thompson, Paul B. 1995. *The Spirit of the Soil: Agriculture and Environmental Ethics.* London: Routledge.

Toqueville, Alexis de. [1835] 1945. *Democracy in America.* Translated by Henry Reeve, Esq. Vol. II, book 2. Toronto: Alfred Knopf

U.S. Government Printing Office. 1989. Harry S. Truman, Inaugural Address. In *Inaugural Addresses of the Presidents of the United States.* Washington, D.C.: United States Government Printing Office.

Walzer, Michael. 1983. *Spheres of Justice: A Defense of Pluralism and Equity.* New York: Basic Books.

———. 1994. *Thick and Thin: Moral Argument at Home and Abroad.* Notre Dame: University of Notre Dame Press.

Warren, Karen J. 1987. Feminism and Ecology: Making Connections. *Environmental Ethics* 9 (1): 3–20.

Weinberg, Bill. April 1994. From an Anti-Authoritarian Perspective: Interview with Insurgent Subcommander Marcos of the Zapatista National Liberation Army (EZLN). Internet: Chiapas-l@ds5000.dgsca.unam.mx

Weinpahl, Paul. 1979. *The Radical Spinoza.* New York: New York University Press.

Wenz, Peter. 1993. Minimal, Moderate, and Extreme Moral Pluralism. *Environmental Ethics* 15: 61–74.

Wilderness Act (Public Law 88–577). September 3, 1964. Available on the Internet at http://www.xmission.com/~uwep/uwepwild.html

World Resources Institute. 1994. *World Resources 1994–95: A Guide to the Global Environment.* New York: Oxford University Press.

Worster, Donald. [1977] 1994. *Nature's Economy: A History of Ecological Ideas.* 2d ed. Cambridge: Cambridge University Press.

Young, Iris Marion. 1987. Impartiality and the Civic Public: Some Implications of Feminist Critiques of Moral and Political Theory. In *Feminism as Critique: On the Politics of Gender,* edited by S. Benhabib and D. Cornell. Minneapolis: University of Minnesota Press.

———. 1995. Together in Difference: Transforming the Logic of Group Political Conflict. In *The Rights of Minority Cultures,* edited by W. Kymlicka. Oxford: Oxford University Press.

INDEX

Deane Curtin, professor of philosophy and the Raymond and Florence Sponberg Chair of Ethics at Gustavus Adolphus College, is coeditor of *Cooking, Eating, Thinking: Transformative Philosophies of Food*. He has lived and taught in India, Japan, and Italy, and has published articles on deep ecology, ecofeminism, and contemporary Gandhian resistance to development.